$20 Per Gall

$20 Per Gallon

How the Inevitable Rise in the Price of Gasoline Will Change Our Lives for the Better

Christopher Steiner

GRAND CENTRAL
PUBLISHING

NEW YORK   BOSTON

Grand Central Publishing
Hachette Book Group
237 Park Avenue
New York, NY 10017

Visit our Web site at www.HachetteBookGroup.com.

Printed in the United States of America

First Edition: July 2009
10   9   8   7   6   5   4   3   2   1

Grand Central Publishing is a division of Hachette Book Group, Inc.
The Grand Central Publishing name and logo is a trademark of Hachette Book Group, Inc.

Library of Congress Cataloging-in-Publication Data

Steiner, Christopher.
    $20 per gallon: how the inevitable rise in the price of gasoline will change our lives for the better / Christopher Steiner.—1st ed.
        p.   cm.
    Includes index.
    ISBN 978-0-446-54954-7
    1. Petroleum products—Prices—United States.   2. Transportation—United States—Forecasting.   3. Economic forecasting—United States.
4. United States—Economic policy—2001–   I. Title.   II. Title: Twenty dollars per gallon.
HD9564.S74   2009
330.973—dc22

                                                                  2009006190

Text design and composition by SDDesigns

for
Sarah and Jackson
&
Gary and Janet

Contents

Author's Note • *ix*

$4 PROLOGUE: The Road to $20 and Civilization Renovation • *1*

CHAPTER $6: Society Change and the Dead SUV • *17*

CHAPTER $8: The Skies Will Empty • *52*

CHAPTER $10: The Car Diminished but Reborn • *81*

CHAPTER $12: Urban Revolution and Suburban Decay • *113*

CHAPTER $14: The Fate of Small Towns, U.S. Manufacturing Renaissance, and Our Material World • *141*

CHAPTER $16: The Food Web Deconstructed • *170*

CHAPTER $18: Renaissance of the Rails • *198*

CHAPTER $20: The Future of Energy • *224*

$20 EPILOGUE • *247*

Acknowledgments • *255*

Endnotes • *259*

Index • *265*

Author's Note

O il and gasoline are mercurial commodities. The year 2008 saw oil prices touch highs that most thought wouldn't occur until decades in the future. The same year also brought prices collapsing to lows that hadn't been seen for more than four years. Gas prices can swing capriciously with the throes and fortunes of the world economy. Predicting gasoline's price, during the short term, is a game of chance. Long term, however, there is only one sane prediction for gasoline prices: *up*.

Most of us can agree, as the facts and considerable bounty of research show, that oil is a finite resource that we use at a gluttonous pace. This book goes beyond the mere acknowledgment of peak oil. This book is the next step in the conversation. This book examines how our everyday lives will change as the price of gasoline gradually escalates. What will life look like with gas that costs $8 per gallon? $10 per gallon? $18 per gallon? Our homes, our cars, our jobs, our vacations—throughout they will all change, step by step, with the price at the pump.

In that spirit, I've worked hard to find people who grasp our futures, people who can map out our lives as they change with the price of gasoline. The following pages form a thought experiment on the *what-ifs* of high gas prices with a focus on tangible changes rather than abstract ones.

February 2009

$20 Per Gallon

$4 PROLOGUE

The Road to $20 and
Civilization Renovation

W e used to turn to the weather when all else failed us as con-
versationalists. Clouds and sun, however, have been relegated
to the backseat of chitchat lulls. Everyone wants to talk about the price
of gasoline. Even if you don't drive, this is fascinating fodder. Yes, the
calamitous increases and the more sudden decreases of gasoline prices
have been interesting to us purely as an economic curiosity—how can
something that's been around for so many years, in such utter abundance, suddenly see its value rise and fall with such confounding volatility? But there's more to our interest than cerebral economics. The
tales of gas price flux have regaled our nation in the manner that J. K.
Rowling or Stephenie Meyer tames adolescents. You cannot open a
newspaper, national or local, that doesn't feature a prominent story
with some angle on gas prices. And as it turns out, we're not lem-
mings tethered to a petrol spigot. We have limits, and some of them
have been reached. During 2008, a year when gas prices touched
historical highs, Americans drove 100 billion fewer miles than they
did the year before. That's the first such decrease in thirty years, and
easily dwarfs the driving decreases during the 1970s oil embargoes.

There's something guttural, something personal, about the
price of gas. Even though we've pared our driving, there's a feeling

1

that there's more to this, more than $2 versus $4, more than the price of our weekly fill-up. At the gas pump, we're egregiously offended by big numbers and comforted by small ones. Big numbers make us sick. But why? The price of commodities, the price of nearly everything we use in abundance, has shot up during the last five years. So what makes gasoline so special? We don't have the same visceral reaction to, say, the price of grain—even though it goes into half of everything we eat and its price has more than doubled in recent years. Why does gasoline set off different, shriller alarms than other things we consistently buy? Perhaps that's our human intuition—an evolved sense that there's more to a situation than the mere face of it.

It turns out that our sense of intuition, honed by millennia of survival, is quite canny. The inexorable rising price at the pump represents several worlds of change beyond smaller cars and more cumbersome gas station charges. The price of oil—and thus, gasoline—affects our lives to a degree few realize. It's not just the BP or Shell portion of your Visa bill. It's the bricks in your walls, the plastic in your refrigerator, the asphalt on your roads, the shingles on your roof, the synthetic rubber in your ball. With every penny that gasoline moves up, so, too, does the price of most things we consume.

Stop what you're doing. Look around. Look on your desk, at your shoes, at your shirt, at your windows, your kitchen—how much of it comes from oil? More than you think. Look out your window— look out at the world—how much of it owes its existence to oil? Again, more than you think. The United States imports 67% of its oil, but only 40% of that goes into our vehicles' fuel tanks. The rest is used to make, fortify, and shape just about anything you can imagine.

Consider Bill McPetroman of Suburbia, USA, 2009

Bill lives like many of us do. He's an American suburbanite with a good job, nice house, nice family. Bill isn't rich, Bill isn't poor. Let's examine a typical Bill morning in 2009 as he gets up for a day at the office. For simplicity's sake, Bill's wonderful wife and children, who, let it be known, enjoy gasoline as much as he does, are on vacation at the family cabin; Bill will be joining them there this weekend.

It's Thursday morning. Bill gets up at 7 a.m. to the sound of his Sony clock radio, which is encased in plastic made from hydrocarbon molecules ripped from sweet crude oil at a Houston refinery. Just about everything plastic in our lives is made in a similar process with one main source: oil and its derivatives.

Bill rolls off his sheets, and puts his feet on the carpeted floor, whose fibers are made of nylon, one of the original and most successful plastics made from petrochemicals. He pads to the bathroom and puts a hand on his bathroom countertop, made of DuPont's Corian, a common household countertop material that is largely acrylic. DuPont makes Corian with a series of bonds between pigments, binders, and polymethyl methacrylate, a petrochemical, which, of course, comes from an oil refinery.

Bill generously lathers his face with shaving cream that smells like a man should smell. The lather, incidentally, is formed by an endless list of ingredients; one of its major building blocks, however, is polymethyl methacrylate, which, of course, comes from oil. Smoothly shaven, Bill pulls his nylon shower curtain back and hops into his bathroom's attractive preformed shower stall, made of chlorinated polyethylene, another one of those ubiquitous petrochemicals. Bill washes his hair with shampoo and conditioners made mostly of goopy hydrocarbons, linked and processed from oil; the same goes for his bar of soap. The plastic bristles and handle on his toothbrush, too, came from black gold.

Bill dresses and heads to the kitchen for breakfast. He shuffles across the kitchen floor, installed during a recent renovation; it's a beautiful engineered oak floor. This kind of floor holds up to all sorts of abuse and features a thin layer of oak, about one-eighth of an inch, glued on top of a rigid and burly pad of plywood. This common type of floor earns higher durability ratings than pure wood. It's held together with binders and glue that come almost exclusively from petrochemical plants processing crude oil.

Bill puts his coffee cup and cereal bowl down on his new kitchen countertop, which is man-made stone called Silestone. It's quite dazzling. The inch-and-a-quarter-thick Silestone slab is made of 95% quartz and 5% polymer resin. The resin, again, comes from oil. There isn't much in Bill's kitchen—in fact, in his whole house— that doesn't trace some aspect of its origins to the grinding cacophony of an oil well.

The same can be said for where Bill lives: a suburb thirty miles from the center of Chicago. His existence, his town's existence, and all of far-flung suburbia's existence, be it in Los Angeles, Paris, Dallas, or Tokyo, owes its life to vast fields in places like the Middle East, the North Sea, and the Gulf of Mexico. Having finished breakfast, Bill walks into his two-car garage and climbs into his Ford Explorer. He rattles down his street's immaculate strip of asphalt toward a six-lane highway that will take him to work, forty minutes away. Bill's normal evening hours are spent shuttling his children from athletic events to tutoring sessions to music lessons to shopping malls, all of which are located in disparate corners of his megaburb, which is more than five miles wide. Bill's Americanized materialistic existence, like all of ours, is wrapped in a cocoon of gasoline and its petro-bred brethren.

But there's more to this than the price of your, my, and Bill's stuff. The mounting cost of gas will dictate cultural changes, housing changes, civic changes, education changes—it will leave nary a spot on the globe, or how we live, unchanged. Not all of the change we face is gloomy. In fact, many people's lives, including many Americans' lives, will be improved across a panoply of facets. We will get more exercise, breathe fewer toxins, eat better food, and make a smaller impact on our earth. Giant businesses will rise as entrepreneurs' intrepid minds elegantly solve our society's mounting challenges as gasoline prices inevitably rise, changing the world economy and our lives forever. The world's next Google or Microsoft, the next great disrupter and megacompany, could well be conceived in this saga. It could be a battery company, a breakthrough solar outfit, or a radically innovative vehicle manufacturer. This revolution will be so widespread and affect so many that it will evoke the Internet's rise in the late 1990s.

But this revolution will be even bigger than that. The Internet allowed us to buy a book online, to peruse information at will and with speed. The rising price of gasoline, however, will reshape your house, your car, your town, your stores, your job, your life. America has never seen so great an innovation spur as escalating petroleum prices. This tale will bring with it all the global impact of a World War and its inherent technology revolutions—minus all the death. Some people even welcome oil's coming paucity and expense as one of humankind's grand experiments. And, in fact, it will be so. The future will be exhilarating.

This book acknowledges that future and embraces it. In these pages we want to tackle that omnipresent and intricate question: How will the rising price of gas affect our lives? There is a two-word, sophomoric answer to the question: a lot. But this is not a simple matter to debug. Oil and gasoline play such integral, piercing parts in our lives. At times their presence is beyond obvious, such as when we're pumping gasoline into our car on a hot afternoon for $3.50 a gallon. And at other times, gasoline's presence is more nuanced, but just as pervading, such as when a New Yorker buys a potato that's traveled from Idaho to her grocer, or when you turn up the thermostat during a chilly evening, or when you wrap leftovers in Saran Wrap, or when your local high school stops playing in statewide tournaments to save money.

The polygonal changes that rising gas prices will bring cut a puzzle that's hard to decipher. But the best—and the most entertaining—way to tame this subject is to section things according to what we pay at the pump. This book's chapters follow the cost of gasoline in the United States: Chapter $6, Chapter $8, Chapter $10, and so on. Each chapter details the changes, consequences, and innovation that each price level will bring. This approach proves to be particularly informative because our lives' adaptations will not arrive all at once, but will filter in gradually as the price of petroleum dictates. Each increase in price will bring with it new pain that will force us to adapt. Each dollar increase in the price of gasoline will crank different gears of change: $8 gas isn't $10 gas, and $12 gas isn't $14 gas. Each extra dollar unlocks new possibilities and ushers out an old product or way of life. Each chapter will focus on one or two major changes brought about by this particular gas price, as well as a coterie of other, smaller events connected to this price. Our lives will transform on innumerable fronts—socially, economically, and so on—as we go from $6 to $8 to $10 and beyond.

Why the Price of Gas Will Keep Climbing (Why the Following Chapters Matter)

The plausibility of these scenarios, these hypothetical worlds that each chapter will project—America at $8-a-gallon gas or $14-a-gallon gas—depends on gasoline's increasing scarcity and, of course, its increasing cost. There still exist thousands of people, some of whom preach from very public pulpits—editorial pages, magazines, television—that say expensive oil will be a temporary blip in our continued and apparently endless path of gluttonous consumption. Gas prices, these people say, are artificially goosed up by nervous traders and reckless speculators; normalcy will return soon, they assure us, as it did in the latter months of 2008. But normalcy, for better or worse, is already gone. Gas prices had to go up, and so they did.

The sunny "this is merely a passing bubble" outlook—unfortunately for Hummer drivers and the airlines—has taken no measure of world economics, demographics, or capitalism. The following two statements, in most sane circles, are accepted as fact:

1. The demand for oil will gradually increase and will continue to increase as the global middle class expands.
2. The oil that remains in the earth will be more and more expensive to locate and extract.

Those two statements lead us to a third conclusion:

3. The price of gas will climb to prices far past where we're at right now.

The swooning momentum of oil prices can be a tricky bull to corral. Wild upward swings in gas prices will usually be mitigated by a downward correction. Oil's price volatility is not anomalous to the ridiculous and heady explosion—and resulting implosion—of housing prices that we've seen over the last eight years. But the oil market moves much faster. A price spike can last several months and its resulting correction another month or two, compared with the years of booming home values and the subsequent multiyear downturn. The difference, however, is an important one: There is always less oil and always more people who want it. We're always building more houses, but we can't make more oil. So while gas prices will swing up and down, season to season, month to month, the consistent, durable trend will be one of increasing price.

Though global oil demand eroded in 2008 and 2009 owing to the world's acute economic malaise, that lull will be temporary. Any future economic expansion in the near term will mean further increases in oil demand. Oil demand has risen—and will keep rising—

in tandem with a burgeoning worldwide middle class, the fastest-growing segment of global population. The world's total population will jump by 1 billion in the coming twelve years, but the middle class will add 1.8 billion to its ranks, 600 million of them in China alone. Researchers at the Brookings Institution estimate that the middle class will comprise 52% of the earth's total population by 2020—up from 30% now. China's middle class will be the world's largest in 2025, and India's will be ten times its current size.

Consider this: The United States has 750 cars for every 1,000 people. China, on the other hand, has 4 cars for every 1,000 people. If China gets to only half the ownership rate of the United States, it means an additional 400 million cars on the road, looking for gasoline.[1] That's almost like adding another two United States' worth of cars to the world. Moreover, even if the price of oil gets so high that it creates serious demand destruction in places like the United States and Europe, the use of oil will still increase in economies such as China's, which is growing at a 10% clip. Growth that size doesn't evaporate overnight. And economies, especially China's, need oil and energy to grow.

What does it mean to be middle class? It means to have a home, to have a regular income, to have consumer freedom, to drive a gas-burning vehicle, and in general, to consume. When people consume, they consume oil. It takes oil to power your car, to make your plastic yogurt cup, to harvest the grain that makes your bread, to transport the livestock that will be your meat. It takes fuel to ship the clothes, gadgets, and items that middle-class people buy and use. It takes petroleum to create the chemicals and compounds that go into so much we use today, including computers, cars, homes, and infrastructure. Car sales may be down or flat in Europe and the United States, and they may remain that way, but places like China, India, and Russia will, over the long term, continue to add cars to their roads.

The Middle Class Not Only Expands, But Also Descends, Thanks to The People's Car

As more people make more money and ascend toward the middle class, globalization works to pull the middle class down toward more people. India's Tata Motors began making a car called the Nano in 2008. The Nano has become an international superstar, burnishing Tata's emergence as a world automotive player and ginning demand for the car before the first one even left the factory. At the 2008 Geneva auto show—usually the glitzy province of strutting Porsches and BMWs—the diminutive Nano stole the show, its displays consistently mobbed by Europeans and international press. The car has a Facebook page that draws millions of hits. Before the vehicle was released, bootleg video clips that caught test models on the highways of India soared in YouTube popularity.

What makes the Nano so popular? It's pushed along—literally, the engine is in the rear—by a tiny two-cylinder, 623-cubic-centimeter engine made out of aluminum. Its dashboard features three things: a speedometer, a fuel gauge, and an oil light. It has one windshield wiper, a small front trunk, and on the basic model, no radio, air conditioning, or power steering. So—again—what's the hype about? It's about the car's cost: $2,500; and its efficiency: 48 miles a gallon, no batteries necessary. That's a new, ultraefficient car for the same price as an upper-end laptop computer.

The Nano and scores of other equalizing products like it (most of them not quite as dramatic) have made being middle class a reality for billions of people traversing the murky zone between poverty and comfortable living. Even with gas topping $4 or $5 or $10, billions of previously carless people can afford a vehicle that costs them a mere $2,500 and gets such fabulous mileage.

Tata has dubbed its phenom "The People's Car." Indeed, millions in India are champing to dump their mopeds and bicycles for

Nanos. One of those people is Uttam Shivhare. He drives a three-wheeled motorized rickshaw for a living in Varanasi, a holy city in Northern India populated mostly by Hindus. The forty-year-old makes $150 a month for weaving his rickshaw taxi in and out of the cramped streets and alleyways of Varanasi, picking up and depositing customers as he goes. Shivhare's rickshaw has a canvas roof but no doors, and if passengers scrunch, as they often do, it can fit three people in its backseat. As an owner of motorized transportation, he is respected. But, Shivhare says, real community respect comes with owning a legitimate automobile—doors, roof, trunk, and all. The cheapest car on the market before the Nano's launch was the Suzuki Maruti 800, at about $5,000, well beyond Shivhare's means. But a Nano, at half that price, makes joining the car-driving middle class possible for Shivhare. Shivhare's teenaged daughter, Shubham, and his son, Samiksha, first told him about the Nano after reading about it in English dailies. "All their friends who are from rich families have cars but we could never afford one," Shivhare says. "Now we can," he beams.

People like Shivhare, who make money and live with fierce desires to upgrade their families' lives with an automobile, exist by the millions. Perhaps even the billions. Those people, through the emergence of their countries' flourishing economies, will get their chance. And they deserve that chance. But it means more people needing more oil. Imagine if the Nano adds a mere 3 million new drivers to the roads across the world and each one of them drives an average of 15,000 miles a year. That creates demand for an additional 1 billion gallons of gasoline a year. And 3 million new drivers is a wildly conservative number, considering India and its neighbor China, with 2.4 billion people together, have more than a third of the world's population, most of whom don't yet drive cars.

Not only are places like India, a net oil importer, devouring more and more oil, but the net exporters, places like Iran and Saudi Arabia, are gobbling up more, and shipping out less, of the resource that their economies are built on. The population of the Middle East has doubled in the last thirty years. That population demands more oil, meaning that less and less of it makes it into world markets each year. Iran and Saudi Arabia actually subsidize gasoline for their populations. Part of that calculus is economic, part of it pure survival tactics by the ruling powers, trying to ensure their popularity with fickle yet subdued electorates.

Saudi Arabia is building dozens of power plants across its sandy expanse to handle the growing demands of its petrochemical business, which turns hydrocarbons into useful industrial compounds. The new power plants don't run on coal or enriched uranium, as they do here in the United States. They run on oil, keeping billions of barrels of oil from gasoline refineries. Iran used to export 70% of its crude, but now sends out only 50%, as their own middle classes have grown and domestic demand has increased. Saudi Arabia's oil consumption has increased 6% a year during the last five years while Iran's has jumped 8% a year; Venezuela, another big exporter, has seen domestic demand spike 10% a year during this time.[2] The Saudis have made a lot of noise about their plans to become a provider of all energy, be it solar, wind, or oil, but those plans are existentially tied to their oil reserves. Nothing the Saudis will do can replace the boggling wealth that pours into their country like oil oozes from its desert. The turn toward alternative energy on the Arabian Peninsula amounts to window dressing for its one real industry: oil.

As the middle class continues to explode in China, India, and scores of other spots circling the earth, hundreds of millions of additional cars will hit the roads, giving rise to more demand for gasoline and other petroleum-based products. People want what Americans have had for decades: easy cars and an easy life. These people will get what they want, but in the process they will catalyze a global economic reformation on a scale never seen, changing our lives, changing their lives, changing the earth.

There Remains Little Easy-to-Get Oil

New people every day get introduced to levels of lifestyle and income that add to the demand for the world's oil. That pressures demand on one side. On the other side, the supply side, petroleum has been getting harder to find and extract from the earth. Of all the statistics telling us oil is getting harder to find, none are so compelling as this: For each six barrels of oil we consume, we find one.[3] The Texas and Saudi Arabia–style gushers of yore are exactly that: the past's myth and lore. There are no more undiscovered fields such as those. We now work harder than ever to get a barrel of oil to the surface, especially from deep-sea wells and aging fields that require all manner of expensive and complicated tricks, such as injecting water into source rock to force out more oil. We have hit what's popularly known as *peak oil*, meaning that global production of crude is at a zenith that will never again be realized. The evidence supporting *peak oil* as a current phenomenon is compelling.

A founded argument for oil's increasing scarcity has been made best and most famously by Ali Samsam Bakhtiari, a former director of the National Iranian Oil Company, who died in 2007. In one of the Ph.D.'s last research essays, he wrote this about the world's oil production:

> After some 147 years of almost uninterrupted supply growth to a record output of some 81–82 million barrels/ day [mb/d] in the summer of 2006, crude oil production has since entered its irreversible decline. This exceptional reversal alters the energy supply equation upon which life on our planet is based. It will come to place pressure upon the use of all other sources of energy—be it natural gas, coal, nuclear power, and all types of sun-

dry renewables especially biofuels. It will eventually come to affect everything else under the sun.[4]

He is not alone in his dire outlook. T. Boone Pickens, a man who has built a $3 billion fortune on oil and gas, said at a Forbes CEO conference, "The world has been looked at. There's still oil to be found, but not in the quantities we've seen in the past. The big fields have all been found and the smaller fields, well, there's not enough of them to replenish the base . . . If I'm right, we're already at the peak. The price will have to go up."

Pickens has taken things a step further. The lifelong oilman is calling for the United States to stop blowing $700 billion a year on foreign oil and has tried to create a pop buzz for wind power, on which he and other investors plan to dump $10 billion for a massive project in the Texas panhandle. Perhaps this is an eighty-year-old trying to cement an eternal legacy. Perhaps this is just T. Boone, the billionaire, trying to make another billion. Whatever it is, the shrewd Wall Street raider wouldn't be jamming himself into this business unless he thought that conventional energy—oil—was on the wane.

It doesn't help that the ten largest holders of oil reserves in the world are state-owned oil companies in countries such as Russia, Iran, and Venezuela, which aren't particularly friendly toward the West.[5] The world's giant independent oil companies, like Exxon Mobil, Royal Dutch Shell, BP, and Chevron, have the most experience and best methods for bringing hard-to-get crude to the surface and for maximizing the value of maturing fields. These companies once controlled more than half the production of the world's crude, but have been reduced to 13% as bouts of resource nationalism have pushed them out of countries such as Nigeria, Venezuela, Bolivia, and Russia, reducing efficiencies in those countries as well as supply out of them. The big multinational oil companies are desperate for places to spend on exploration, but have few promising places to do it. As a result, these companies spent only $11 billion on exploration in 2007, while spending $58 billion on share buybacks, five times what they spent on exploration.[6]

The United States has now burned through 70% of its oil.[7] But we're so desperate that we're drilling at a pace we haven't approached in more than two decades: 40,000 wells a year. No matter, our production continues to decline. But that's hardly surprising to most people. What's jarring: The declining production of half of the twenty largest oil-producing countries. These countries comprise 85% of all oil produced.[8] What's more, half of the world's oil is supplied by just .03% of its oil fields. This underlines the importance of the megafield—when the megafields' productions start ebbing, then it's likely the world's supply has begun an irreversible decline.

Production in many of these fields, such as Mexico's mammoth Cantarell Field, has already begun slipping, according to Pemex, Mexico's national oil company. Many experts also believe that Gharwar, Saudi Arabia's monster field and the largest in the world, has begun declining as well. Oil fields typically go into decline after fifty years of use. The average age of the world's fourteen biggest oil fields: an alarming forty-nine years.[9] Oil from these sources can cost as little as $1.50 a barrel to produce. Easy production from places like these helps alleviate price pressure from newer, more expensive sources like Alberta's tar sands, where oil can cost $60 a barrel or more to produce. Even at $5 a gallon (a mere 31 cents a cup), people don't realize how inexpensive gasoline really is. Compare that price with Budweiser, at $13 a gallon, or Coke at $8 a gallon, or Evian water at $7.50 a gallon. The decline of old and cheap sources of oil will push the cost of gasoline, which handles the incomparable task of moving us around the world, well past the price of a gallon of bottled French water, which is no better for you than what comes out of the tap in America for mere pennies.

Our Oil Infrastructure Is Crumbling and It Needs More Than Rustoleum

In addition to the simple economics of rapidly rising demand and decreasing supply, there exists another future pressure on gasoline and energy prices: deteriorating infrastructure. Matthew Simmons, founder of Simmons & Company International, one of the world's premier oil investment banks, says that 80% of the world's refineries, pipelines, drilling rigs, and storage tanks are corroded, rusted to the point where replacement and retrofitting must begin soon.

This problem manifested in 2006 when BP's thirty-year-old Alaskan pipeline carrying Prudhoe Bay crude sprung a leak, spilling 270,000 gallons of oil into the pristine Alaskan bush. The pipeline sprang another leak in 2007. Our aging refineries face the same problems. In 2005, hydrocarbons spewed out of a breach in an isomerization tank at a BP refinery near Houston. The gushing stream ignited when it hit the air and killed fifteen people. Later that year at the same plant, a hydrogen pipe blew up. Again in the same year, at a BP plant nearby that handles hydrocarbons derived from crude oil, a fire engulfed part of the facility, its flames bursting fifty feet from the ground. The blaze couldn't be tamed; it burnt itself out after three days.[10]

Simmons says without rebuilding, failing infrastructure will bring massive declines of supply in the next decade as more and more pipelines, tanks, and refineries fail. Rebuilds and repairs could cost a boggling $50 trillion. Those are costs that, whether through decreased supply or through money spent on direly needed renovation, will be passed through the system to end users—us—and of course, will increase the price of petroleum at the pump.

As Oil's Price Climbs, So, Too, Will the Costs of All Energy

The costs of other energy sources, such as coal, natural gas, ethanol, and even nuclear power, will march up in price with oil. These cousins are indelibly melded together as part of the global energy grid. When the price of oil climbs, so, too, do the costs of coal and crop-based fuels. The dynamic functions as a market. If the price of oil quickly outstrips the price of all other energy sources, businesses and commerce will find ways to migrate their consumption toward energy not derived from oil. Effects aren't immediate, to be sure. If the price of oil doubles, causing heating oil to appreciate similarly, heating oil consumers won't rapidly switch to natural gas–fired furnaces.

It's important to remember that a future of higher gasoline prices means higher energy prices across the board. The provoking conundrum here, and what this book explores, is how will we adjust to this—not only to higher gas prices but also to scarcer and higher energy prices across the board? Expensive energy, for some, will be strictly a burden. For others, it will be an opportunity for innovation. How will our lives be different, worse or better? Where will we capture the efficiencies needed to sustain our elaborate civilization? Will our homes look the same? Our offices? Our vehicles? Our neighborhoods? Our food?

It will all change. The price of gas will leverage change, fundamentally altering nearly every facet of our lives.

CHAPTER $6

Society Change and the Dead SUV

A t $4 a gallon, Americans cut back their driving by billions of miles. SUV plants were shut down. Hybrid cars became best sellers. Detroit's sales lots became lonely places. Families cut back on vacations, rationed car use, and left their 4Runners and Explorers in the garage in favor of driving their sedans. The economy stalled. Four-dollar gas sharply pierced American psyches with the realization that our lives must change, that the old way of living, the way we've built our society since World War II—bigger, bigger, better—could actually be in peril. The effects of $4 gas mimed those of the Arab oil embargoes in the 1970s. Except this time, there was no embargo. Just more demand. Just billions more people, from the African continent to central Asia and the Far East, realizing their economic ambitions and rising to become oil consumers of consequence. And those people aren't going away. Their ranks will only grow. To be sure, investor speculation in the oil market played a role in crude's swift rise, but that speculation was backed by a voracious global demand with roots in global economic expansion. That demand can be muffled by global recessions and regional slowdowns, but it will always reemerge intact, as more people demand more energy.

17

With so many changes precipitating with gas prices at $4, it's clear that $6 gas will bring even more dramatic change. This price will set massive gears gnashing, gears that will eventually change nearly every aspect of our lives, some for bad, some for good. Six dollars will be a calling card, a dawn, a pendulum rocker. At $4, there remains hope in many people's guts that expensive fuel will recede far into the past and that prices of $2, or even $1.50, will return for good. Those hopes, misbegotten and childishly optimistic, will be finally dashed at $6. The lusty days of $2 gas will be firmly in the forgotten past as our new world unfolds. At $6, our lives, our businesses, our families, will all be caught, unready for the coming cavalcade of evolution and adaptation that rising gas prices will bring.

Monthly gas station bills for families that were $400 at $2 will be $1,200 at $6. Our economy, and even our societal fabric, will suffer a stiff jab to the mouth when gas tickles $6. Changes that were merely budding at $4 will bloom in full. The $6 price level will activate change like no other. It will serve as a bellwether to American society that the way we consume energy is unsustainable.

What happens at $6 will be a prelude to $8, $12, and $20. It's here where Americans will be truly shocked and deeply affected. But it's also here where Americans will pause, take measure, and accept a future of higher energy costs. Denial still runs deep and swift at $4; people can convince themselves that cheaper gas— normalcy—will return. That moat of unfounded reasoning will quickly dry out once prices reach $6. Energy will cost more, but we'll use less and we'll use it smarter.

But our acceptance of things will not shield our economy and our lives from the pain that comes with more expensive gas. We will not be prepared. Our shipping services won't be prepared, nor will our homes, our food, our children, our jobs, or our cars. Four-dollar gas made life more expensive. Six-dollar gas, however, will mark the beginnings of true change. Four-dollar gas meant our public transportation systems saw 300 million more trips in 2008 than in 2007. San Francisco's rapid transit system, BART, once a neglected novelty, removed seats from its trains to make room for more people to pack on and stand.[1] In Boston, the number of cars on its infamous Mass Pike dropped by millions in 2008 and public officials implored mass-transit passengers to travel during off-peak times to mitigate crowding problems on the city's "T" subway system. In Chicago, riders swamped "L" trains even more than usual, despite the fact that, owing to massive overhauls on many tracks, some trains were running at their all-time slowest. At $6, public transit will be the absolute belle of the ball. Our subways will overflow further, trains will be added, and new routes proposed. But that's not even half of the $6 story.

The Big Snowball: What We Drive, and How We Drive It, Will Change Indelibly

Six-dollar gas, though its specter may sound implausible, isn't too far away, says Jeffrey Rubin, a respected economist and the chief strategist and managing director of CIBC world markets. Rubin says gasoline will likely cost $7 a gallon by 2010. As a result, he says, "Over the next four years, we are likely to witness the greatest mass exodus of vehicles off America's highways in history. By 2012, there should be some 10 million fewer vehicles on American roadways than there are today—a decline that dwarfs all previous adjustments including those during the two OPEC oil shocks."

No realm of our lives will be affected faster, and no corner of big business will be rocked harder, than that of the vehicles we drive. Of those 10 million vehicles that Rubin predicts will come off U.S. roads, many will be SUVs. In fact, if you examine things with an eye toward a kind of natural selection of automobiles in a world of $6 gas, it's pragmatic and reasonable to expect that most of the vehicles coming off the road will be the guzzlers, the SUVs, the nonessential pickup trucks, the low-end sports cars. Those are the cars that people won't want.

Small cars will be worth money. Large cars will be worth very little. Prices of nimble fuel sippers will hold up incredibly well. We've already seen this effect, in fact, when gas was $4 a gallon in 2008. Two-year-old Honda Civics, in demand for their brisk fuel economy and low-maintenance reputations, were selling for $16,000, or 85% of what a new Civic cost at that time, according to J. D. Power & Associates. A similar two-year-old Toyota Prius, the hybrid car that's becoming ubiquitous in American cities, ran 87% of the new-model price. Used cars of that age normally cost 50% to 60% of what a new model costs.[2]

When gas hovered at $4, our beloved SUVs rapidly depreciated. They were impossible to sell; nobody wanted a car that seemed to be facing its twilight. When gas reaches $6, our SUVs will look like scrap metal in our minds' eyes. They will be intractably obsolete testaments to a time when oil came easy and cheaply. The whole country will sit up, take notice, and realize that, in driving our SUVs, we have been piloting vehicles that were simply unsustainable luxuries unique to this time in history. The SUV's traction in the auto market teetered ominously when gas cost $4 a gallon. At $6, the SUV will die.

Many people enjoy slathering the blame for our bloated domestic vehicles squarely on the big three Detroit automakers. We bemoan them as out of touch and foolish when compared to their nimble counterparts from Japan. "What a bunch of morons," we say. "Didn't they learn anything from the 1970s and 1980s?"

They did. As consumers, we learned a few things, too. But we rapidly jettisoned these lessons of scrimp and economy with the gas-and-go 1990s amid blistering economic growth and ridiculously low gas prices. Detroit merely followed our lead; they made what we wanted. As consumers, our tastes for giant vehicles created the demand. Detroit simply filled that demand. And in the process, Detroit made a ton of money. And isn't that the whole point, when it comes to a corporation? What should Detroit have done? Neglect their shareholders and the capitalist model to stubbornly crank out small cars that nobody wanted? No. They did what they did to make money. Toyota and Nissan noticed. They jumped in with their own giant vehicles, chasing the same customers. And it worked. It worked until the SUV party stopped bumping when gas prices sped past $3 a gallon in early 2008. Gas prices have since been tempered by floundering demand and a struggling global economy, but those conditions won't last forever. Even with the downturn in gas prices, SUV sales have not perked up much; Americans have developed a sense of inevitability regarding the SUV's ultimate doom.

The tale of the SUV and America is an incredible economic parable. It's a study in elastic demand and its wild swings of enriching glory and muddy tragedy. It's a story framed by lust, vanity, money, and—playing the role of protagonist, or antagonist, depending on one's view—the price of gasoline.

How America Got Hooked on the SUV

To understand how we've gotten to become a nation of gasthirsty, steel-craving gasoline munchers, it's important to know how the last twenty years have unfolded. The last two decades have featured a collision of storms, economic and societal, that have shaped Americans' tastes and stretched the limits of consumption. Some of the cheapest oil in history coincided with the rise of SUVs, which engorged the bigger-fatter-better trend to an exponential degree here in the United States. Our society evolved from being one of savers, scrimpers, and pragmatists to being one of flaunters, competitors, and cravers. The gross enlargement of the standard American vehicle came even after the severe oil scares in the 1970s and early 1980s deflated the size of most Americans' cars. We blithely forgot—even with those memories of long gas station lines lodged somewhere in baby boomers' heads—how volatile the gas pump can be.

The SUV's early roots can be traced back to the middle years of the twentieth century, when companies such as Willys, Kaiser Jeep, and Chevrolet were turning out boxy passenger carriers bolted to pickup truck frames.[3] The vanguards were the Wagoneer and the Suburban. Ford joined the fray in 1965 with a burly two-door Bronco model. Chevy added the Blazer soon thereafter. These vehicles were aimed at niche customers who needed robust ground clearances and superior traction to drive where they had to drive—and that didn't mean to the supermarket for cold cuts and ice cream sandwiches. SUV owners were farmers, ranchers, and government land stewards. The trucks had little appeal to suburban families, who preferred their smooth-riding station wagons. Four-wheel drive existed, but it didn't carry the cachet or desirability with the general populace that accompanies it now.

The modern SUV's true birth came with the 1984 Jeep Cherokee. Its success with consumers as an alternative to the station wagon or the nascent but popular minivan induced Chrysler to acquire AMC, the owner of Jeep, in 1987. The Cherokee continued its success with baby boomers eager to differentiate themselves from those driving homey wagons and vans. But the Cherokee was only a snowflake to the coming avalanche: the Ford Explorer. The Explorer, debuting in 1990, got its owners 15 miles per gallon in the city and 20 mpg on the highway. That mileage came with its original V6 engine. In ensuing years, Ford made a V8 model available, which got even lower mileage. But that didn't hurt its popularity. Even with the first Iraq war raising oil prices and a short recession blanketing the country, there was no dampening the phenomenon of the Ford Explorer, the undisputed champ of the SUV age. Ford has sold more than 6 million Explorers during the last eighteen years, making it, by far, the most popular SUV to growl across American roads. In 2000, the truck reached its pinnacle as Ford sold a record 450,000 Explorers. That was the same year Toyota debuted its Prius hybrid in the United States, selling fewer than 15,000 of the fuel miser. Things have changed: Annual sales for the Prius passed the Explorer in 2007. Toyota has now sold more than 1 million Priuses.[4]

The Explorer and its 1990s contemporaries exploited federal fuel-economy laws that said an automaker's car fleet had to average 27.5 mpg, but light truck fleets needed only to average 20.5 mpg. The Explorer and others of its ilk, such as the Jeep Grand Cherokee, were, thanks to the tireless work of Detroit's high-paid Washington lobbyists, classified as light trucks. That illustrates the power wielded by well-funded lobbyists; nobody with a string of integrity could honestly argue these vehicles were light trucks meant to transport materials and goods. SUVs, clearly, are passenger vehicles. Anything with eight seats and twenty-seven cupholders is not a light truck. As the 1990s wore on, Ford improved its Explorer design—and made it even bigger—and customers kept flocking. Toyota crafted its 4Runner to fit the segment, Nissan launched the Pathfinder, GM rolled out a redesigned Blazer, and Chrysler kept pumping out Grand Cherokees and its new entrant, the hulking Dodge Durango. Each updated model, be it for the Explorer or the Blazer, got more luxurious and, more importantly, bigger.

Consumers' appetite for larger, brawnier SUVs led to a new animal: the full-size SUV. To somebody paying attention to automobile nomenclature, this may have been bewildering. So-called full-size SUVs already existed. Explorers, Blazers, Cherokees, and similar trucks—they were full-size. But this existing full-size segment, suddenly, had been relegated to mid-size status. The new full-sizers—the Chevy Tahoe, the Lincoln Navigator, the GMC Yukon, the Cadillac Escalade, the Toyota Sequoia, the Lexus LX-450, the

Hummer, and the Ford Expedition—were moving in. And Americans loved them.

No example better illustrates our obsession with monster vehicles than the story of the Ford Expedition. Its tale will be recounted in economics classes for generations. Ford's Michigan Truck Plant, a Ford factory outside Detroit in the town of Wayne, began assembling the Expedition in the summer of 1996.[5] Ford thought the giant Expedition would be a nice, profitable niche vehicle to go with its smaller, more mainstream Explorer. At 12 mpg in the city and 17 mpg on the highway, the Expedition, Ford thought, couldn't appeal to a wide swath of customers. Ford was wrong. The Michigan Truck Plant originally was going to spend half its time producing F-150 pickups in addition to making Expeditions. That arrangement lasted a few months. Americans went bananas for the Expedition and Ford couldn't keep up. The Michigan Truck Plant began making SUVs exclusively within a few months of the Expedition's debut. Soon, the factory was running twenty-four hours a day, six days a week. Some unionized autoworkers were pulling down $200,000 a year with overtime. In 1998, the plant's revenues—just this one building—were $11 billion, about equal to McDonald's global revenues that year. Each year the plant was churning out 300,000 Expeditions and Navigators, generating as much as $15,000 in profit on each of the monster SUVs. Ford had fifty-three assembly plants across the globe in 1998, but the Michigan Truck Plant accounted for a third of the company's profits by itself,[6] nearly $4 billion. It was the most lucrative factory in the world.

The SUV revived the moribund American auto industry, which had been getting whipped by Japan's more dependable and more fuel-efficient fleets. In 1998, just after Daimler and Chrysler had merged, the three largest companies in the world by sales were GM, Ford, and DaimlerChrysler, not in small part due to the SUV. Here was a vehicle that Detroit had been making for decades—the pickup truck—and to sell it for twice the normal price, all Detroit had to do was slap on a few more doors and a couple rows of seats. And why not roll out some luxury models? The most successful, the Cadillac Escalade, was nothing but a GMC Yukon spiffed up with additional sound dampening, some chrome, and a few minor modifications. And the GMC Yukon, of course, was nothing but a slightly nicer Chevy Tahoe, which was, of course, a Chevy Silverado pickup truck with some seats and a roof. GM made the Escalade for $25,000 and people scrambled to buy them for $50,000. Most carmakers—Toyota, Ford, Chrysler, and GM—got into the luxury SUV game; it was simply too profitable not to. In 1990, cars made up 90% of the luxury market. By 1996, cars had been relegated to 44%, with SUVs scooping up the majority.[7]

The giant SUVs were expensive, inefficient, gaudy, and perhaps worst of all, unsafe. In his book on the SUV popularity surge and its dangers, *High and Mighty*, *New York Times* writer Keith Bradsher compared driving an Escalade to "a pig on stilts." So be it, Detroit said. "If pigs are big and popular, I guess we'll make pigs," quipped Harry Pearce, vice chairman of GM in 2000. So the pigs, which were prone to rolling over and hard to maneuver, kept coming.

The dazzling rise of SUVs had roots in many things, not the least of which was Americans' mercurial psyches. According to some of American automakers' own market researchers, the type of people who tend to buy SUVs are insecure and vain. They're people who frequently are nervous about their marriages and uncomfortable about having become parents. They have little confidence in their skills as drivers. And more than anything else, they're self-absorbed and narcissistic, with little interest in their communities and neighbors.[8] Those aren't my own observations. They come straight from marketing folks on Detroit carmakers' payrolls, who recounted their research to Mr. Bradsher. The carmakers, in this sense, can be depended on. Their market research is exhaustive, detailed, expensive, and massive in its scale. Perhaps you're reading this and appraising your own character right now, on account of something you may park or have parked in your garage. I know the feeling. I drove an old Toyota 4Runner all over the country for a decade—running the odometer past 240,000 miles—and I loved it.

Oil Prices Enabled the SUV to Thrive, but They Will Ultimately Bury the SUV in its Grave

We can't fully blame ugly American attitudes for the rise of the Jeep Grand Cherokee, the Expedition, and the rest of their brood. SUV mania and Detroit's renaissance rose, not coincidentally, with the lowest oil prices the modern world has ever seen. Oil in 1998 averaged $15.35 a barrel in today's dollars. The next cheapest year was 1946, when oil sold for $17.26. Many parts of the country in 1998—just a decade ago—saw gas prices of well below $1. Driving from Illinois to New Orleans on a trip with friends that year, I paid 59 cents a gallon at a gas station in Missouri. I filled the tank for 7 bucks. Gas wasn't free, but it was close. Roaming the country was limited by one's stamina and caffeine tolerance, not by money.

Low oil brought casualties, too. Amid the record-low oil prices in 1999, GM trashed its ballyhooed electric car, the EV1, which it had spent billions to develop during the 1990s. The car had just started rolling off a Lansing, Michigan, assembly line in 1996.[9] Electric cars and subcompacts were of little use to Americans with gas at a buck or less.

Cheap gas also fueled a pickup truck boom. Ford sold 939,000 of them in 2004, a record. Pickup trucks, because of their functionality, will persevere at $6, but normal people won't consider them for a spot in the garage, as they have in the past. The days of driving a truck purely as a statement of machismo, or a subconscious sense of insecurity, will be gone. These feelings can't be indulged at $6 a gallon.

Gas prices of $4 during 2008 gave us a clear vision of what to expect when gas reaches $6. Trucks, vans, and SUVs comprised two-thirds of Ford's 2004 sales in the United States. Things have changed since then. Amid rising gas prices, Ford lost $15.3 billion in 2006 and 2007 combined. In the summer of 2008, Ford shut down production at its Michigan Truck Plant for more than a month before announcing that the famed factory would stop making Ford Expeditions and Lincoln Navigators altogether. Ford is spending $75 million to make its truck plant into a compact car plant. The factory switched to producing the Ford Focus, and some employees even worked overtime at the plant during 2008 to keep up supply of the compact car, whose sales boomed amid $4 gas.

Mirroring what will surely be more severe effects when gas reaches $6, $4 gas sent our carmakers to the brink of death. Expeditions, Navigators, Tahoes, and Jeeps piled up at dealerships, with few takers even with giant incentives and discounts. GM will shutter at least four SUV and truck plants by 2010. When gas reaches $6, all SUV plants will close. GM, the fallen icon, lost $39 billion in 2007 and $15 billion just in the second quarter of 2008 amid growing American rejection of its giant and profitable trucks. When gas reached $4, Chrysler, with few compact offerings, was reduced to proffering lame promotions such as guaranteeing Jeep buyers $2.99 a gallon gasoline for the first two years they own their vehicle.

As our cars morph smaller, so will some of the companies who sell them to us. By the time you read this, one or more of the big three American carmakers may have already succumbed to the combined effects of high 2008 oil prices and an economic slowdown. Six-dollar gas will further challenge the survivors, perhaps reducing the Big Three to the Big One.

"Six-dollar gas will wreak havoc on the industry, no doubt," says Mike Jackson, director of North American vehicle forecasts at CSM Worldwide, an international analyst firm. "It will signal a whole new era for carmakers. They will change or they will perish."

Americans Will, at Long Last, Embrace Diesel When Gas Reaches $6 a Gallon

Diesel engines, long ignored and often maligned in North America, will begin to settle in at the American table when gas goes to $6. Ford has a car for sale in Europe right now that gets 65 miles per gallon. The car is attractive, seats five, and has an onboard navigation system. And it's a diesel. It's called the 2009 Ford Fiesta ECOnetic.

Volkswagen, Mercedes, and BMW have plans to get new cars utilizing clean diesel technology to the North American market starting in 2009. Diesel engines, invented by Germany's Rudolf Diesel in the late 1800s, can get as much as 50% more mileage out of a gallon for two reasons. The first is that a gallon of diesel fuel contains about 17% more energy than a gallon of normal gasoline. The hydrocarbons in diesel fuel are made out of longer chains of hydrogen molecules, making the fuel heavier and more dense with energy. The second reason diesel engines do better revolves around how they explode fuel. A conventional gasoline engine takes in air and gasoline, compresses the mixture with a piston, and ignites it with a spark plug. The resulting explosion pushes the piston down, which ultimately drives the car's wheels. A diesel engine's pistons compress air alone, no gasoline, to a pressure about double that of a conventional engine's compression. The air in the diesel engine rapidly heats up when it's compressed. When the temperature of the compressed air is near its peak, the diesel engine injects the fuel, which explodes from the heat of the air, forcing the piston down. Diesel engines have no spark plugs. The higher compression rate leads to higher efficiencies and to additional power. Here's a simplified way of looking at the diesel advantage: When all of the oxygen molecules are packed so closely together in high compression, the fuel stands a greater chance of quickly reacting with the air, making for a more efficient explosion.

Diesel cars, like Ford's ECOnetic, will see their fortunes burgeon when gas reaches $6. Car shoppers in the United States aren't going to care much about diesel knock, the rattling noise a diesel engine makes, or their slower accelerations. And many of those quirks have been smoothed out, in fact, in some of the new-generation diesel engines being released by VW, Ford, and Mercedes. The other big and legitimate snipe on diesel engines in the past is that they're dirty and fundamentally worse for the environment than our standard gasoline engines. That used to be true. But the new, so-called green diesel engines hitting the market now run just as clean as a gas engine, in some cases cleaner. Improving the distribution infrastructure for diesel fuel won't cost much because it's largely already in place—our trucks and semis have long leveraged the advantages of diesel engines.

Six-Dollar Gas Will Mean Fewer Lives Lost to Crumpled Steel and Unyielding Pavement

There will be painful economic adjustments. But not all of our adjustments will be agonizing. Some of the first dominoes to tumble will be beneficial for all of us. The graph representing the number of miles driven by Americans annually is a consistent set of stairs, each stair reaching higher than the previous stair. Anybody climbing those stairs would be in for a surprise when they reached for the tread of 2008—because, as was mentioned earlier, that stair was *lower* than the previous stair for the first time in nearly thirty years. High gas prices compelled Americans to drive 100 billion fewer miles in 2008 than they did in 2007. That's a good thing. In some ways, it's an excellent thing. Harvard and the University of Alabama determined that for every 10% gas price increase, there's a resulting decline of 2.3% in the number of driving deaths nation-wide.[10] That means a shift from $4 gas to $6 gas would save 4,000 lives. That's a third more people than America lost in the 2001 attacks on the World Trade Center.

David Grabowski, a professor of health care policy at Harvard Medical School and one of the study's authors, says that, when putting the paper together, they didn't examine gas prices as high as $4 or $6, because they were limited to available data sets of historical prices that hadn't yet reached those heights. But he believes that, starting at $4, the tale of statistics will become even more dramatic. "There's plenty of evidence that these higher prices of six and eight dollars will bring about change even faster than increases in the past," Grabowski says.

Grabowski has done some complicated extrapolations, however, to plot his data according to theoretical $4 gas prices. Assuming the prices are sustained for a year, gas prices of $4 would save 1,000 lives every month compared with the current driving fatality rates. That's 12,000 people annually, almost a third of those killed on U.S. roads every year.

"In the short run, the changes we make in our lives according to gas prices are very superficial," Grabowski says. "But in the long run, the changes add up and the results are staggering."

Taking things further, to our world of $6 gas, Grabowski sees changes sustained and habits reforged, a civilization adapting its lifestyles and modes of transportation. He expects 15,600 lives to be saved annually at $6 gas (compared to $2.50 gas). At $8, 18,000 lives saved a year; at $10, 20,000 lives.

Those numbers could even be conservative, Grabowski says. "I think it's not going to be a purely linear progression. We will probably see accelerating rates on things like this," he says. "People really aren't able to make major changes to their lives when gas just spikes in price. But when those prices are sustained for years, that's when people change their lives."

The numbers in Grabowski's study reflected gas prices rising at a time when, for the most part, the number of SUVs on the road was rising or flat. His numbers reflect, merely, the effect of fewer cars crowding our roads. Grabowski's calculations do not account for the fact that many of the cars that will be leaving our roads when gas reaches $6 will be the most dangerous ones. SUVs, when it comes to accidents, are decent at protecting the people inside the SUV, but in all other respects, their effect on the safety of our roads is a negative one. The obvious problem is that SUVs inflict colossal damage on those they hit. "Nobody wants to be in the Yugo," says Grabowski. "They want to be in the Range Rover."

The real problem with an SUV stems not from how it protects its passengers, but from its inability to avoid accidents. SUVs flip easily and can't easily swerve to avoid contact. A driver of a small Toyota Corolla, seeing a pileup accident suddenly forming ahead of him, may veer to another lane or a shoulder in time to avoid smashing through the tailgate window of the kid-filled station wagon ahead of him. Because of its mushy handling and outsized momentum, the Range Rover—or Explorer, Grand Cherokee, or Tahoe—is far more likely to barrel into the back of the station wagon, bringing its full girth to bear on the pileup crash.

When gas hits $6, fewer SUVs on our roads will mean fewer accidents and fewer people dead. The same can be said for pickup trucks. Safety statistics compiled by Tom Wenzel, a scientist at the Lawrence Berkeley National Laboratory in California, and by Marc Ross, a University of Michigan physicist, bear out the theory that SUVs can wreak more death on our roads than normal cars. Their research expresses the numbers of driver deaths per million vehicles of a given model. In a separate statistic, they also determined how many other deaths resulted from accidents involving those models of cars.[11]

For example, for every million Toyota Camrys on the road, 41 Camry drivers perish in crashes and an additional 29 people die in accidents involving Camrys. That makes for a total of 70 people killed per million Camrys on the road. Drivers of the Ford Explorer, however, which would slice through a Camry like a spoon through an avocado, die at a much higher rate: 88 drivers per million vehicles. And perhaps because they're so big and inflict so much damage, 60 people die in accidents involving Explorers, for a total of 148 deaths per million vehicles. But why more driver deaths if the Explorer is so much bigger? Because, again, it's more difficult for an Explorer to avoid accidents than it is for a nimbler Camry. These aren't isolated examples. Consider the Toyota Avalon, with 60 total deaths per million vehicles, or the Volkswagen Jetta, with 70, or the Nissan Maxima, with 79, compared with these SUVs: the Toyota 4Runner with 137 deaths per million vehicles or the Chevy Tahoe with 141 or the GMC Jimmy with 114. Or consider some of the worst performers in this vein, pickup trucks. Drivers of the Ford F-Series pickup died at a rate of 110 drivers per million vehicles with a gruesome 128 others killed, for a total of 238 deaths, or the Toyota Tacoma with 171 people killed per million vehicles. Those rates are three and four times the numbers for a Camry. With gas at $6, there won't be many people driving hulking Ford F-250s and 350s who don't absolutely have to. It's bad news for Ford, but good news for the rest of the vehicles and travelers on America's highways.

With all this data in hand, would it be cataclysmic for a politician to suggest higher gasoline taxes, if not in the name of raising government spending or weaning our nozzles off foreign oil, then in the name of saving lives? "A tax rate that yields a real increase in the price of gasoline, sustained over time, will reduce fatalities and air pollution substantially," Harvard's Grabowski says. And higher gas taxes wouldn't be outlandish, in the world scheme of things, Grabowski points out.

Gas taxes make up 75% of the price of fuel in Italy; in Canada, Australia, and New Zealand, taxes make up about 50% of the cost of gas.[12] In the United States, taxes account for only 20% of the cost of fuel. If the normal price of gas were $4 a gallon in the United States and fuel taxes were increased so prices were $6 a gallon, the taxes would still only account for 46% of the price of gas, still less than most of the Western world. And think of the rail lines and the improved roads that could be built with that kind of tax increase. It's a luxury that Europe has already known for decades.

Rising Gas Prices Also Mean a Physically Skinnier America

The United States, by just about any measure, has managed to make itself fat. Since 1979, the percentage of U.S. adults who can be classified as obese—the condition of weighing substantially more than the medical optimum—has risen from 15.1% to 32.2%.[13] That's more than a doubling, an astounding rate of change. Moreover, a full two-thirds of American adults are now overweight, perhaps on their way to becoming medically obese. Our fatness costs us a lot of money: $117 billion per year in early mortality and extra medical expenses, according to the U.S. Department of Health and Human Services. That's enough money to buy all of Nike, Yahoo!, Boeing, and Starbucks with billions to spare. And, of course, our fatness costs lives: 112,000 deaths related to complications and diseases stemming from obesity. That's the same number of people who live in Ann Arbor, Michigan, or Peoria, Illinois, people who die every year because they're fat.

There's a bevy of factors behind the surging waistlines of Americans: processed foods, television, video games, computers, fewer laborious jobs, more service-oriented jobs. But one factor floats just below the oily surface of our largesse: cheap gas.

Charles Courtemanche, an economist at the University of North Carolina at Greensboro, has produced a study suggesting that permanent hikes in gas prices may slash obesity rates. The amount is hardly nominal: A sustained $1 increase in gasoline equals a 10% dip in the nation's obesity rate—that's about 9 million fewer obese people clogging up health care systems and costing society, and themselves, money. "The price of gas is a powerful lever when it comes to medical expenses and mortality rates," Courtemanche says. "There's a savings in this for all of us."

Courtemanche's study used a common federal government data set that has sampled citizens' health care statistics every year since 1984. He divided the data by state and compared each set of health and weight statistics to gas prices in each of their respective states. By breaking it up by state, Courtemanche could parse the relationship between obesity and gas prices even further because gas prices can vary state by state and can be affected by local taxes. A gas price increase in Missouri may be more or less pronounced in Tennessee or Arkansas. When Courtemanche finished, he had more than 1 million different data samples. "I feel confident in saying that it's a causal relationship," he says of gas prices' effect on obesity rates.

Courtemanche found evidence in his data that rising gas prices resulted in more Americans walking and more Americans bicycling. Perhaps just as important, he noticed that, as gas prices increase, people eat out at restaurants less. In addition to more strolling and cycling, people use public transportation more, Courtemanche says, and that, too, burns far more calories than sitting in a bucket driver's seat, sipping coffee, and flipping through radio channels. People who use subways, buses, trolleys, or commuter rail services need to get to and from mass transit stops and that probably means more walking on both ends. A $1 rise in gas means 11,000 fewer lives lost to obesity-related causes and $11 billion per year saved on health costs, Courtemanche says.

Something even more interesting may happen, Courtemanche thinks, when gas prices climb from $4 to $5 to $6 and up. "As we go up from $4, the effect gas prices have on obesity might even accelerate," he says. "Now you're not only talking about more biking and walking, you're talking about people actually starting to change where they live and more people moving into cities."

Courtemanche, for one, has cast his lot with the urban crowd. He and his wife have decided to buy an attached townhome in central Greensboro rather than a larger single-family home a little farther out. "We want close-by shops and restaurants that are walk-able and bike-able," he says. "I think that's the direction we're all going in."

High Gas Prices Will Clean Up Our Skies, Clear Our Vistas, and Scrub Our Lungs

There are few niches of urbanity that inspire a sense of clean, opu-lent living like Santa Monica, California. Driving north up the Pa-cific Coast Highway here is like straddling the beach, Hollywood, and the French Riviera. It's a green and lush spot, where sunshine rules and where it always seems to be 78 degrees. The cars are waxed, the people coiffed, and the ocean views resplendent. Surf-ers climb up the sea cliff stairs from the beach and joggers trot beneath giant palms on a winding sidewalk snaking between two perfect runways of green grass. People here can catch a sea view by just craning their necks westward. There are few better fusions of landscape and human inhabitance. It's a merry tune that plays here. Merry until you go to snatch a view of the San Gabriel Moun-tains, which rise more than 6,000 feet to the north and east. That's when the magic ends. It's hard to see those mountains. It's akin to trying to view the New York skyline through a scratched and grubby window on an elevated train in Queens. The grandeur is half ap-parent, but it's not at all satisfying.

We've added the smog rampart in our lives with our industry, our fires, and our cars. It would seem to make sense that higher gas prices, which mean fewer cars on the road driving fewer miles, would mean less pollution. But how much damage do our car engines wreak on air quality compared with belching coal power plants, steel mills, and antiquated factories? How much of that urban fog that cloaks many of the globe's finest views comes from our vehicles? Quite a bit, says J. Paul Leigh, a professor of health economics at the University of California, Davis. And that murk doesn't only harm our views.

Some of the worst, most damaging air pollution to humans comes as particulate matter, airborne particles from 10 micrometers down to below 2.5 micrometers. How small is that? A human hair typically has a thickness of 70 micrometers, which makes it thirty times larger than the smallest particulate matter we breathe. Our vehicles spew about 50% of the ambient particulate matter in the air, Leigh says. That's a staggering amount. What makes particulate matter so damaging is that, when inhaled by humans, their teeny size allows them to lodge into lung walls and even to enter our bloodstreams. Particles can cause a spectrum of health problems from coughing, chronic bronchitis, irregular heartbeats, and nonfatal heart attacks to premature death for people with heart or lung disease.[14]

Fine particles—those that are smaller than 2.5 micrometers and the deadliest to humans—are also the major cause of haze in parts of the United States, such as the fog that plagues Los Angeles' mountain views. The grimy soot of particulate pollution also makes our streams and lakes more acidic, changes the balance of nutrients in coastal waters, and can alter the diversity of ecosystems. Their most damning scourge, however, is their effect on human life: An estimated 25,000 people in the United States die every year from particulate pollution.[15]

Leigh conducted a study, concluding in 2008, that tried to pinpoint the effect a 20% jump in gas prices would have on air pollution, especially particulate levels. "It's clear that higher gas prices have public health implications," Leigh says. "There is overwhelming epidemiological evidence of air pollution causing heart attacks and other factors leading to deaths. When you find spikes in air pollution, you find spikes, within just a couple of days, in heart attacks in seniors and generally in people who have a history of heart disease."

Leigh found that a 20% increase in the cost of gas, sustained for a year, would save, conservatively, 694 lives because of decreased air pollution. Leigh's study used gas prices and data available from earlier years when the price of gas was more modest than recent times. But we know that as gas has approached $4, people have dramatically altered their behavior. Leigh suspects that when the price of gas climbs past $4 to $6 and beyond, more lives will be saved than the linear line his study suggests. "It's quite credible to think that, as people are affected more and more by high gas prices and as some even switch to hybrid and electric cars, this trend in lives saved would accelerate as the price of gas goes higher."

Moreover, Leigh says his study focused only on the near-term effects of pollution from cars relative to gas prices, which is the only feasible way to measure things. "But the real damage from air pollution accumulates over the long term," Leigh points out. "These studies are understated because the long-term effects are so hard to track."

Six-dollar gas will usher in a new sense of conservation. A sense of cash conservation, not ecological. Nothing motivates change like money. But all these meatballs come from the same loin. More expensive gas will mean less gas burned, which means better views of the San Gabriels in Los Angeles, the Wasatch Range in Salt Lake City, the Cascades in Seattle, and the Rockies in Denver. More important than the improved sharpness of our mountain views, however, will be the *multiple thousands* of lives saved by fewer particulates invading our air. With gas prices at such a premium level, our tailpipes will finally emit judiciously rather than on mere whim. Our lungs will be grateful.

Six-Dollar Gas Will Spark an Infrastructure Revolution and the Era of Widespread Tolling

Our pullback on gasoline use when prices reach $6 will create some unintended, tangential costs. One of the least considered costs: the price of sustaining our infrastructure. As Americans drive fewer miles and buy less gasoline, we pay less in federal fuel taxes, which are levied at 18.4 cents per gallon. At the 2008 prices of $4 a gallon, because Americans drove fewer miles and bought less gasoline, there were less road taxes collected. At $6 a gallon, the federal government will collect an even smaller amount for road taxes, even though the cost of maintaining the roads, thanks to the high price of gasoline, will go up. Those gas taxes are the main source of funding for highway and mass transit systems, networks in dire need at the moment.

A quarter of U.S. bridges are either "functionally obsolete" or "structurally deficient." One out of every seven miles of U.S. pavement is rated "not acceptable," according to the National Surface Transportation Policy and Revenue Study Commission, which assesses infrastructure and recommends fixes.[16] It will take $1.6 trillion to get all of our roads, bridges, and tunnels up to safe, acceptable conditions, according to the American Society of Civil Engineers.[17] Based simply on our system's current decay, it's clear we weren't even generating enough taxes to keep up our roads with lower gas prices; higher gas prices and less driving will exacerbate this problem. It's a conundrum that can be seen no farther away than your closest viaduct, bridge, or overpass.

"Look at this right here, at least fifteen percent of the concrete has simply fallen off," Joseph Schofer points at a crucial support arch underneath a train overpass that stretches across Hollywood Avenue on the north side of Chicago. "You have a lot of spalling on this concrete," he says (when outer layers of concrete chip, crack, and slough off, it's called spalling). "But spalling is not necessarily a terrible thing and it's not unusual in concrete. What you don't want to see is spalling so bad that the concrete's reinforcing steel is exposed," he says. Then he extends his finger, wagging it. "But there's the steel staring us right in the face." The outer rings of steel rebar form a set of rust-colored veins around several of the bridge's most decrepit arch supports. The exposed steel's one-inch thickness is already badly eroded itself, lost to oxygenation.

Professor Joseph Schofer has been teaching civil and environmental engineering at Northwestern University for forty years. He says the United States was already heading toward problems because of the general age of our country's infrastructure, but the recent rise in gas prices has pressed the problem to the fore. "We're now reaching a point with our infrastructure where something has to be done in terms of how we finance it," he says. "We're going to run out of money. This is a crisis, let there be no mistake."

Billions, if not trillions, will be needed to fix bridges like the Hollywood Avenue span just four blocks from Chicago's Lake Shore Drive. Under the bridge, small piles of rubble have accumulated, like an ancient limestone cliff shedding its layers, where the concrete is deteriorating quickest. The Chicago Transit Authority, which runs the rapid transit L trains that traverse the four tracks above, has buttressed the bridge's arches with steel girders, shoring them up in case the concrete fails. "Usually, when we talk about shoring and bridges, we're talking about temporary shoring," Schofer explains. "These," he says, fingering one of the yellow-painted trusses, "are not temporary. This is heavy-duty stuff. Is this their permanent solution?" Schofer wonders. "It very well might be."

In fatter times, the CTA would likely rebuild the bridge, fully replacing the most battered sections and repouring structural concrete. The bridge's deck, the horizontal structure that the tracks rest on, is also made of reinforced concrete. Several large areas of the deck's underside, each roughly fifty square feet, have already deteriorated, exposing their lower rungs of steel rebar, now flaky with rust.

"They haven't done anything there yet because there's probably a lot more steel in that deck than they need—there's a lot of redundancy built into these bridges," Schofer says. "But this ought to be on somebody's list. I have to wonder how often they look at this."

It's tough to add things to lists when there's little money, which explains how quick, cheap fixes, like the steel jammed underneath this concrete Chicago bridge, get tacked up and approved. The way we levy infrastructure taxes has to change and will change. Soon. Basically, the faster gas prices reach $6, the faster our current infrastructure rubric will collapse. "I think we're going to see big alterations in how we pay for roads within the next five years," Schofer says. "This is not a faraway problem."

There exist many theories on how to raise the necessary capital so we're not driving, walking, and pedaling on packed dirt twenty years from now. None of them would be popular. "To have people pay directly for things that they may have felt they were getting for free before, even though they weren't, is a very hard thing to do," Schofer says. One of the simplest ways to fix the problem would be to change the tax on gasoline from a flat fee to a percentage. The federal government has charged the same 18.4 cents per gallon whether gas was $2.70 or $4.50, even though the jacked-up price of gas affects nearly everything that goes into building roads. The price of building roads has increased, essentially, at the same rate as the price of gas, but the government has been collecting the same amount of money—18.4 cents a gallon— even as the number of roads and bridges needing work piles up. If the government charged, say, 10% on every gallon of gas, then it would collect 20 cents on $2 gas and 40 cents on $4 gas. A simple solution, and a needed one, because, as Americans demonstrated during 2008, we buy fewer gallons when the price of gas goes up.

But getting that measure into place is next to impossible politically. There are few incumbent politicians who want the bull's-eye of raising gas taxes on their backs.

Schofer believes the likelier solution will be some kind of usage tax on our major roads, similar to a toll, but widespread and sliding, so that rush-hour drivers get dinged for more. "People have to be reminded with higher tolls that certain behaviors, traveling at off-peak times, are better for society," he says. It can be done. Models with such things in mind have been successfully implemented in the central city areas of London and Stockholm. "These systems were put in place with strong leadership at the top," Schofer says. "I just don't know if we'll get that leadership."

London's problem proved particularly knotty. In 2002, about 250,000 vehicles entered London's central business district every day. Those drivers, it was estimated, spent a full 50% of their time stuck, going nowhere. The city's bus system, also part of the vehicle-choked roads, was considered slower than walking during peak travel times near the central city. In 2003, Mayor Ken Livingston, who campaigned on congestion issues in the 2000 election, installed a camera system that captures license plates at all 174 entry points to London's business district, charging drivers $9 to enter. That toll was raised in 2005 to $14.[18]

London's experiment has been, by nearly every measure, a success. Congestion has shrunk 30% and the average speed of vehicles inside the district has increased 25%. The system makes a net profit of roughly $200 million. That money goes to pay for improvements to the network and then to pay for public transit projects. A bus system improved with toll revenues and by less congested roads now carries 37% more people entering the central business district during peak times. Bus riders' waits citywide have decreased 24%. A full 85% of peak travelers entering the district now use public transportation.

The scheme has led to a drastic reduction in air pollution, too, within London's heart. Levels of nitrogen oxide, which causes smog, have dropped 18% and disease-causing particulate matter is down 22%. Fossil fuel use and carbon dioxide emissions within the zone are down 20%. The public has responded well, despite early skepticism and some outrage. Many shops and businesses have benefited from decreased travel times to their locations; of proprietors in the district, 71% say the system has not hurt business whatsoever.

Stockholm put in a system similar to London's in 2006, when only 31% of the population favored such a move. After a six-month trial, the system gained permanent status through a referendum where voters gave it approval. Now, a full two-thirds of the city agrees that the system has been a positive change. It has led to 15% less traffic and a 14% decrease in CO_2 emissions.

Congestion of this magnitude does not plague every American city, of course, but the idea of charging drivers for road usage, and on a sliding scale determined by time of day, is quite applicable—the London and Stockholm implementations prove it can be done successfully. New York's Mayor Michael Bloomberg proposed a similar measure for lower Manhattan, hoping to charge drivers $8 or more to enter the southern half of the island, where traffic is worst. His proposal didn't pass the city's political phalanx and was quite unpopular with local businesses who depend on getting their vehicles into the city every day. But these kinds of measures will sprout up in the United States eventually, with New York likely leading the way. Other probable tolling spots: Chicago's central Loop; Washington DC's core; San Francisco's financial district; and Boston's business center.

A system similar to these, but on an even grander scale, could work for the entirety of the United States in a future of higher gas prices. And the U.S. system would be implemented for reasons beyond congestion; it would be installed for the very sustainability of our road systems. Schofer pictures electronic tolling throughout our infrastructure, similar to the full-speed tolling systems in place on some roads today. People would, in essence, pay for every mile they drive. "For this to work, we have to explain to people how dire the situation is," Schofer says.

When the price of gas hits $6, asphalt will be more expensive than ever. The sticky, black component of asphalt comes directly from oil refining. It's the gunk left at the bottom of the refining tank after the more valuable resources—jet fuel, gasoline, diesel, and propane—have been skimmed from the top. So the price of asphalt rises and falls almost identically with the price of oil and gasoline. Higher gas prices mean higher prices for asphalt, which makes up a huge majority of our roads. Even with gas at $4, municipalities and governments have paved less and have let streets reach levels of disrepair unthinkable a decade ago because material costs, especially those of asphalt, have become exorbitant. The expense of paving materials coupled with a severe loss of gas tax revenue will result in fewer road projects getting completed and fewer roads maintained in good condition. "Something will have to be done—but it probably won't happen during an election year," Schofer laughs.

High gas prices could, perversely, bring higher tax levies on gasoline—and thus, higher gas prices—to ensure we have enough money to fix our infrastructure and to avoid disasters such as the 2007 Mississippi River bridge collapse in Minneapolis that killed thirteen people.

Without changing how we pay for roads, gas prices touching $5 and $6 could bring us persistent bridge and road closures. "No state transportation department wants to have the next collapsed bridge on national television," says Richard Wallace, a senior project manager at the Center for Automotive Research in Ann Arbor, Michigan. "So if you don't have the money to fix it, what are you going to do? You're going to close it."

As the price of gas increases toward $6, Wallace says, states will effectively have 25% to 30% less money to fix roads and "it doesn't take long before your whole system is below-grade pavement. They're trying to keep the whole thing together with baling wire right now."

One result of this circuitous cycle of less driving, higher taxes, and poorer roads will be more privately run roads and bridges. Legislation is on the books in about half the states to allow private entities to manage, toll, and maintain roads and bridges. Usually, there are statutes limiting how much tolls can be raised by the roads' private managers, and the byways' surface and structural conditions are subject to public review and held to minimum standards. The surface conditions on Chicago's Skyway, a giant series of bridges linking Northwest Indiana to Chicago's South Side, have actually improved since Australia's Macquarie Infrastructure Group and Spain's Cintra took over the road in 2005.[19] The two companies paid Chicago $1.8 billion to lease the road for ninety-nine years. The road charges a toll of $2.50 to cars that cross its eight-mile stretch, which offers views of Lake Michigan and the battered remains of yesterday's leviathan steel mills.

State and federal governments face tough choices in coming years regarding our roads. These choices will be punted around by Washington's procrastinators until something drastic—like $6 gas and spreading bridge closures—compels them to find a solution. Tax codes will be overhauled, tolls doubled and tripled. Tire-swallowing potholes and dead ends will become permanent parts of the American driving experience. A solution, be it tolling, taxing, or otherwise, will come, but it will need a dramatic catalyst: $6 gas.

The Ubiquitous Yellow School Bus Will Largely Disappear from America's Roads

Few things touch as many people's lives as our roads. But our country's education system ranks as high as anything on most people's priority list. High energy prices won't change the way we teach our students, but this new expense will definitely affect how students, from kindergarten through college, get to school every morning.

Montgomery County, Maryland, is home to the bustling belt-way corridor outside Washington DC. The county oversees a giant school district that buses 96,000 children to school every day. In moving all these kids around, the district's yellow buses burn up 3.3 million gallons of diesel fuel a year. During the high gas prices of 2008, the county faced prices greater than $4.50 per gallon. For every penny diesel fuel goes up in price, Montgomery County has to spend another $33,000 to sustain their busing program.[20] When the price of gas rose more than $2 during the past few years, Montgomery had to come up with an additional $7 million. Things are doubly hard when, on the yearly education budget, gas is accounted for as a fixed price item when it's clearly not.

School board officials authorized Montgomery's superintendent to impose greater maximum walking distances on students. Generally, students who live inside the walking limits are expected to hoof it to and from school. The limits currently are 1.5 miles for middle school and 2 miles for high school. The district last raised the limits in 1996, when it increased the high school limit from 1.75 miles to 2 miles. That move, with gas prices at little more than $1, saved the district $250,000. A similar move now would save four or five times as much. When gas prices inevitably flirt with $4 again and head up near $6, the walking distances all over the country will surely be extended.

Fairfax County Public Schools in Virginia, which transports more students than any school system outside of New York's, set its fuel budget at $8.4 million in fiscal 2009, double the 2005 level.[21] Faced with cost increases such as these, America's schools have tough choices ahead of them. When gas reaches $6, the crisis will be an exploding one across the nation. Parents will be outraged at the possibility of losing bus service for their children, but school systems will have to cut somewhere, and perhaps rightly, those cuts are likely to come in the form of fewer buses, routes, drivers, and gasoline rather than fewer teachers, classrooms, and sports.

It could be that, for at least a time—until technology brings us cheaper-running buses, and it will—many school districts across the country will abandon busing except in the most rural of cases. In fact, many states don't require districts to supply transportation to students, including California, where the Capistrano United School District in Orange County recently eliminated forty-four of its sixty-two bus routes, saving the district $3.5 million.[22] The cuts affect 5,000 students and have many parents frothy mad, threatening lawsuits. Challengers say that the cuts mean hundreds of more cars on the roads because parents will have to drive their kids to school. Those parents are paying for gas, too, however, and can't be pleased at the prospect of adding more miles to some of their already circuitous Los Angeles commutes. But in a place as nice as Orange County, weather-wise and community-wise, it only makes sense that children should hop on their bikes or take a pleasant walk in the Southern California sunshine to get to school.

High Gas Prices Will Temper the Major League Traveling in Youth Sports

The face of school athletics, an arena quite near many parents' hearts, will undergo large changes, too. Kids today, whether they hold the promise of being an elite athlete—a future Michael Phelps—or just that of a decent jump shooter on the basketball court or an average midfielder on the soccer pitch, travel more like professional athletes than ever before. They play in tournaments on both coasts, sometimes missing school and catching red-eye flights to make games on back-to-back days, three time zones apart.[23] Parents, in many cases, are all for it. Many travel with their kids, rooting them on from the stands in disparate reaches of the country. One team from Artesia High School in Lakewood, California, recently played five games in six days on opposite sides of the country with a six-hour red-eye flight jammed in the middle. All this during final exams week.[24] This level of coddling and travel has been made possible by two things: overzealous parents bent on making their children stars *and* cheap oil. Parents may not change, but the price of oil certainly will.

Transportation costs are a huge chunk of any high school's sports budget and the adjustments that, at $3 and $4, were just filtering in, will come en masse when gas hits $6. Most school buses get about 6 miles to the gallon, so it can take a lot of expensive diesel fuel to get anywhere. States will implement changes that will mean more than merely fewer multiday tournaments and trips to play elite teams from other states. The changes will alter how states conduct playoff tournaments and, in some cases, will even skew competition, sectionals, and playoffs unfairly.

In 2008, the Illinois High School Association made a change that would require teams and fans to travel less for early rounds of state playoff tournaments. The changes affect sports from basketball to baseball to soccer for schools in the parts of the state south and west of Chicago, where the population is less dense. Previously, the playoffs' early rounds, which are called regionals, were seeded by teams' performances, usually ensuring that the best teams wouldn't meet until later rounds of the playoffs, called sectionals. Now, some of the early rounds will be based purely on proximity, which means schools play the schools closest to them early on, even if the consensus says the two schools are No. 1 and No. 2. "It was pretty apparent that we had to do something to mitigate energy costs for schools," says Marty Hickman, executive director of the IHSA.

The change has been welcomed by schools and fans who, in some cases, have been driving two hours across the state for an early-round playoff game. "We know the price of energy has affected how people spend their money and we'd rather give parents and grandparents an easier chance to see their kids play rather than stretching the tournaments all over the place like we used to," Hickman says. "Even people who aren't crazy about it knew that we had to do something," he says. "I think changes like this are going to become more common across the nation."

Indeed. Tennessee has implemented changes similar to those made in Illinois, with the same mixed response. Mississippi simply cut sports schedules across the board by 10%.[25] A school district in Fort Mill, South Carolina, recently started charging high school and middle school athletes $50 to help pay for gasoline. A school district in Florida recently forbade JV teams to travel outside the county. Another one eliminated middle school sports altogether, similar to a school in Lansing, New York, that eliminated its JV football team and its JV girls soccer team. Many schools across the country are trying to coordinate schedules among several sports so that different teams, say soccer and field hockey, can be jammed onto the same bus. These were changes made with gas prices briefly touching $4; when gas climbs to $6, the changes will be bigger and they will be permanent.

One of the ancillary benefits of changes such as these, Hickman adds, is that it keeps athletics in perspective. "There's a little less emphasis on winning and losing and more of an emphasis on local competition, keeping a community together and keeping things affordable for schools and for fans," he explains. "The coaches may disagree with me, of course."

College teams, especially at the high Division I level, won't feel the pain as acutely. They operate like professional franchises and will continue to do so. But travel for college teams on the Division II and III levels will be altered indelibly. Schools at that level will not and should not come up with the money necessary to sustain complicated athletic travel schedules.

The Return of the Foot Patrol

Companies and governments with large car fleets will be the first to adjust their behaviors to account for high gas prices. When you have 1,000 cars instead of just one, $1,000 extra for gasoline per car means $1 million.

Who drives thousands of cars at all times of the day and night? If you said the post office, you're right. But the post office can raise prices for their stamps, and they've done exactly that many times in the past several years as the price of moving our mail and packages has steadily climbed. Police departments, however, can't raise prices; they can only ask municipalities, whose budgets are already stretched, for more money. And those new funding allocations, if they ever come, take time. Police departments need to cut spending now, so many have already started to reduce their gasoline use immediately. The Houston Police Department blew past its gasoline budget of $8.7 million in 2007 and spent more than $11 million on gas in 2008. San Diego figures to spend more than $3 million more than it budgeted on gasoline.

Americans may be seeing fewer police cars, but they're not seeing less police protection. Police have taken to the sidewalks once again, much like they did a century ago on America's tight and dense city avenues. The modest police department in Suwanee, Georgia, budgeted $60,000 for gasoline in fiscal 2008. Its 2009 budget ramped up its gasoline allowance to $163,000. Michael Jones, chief of the Suwanee Police Department, which has thirty-six officers, says rising gas prices have enabled him to change the way Suwanee is patrolled for the better. "When my father had his beat fifty years ago in Rome, Georgia, he walked it. Everybody knew him. He got Christmas gifts from just about every person in his patrol area. They didn't give him gifts because he was a police officer, they gave him gifts because he was part of the community and he was their friend. That's the kind of thing we want to get back to here," Jones says in his Southern-soaked drawl. "Years ago nobody thought about conserving gasoline but now we're forced to do things differently. When all we do is drive around, you have an effect that we call the legless police, because people only see their officers from the shoulders up. But now we're putting people on the ground where we need them instead of having them just randomly riding around. Whereas before people only saw officers in negative situations, when something has gone wrong, now they see us every day, in positive, normal situations," Jones says. "Even if gas goes back down to a buck, I want my officers to get out of their cars and to be amongst the community."

These types of changes have rippled across the country. Some sheriff's deputies in Illinois's Cook County have ditched their squad cars for bicycles in and around Chicago. The Chicago Police already have a large contingent roaming the streets on Segway scooters and horses. New York City has upped foot patrols and bought twenty hybrid police vehicles last summer.[26] Police in Shelby, North Carolina, have been ordered to park their cars for fifteen minutes every two hours; police there have also been asked to stop taking patrol cars on lunch runs.

"If you add more foot patrols, citizens notice right away. And they feel more at ease and safer, even if, in total, there aren't more police on the streets," says George Kelling, a professor of criminal justice at Rutgers University. Officers on foot are able to pick up all manner of knowledge that they wouldn't be able to pick up in a car. They duck into stores, restaurants, and bars, learning the managers' names and what they're concerned about. "I think the days of police sitting in their air-conditioned or heated cars and watching society from afar are ending. People want the police amongst them, involved, and these high gas prices have made that possible," Kelling says. "The idea that patrolling can be done by car is a bad idea and it just doesn't work."

Kelling recently spent a day pedaling about the Boston Common with two Boston police officers. "They're on those bikes anytime the weather allows it and the citizens are very aware of them being there," Kelling says. "Once you get the police walking or biking around, citizen appreciation goes way up and their fear of crime goes down. When the fear of crime is low, people reclaim ownership over property. Drug dealers get forced out, marginal characters get forced out, and pretty soon there's families and children on the streets again."

Kelling says research suggests that people don't notice when police departments add or take away car patrols driving around. But they notice foot patrols right away. "I don't care where you go—Boston, Philadelphia, Milwaukee, Los Angeles—more departments understand the benefit of getting the officers onto the pavement and out of the car. I would expect to see more of it," Kelling explains. "And the gas savings is a nice benefit. It gets our officers in great shape, too."

CHAPTER **$8**

The Skies Will Empty

Mike Potter is an undertaker of sorts. His cemetery sprawls across a swatch of baked sand in the heat of inland California. It's filled with planes that, at least for the moment, have been deemed more valuable as parked albatrosses than fuel guzzlers plying the skies and ferrying passengers. The gritty desert floor here has been lightly rutted by landing gear, marking the paths of erstwhile aviation giants, now old and unwanted, cast away for lack of money or for younger, shinier versions. Potter gives these outcast birds a home. His business of housing these invalids surges with the airlines' misfortunes. But Potter also profits when the airlines grow and shed old aircraft for new. The old planes have to go somewhere, and Potter is usually the guy who gets them. Those in the aviation industry call Potter's operation the boneyard.

On one side of his boneyard, Potter has a dozen DC-9s lined up like regal veterans champing for one last fight. But these DC-9s will probably never fly again. They sit, waiting to be scavenged for their parts or, when they're finally stripped to stud and gunwale, to be sent to the scrapper, their aluminum skins worth more than their role in an airborne fleet. On another side, Potter has arranged seven Boeing 767s, the king of the transatlantic hop and a widebody legend. They belong to Air Canada, who, Potter says, isn't quite sure what to do with them, so they leave them with Potter at his desert outpost. He's happy to have them. He has plenty of room. And he collects rent.

Potter owns P&M Aircraft, a dusty strip of desert seventy-five miles north of Los Angeles on the edge of the Mojave Airport. When calamity strikes the airline industry, Potter ensures that every displaced plane will have a patch of dirt to rest its landing gear. At sixty-four, Potter still likes to go by Captain Mike, a nod to his own glory days, when he piloted the earth's airspace for TWA. At twenty, he was the youngest pilot to fly for a U.S. airline. At twenty-three, TWA made him the youngest captain and awarded him command of a TWA Convair 880, and later a Boeing 707. Potter, who has plenty of stories, likes to talk about the times when he flew for Howard Hughes when the magnate still owned a large part of TWA. He often dons a captain's hat when making the rounds at P&M. Potter retired from flying for the airline in 1981 after being diagnosed with diabetes. A large man with a dense gray beard, he bears a resemblance to Santa Claus, if Saint Nick took to summering in the California desert and flying jet-propelled planes instead of reindeer-pulled sleighs.

Potter now makes his curious living out of storing, buying, and selling wayward airplanes. He sells them cheap and buys them cheaper. He might buy an old 737, he says, "an absolute guzzler by today's standards," for $100,000. "Then we'll sit it out there in the yard, get rid of the engines for seventy thousand each, and then pull parts off of it as people call in orders. It takes time, but if you have the patience, you can get about $300,000 when you're done."

Potter first trod the salvage path in 1978 when he flew some TWA 880s to the desert for mothballing. He later got his own patch of Mojave and took planes from whoever didn't want them. He's had a little bit of everything land on his strip: Fokker 100s, Convairs, 707s, 727s, 737s, 747s, 757s, 767s, MD-80s, DC-9s, and DC-

10s. He'll sell anything. Seats, flaps, engines, doors, panels. When a plane has been thoroughly scavenged, he lets commandos from nearby Edwards Air Force Base practice hostage-saving techniques with the planes. "They blow all four doors off, sometimes they use rockets, sometimes they use C-4, and sometimes they use things we aren't allowed to see," Potter laughs. "They'll tell us, 'Go take a long lunch, fellas.'"

Potter often rents some of his wrecks to Hollywood directors, giving them a plane body to spectacularly blow up or shoot full of holes. He's furnished props for movies from *Speed* to *Pushing Tin* to *Twister*. Kiefer Sutherland and Fox's *24* shot part of season six on P&M's lot. Dr. Dre led a dance party of several dozen revelers in one of Potter's Convair 880s for the video of "Keep Their Heads Ringin'." Potter proudly displays the video on his Web site.

Potter is known throughout both the film industry and the airline industry as a man who can get you what you need. The bizarre business of Hollywood catering and used airplane dealing has been good to him. He owns a sailboat and a slip in Santa Barbara and gets out on the water whenever he can. Potter probably keeps his captain's hat on when he pilots his boat, which he's registered with a familiar moniker, *Trans World One*, allowing him to rove the radio and ocean waves using his airline call signal from long ago.

Potter's operation forms part of a loose network of plane graveyards scattered throughout the dry air of the American West. Of all the fascinating things that satellite imagery lets us peer at, and there exist many, some of the most peculiar sites have to be the half-dozen or so plane graveyards throughout the West. One, of course, is Potter's Mojave spot; another, Pinal Airpark, is outside Tucson; another is in Victorville, California. More than a dozen 747s jam the confines of the Pinal site in Arizona. Their massiveness coupled with their red-topped Northwest Airlines' paint jobs makes them look like a grill half full of giant Italian sausages (747s), while the rest is occupied by smaller Northwest red hots (737s and

DC-9s). The graveyard that evokes the most gawking, however, is the U.S. military graveyard southeast of Tucson at Davis Monthan Air Force Base. Google Maps will glide right to it if you enter *Davis Monthan AFB* into its address bar.

There you can see thousands of decommissioned fighter jets, bombers, tankers, and cargo planes. From F-4 Phantoms, C5s, marine harrier jets, AWACS radar planes, and the venerable and enormous B-52, almost everything the United States flies rests permanently here in the dry air and alkaline soil (less corrosive) of the Arizona desert. It looks more like a field of toys or plastic models arranged on a furry brown carpet than what it really is: a neatly arranged mess of our country's airborne military history. Even the supersonic bomber, the B-1B Lancer, which only began flying in 1985, can be seen. At least fifteen of those bombers, which cost American taxpayers $300 million each, can be clearly picked out, their engines peeking out behind their retractable wings, destined never to fly again. How much of America's wealth was spent here, in this graveyard? Hundreds of billions, to be sure.

The open-air cemeteries for the world's commercial airlines, too, hold billions of dollars' worth of metal, technology, and history, and their fences will brim with even more as gas prices approach $8. Viewing their contents from above will get more interesting with each day that gas prices settle at $8 or more. Here's hoping that Google and other map sites keep their photos updated so we can see the metamorphic dismantling, plane by plane, of the American airline giants.

But back to Potter. He has never seen more big planes come through his operation than in the early 1990s, when his lot was crammed with beached whales that carried two of the more famous airline insignias ever to fly. In 1991, both Eastern Airlines and Pan Am capitulated to the pressures of increasing oil prices and low-cost competitors. Both airlines had struggled for many years before their antiquated business models and flight networks took them down permanently. The aircraft aftermarket became awash in cheap planes. "That was a good time for us, no doubt," he says. "Probably the best of times, if you're talking about our parts and reselling business."

Potter knows that the days of excess for him will return. He may have a problem finding buyers, but his desert parking lot will soon overflow with the winged mavens of cheap-oil capitalism. Potter has about fifty planes now, "but there's more coming soon," he says knowingly.

When gas inevitably climbs to $8, the airline carnage will be vast and it will come swiftly. Potter's yard will be drowning in familiar logos and planes, as will every desert graveyard. Potter will have to expand. To keep their testaments to human genius flying 500 mph at 40,000 feet, airlines use fuel that's classified as Jet A-1. Jet fuel is basically kerosene, and jet engines burn it like flash paper. A 737 burns about 13 gallons a minute. Plane people talk about fuel in pounds, not gallons, however, so that's 91 pounds a minute. A 737 flight from Chicago to Los Angeles burns about 25,000 pounds or so; a 747 on the same route will burn more than 100,000 pounds. Jet fuel comes from the same oil-refining process that produces gasoline, diesel, and asphalt, so its price is as volatile as gasoline's.

The world's airline executives stare at the very real possibility of disaster every day. If they don't outwardly acknowledge that they're living on leased time, they think it. They think it every hour of every day that they show up for work. Everything that airlines have done in the last five years—paring their workforces; charging for checked baggage; stripping away in-flight meals; raising mileage requirements for reward flights; asking $4 for a tiny package of Oreos; and generally thinking up fees for anything they can—has been done to offset the concrete baluster of fuel prices steadily dragging them toward extinction. When the gas station marquees start reading $8, the airline jig will be up. The airlines, trees of unending bureaucracy and unions, won't all fall in a month. There will be the obligatory rounds of Capitol Hill hand-wringing and perhaps even some imprudent measures such as federal loan guarantees. But in the end, the rising price of gas will gut our extensive air network, leaving less and less behind as the price marches past $8.

Names we've been programmed to recognize and associate with flying and leisure will disappear forever, following Eastern and Pan Am into corporate oblivion. Flying won't be impossible, of course. There will still be airlines, but far fewer, and those that survive—I'll tell you who—will charge fares most of us won't be paying on any kind of regular basis. The days of swinging out to the West Coast to see Aunt Jolene and Uncle Freddy, or flying home for Thanksgiving because it feels good, will be over, except for those with cash to burn. For them, a jet engine will always hum. But for most people, flying will be a luxury indulged once every year or two. Flying the whole clan down to Disney World, ensuring that a few more American kids undergo this baptism in consumerist values and marketing genius, won't be economically possible.

There has been no industry in the history of the world that has defied the simple laws of economics as long as the airline business. How do the major traditional carriers of the United States—United, American, US Airways, Delta, Northwest, and Continental—survive year after year? American stock market investors have a strange affinity for airlines. The airline model, which, even in the best of times, has small profit margins, clearly loses relevancy with every cent gasoline goes up in price. Yet people seem drawn to airline securities, as if owning a few shares of United is somehow sexier than owning equity in Kraft or Coca-Cola. It makes no sense. For the last eight years, all these airline companies have managed to do is lose money. Lots of it. Since 2001, the airlines have hemorrhaged $45 billion. Their fortunes in 2007 turned out decently, actually, when they turned a profit of $5.6 billion. But fuel prices smashed that party quickly, and the industry surrendered those winnings in 2008 when they spent $186 billion on jet fuel. Usually, when an industry performs this badly for this long, it either disappears or radically changes. Most people do not realize how close we are to a total reformation in the skies.

In 2003, a mere six years ago, jet fuel made up less than 13% of airlines' costs. When gas prices reach $4 a gallon, as they did for part of 2008, jet fuel makes up 40% of carriers' costs. That's an astounding number. Almost half of airlines' costs—including the price of planes, ground crews, pilots, insurance, airport fees, maintenance—comes from the hydrocarbons needed to keep these sleek, purring machines aloft. When gas reaches $8, carriers will be throwing down 60% of their operating costs for fuel. That cannot be sustained. The ultimate contraction awaits.

The airlines know it. "The crisis is reshaping the industry in more severe ways than the demand shocks of SARS or 9/11," says Giovanni Bisignani, CEO of the International Air Transport Association, which represents most of the world's airlines. "When fuel goes from 13% of your costs to 40% in seven years, you simply cannot continue to do business in the same way. Fundamental change is needed."

The Flawed Precedents of the Late 1990s and Its Cheap Oil

For those who exited college from 1998 through 2000, the world seemed to offer infinite and simple paths to fat paychecks and glossy lives. Fortunes could be made easily, we thought. People didn't gamble in the stock market; rather, we printed money in the stock market. If it wasn't Yahoo!, it was Dell or AOL or Microsoft. Everything came with little effort. History offers no time with more boundless enthusiasm, easy money, or widespread hubris than the latter years of the 1990s. San Francisco in 1999 was the unequivocal epicenter of the Internet madness. Just about everybody who lived there knew somebody who had circled a date on their calendars, the date they would become rich. Any company with an ink-jet and a couple of engineers could wrangle up a business plan to draw millions of dollars from outside investors.

While the stock market rocketed on the strength of the tech explosion, the rest of America felt rich, too. Corporate America romped in the greatest economic expansion of our time. Pay was fat and perks plenty. Expense accounts became portals to decadence. And, of course, the galloping businessmen of the era had to travel to make all these fabulous dates in the name of capitalism. A coach seat? No. When you're doing business, you need a business-class seat, obviously. Companies small and big regularly snapped up last-second tickets in business or first class for their employees, sending them to this conference, that client, and this clinic on a whim and on many, many dimes. If an airline had a plane that wasn't making money, it was doing something woefully wrong. Airlines commonly had more than half of the first and business class sections full with flyers paying more than $1,000 for their ticket, whether it was from Los Angeles to Chicago or from San Francisco to Atlanta. (Those seats now are filled with frequent flyers who upgrade at no cost.)

Airlines defined their future plans assuming things would roll on just as lustily. They added capacity, bought new planes, built terminals, furnished high-end frequent flyer clubs, and paid their union employees extremely well. These joyous industry times happened to coincide, not coincidentally, with the cheapest oil the modern world has ever seen. As mentioned in Chapter $6, gas prices in much of the United States went under $1 per gallon during 1998. Jet fuel was no different. Thanks to that and thanks to carefree corporate spending, U.S. airlines hauled in $9.3 billion in operating profits in 1998, $8.4 billion in 1999, and $7 billion in 2000. Jackpot. During these times, airlines flew with only 70% of their seats filled. In industry jargon, that's called the load factor. These days, load factors run closer to 85% and airlines are battling to get them even higher to help stave off extinction.

The empty seats and the frivolous business spending, as it happens, were a boon to the common man and the leisure traveler. During the late 1990s and early 2000s, we were able to fly anywhere we wanted, whenever we wanted, for mystifyingly affordable prices. Those cheap flights we enjoyed were a direct result of the exorbitantly priced business seats that American businesses had been snapping up with abandon. When you get fifteen seats occupied by Joe Executives paying $2,000 a pop, selling out some of the plane for $178 works just fine. Back then, 80 million passengers a year paid three to four times the normal fare on domestic flights, sometimes even more than that. That number has now been halved and it decreases further every day.

The economy crashed along with the dot.com boom beginning in late 2000. The terrorist attacks of September 2001 accelerated an already dire situation for the airlines as business travelers, who had begun bailing before 9/11, stayed home along with leisure flyers who were scared and broke. Many planes flew around the United States with less than half of their seats filled. Those types of loads persisted as U.S. airlines lost $10.3 billion in 2001 after enjoying what will surely be the most profitable stretch in U.S. airline history, when they made $50 billion in five years.

The airlines did not learn much from the dark years of 2001 through 2004, however. At a time when there should have been airline failures and liquidations, there were government-backed loans and Chapter 11 reorganizations that allowed capacity to remain largely unaffected, and enabled airlines to chase customers with ever-lower fares with no eye toward profit. In 2005–2007, the airlines reclaimed a semblance of solvency during an economic expansion fueled by low interest rates and a booming housing market, the same factors that led this country to the edge of financial anarchy during the latter months of 2008. Things will continue to get much darker for the airlines. Their fate may be artificially postponed by an economic slowdown that tempers oil prices. But the only given in the future is that oil prices will continue their ascension. And in doing so, they will dismember the airline industry, one carrier at a time.

The Airline Dinosaurs Meet Their Asteroid of Death: $8 per Gallon Gasoline

The so-called legacy airlines, the carriers that emerged from deregulation in the 1970s—United, Northwest and Delta, American, Continental, and US Airways—stand to lose the most and the fastest in a new world of higher energy costs. These airlines suffered hardest after the 9/11 attacks, too, because their skimpy margins leave them no room to wriggle. Their tight quarters are borne out of old workforces, union contracts, expensive airport hubs, and expensive fleets. Their debt loads are so heavy that any spare change they have, should they somehow eke out a profitable year, has to go toward paying down their loans rather than into more new planes, terminal upgrades, or plane refurbishing.

"It's obvious that some of these airlines are just going to have to go out of business," says Vaughn Cordle. Cordle isn't a normal Wall Street pontificator. He's a pilot who flew, among other planes, a Boeing 777 for one of the largest U.S. airlines for more than twenty-five years. Cordle, who is a certified accountant, began digging into the hard economics of the industry in the late 1990s. Fascinated, he immersed himself in the metrics and operating complexities of large airlines. His expertise manifested in a consulting business, AirlineForecasts, which proffers advice to banks and other large investors examining their airline holdings. Cordle recently quit his pilot gig to focus on his consulting work, which has ramped up briskly—and lucratively—with the increasing turbulence facing U.S. carriers. If you ever catch analysis of the airline sector on CNN, Fox News, MSNBC, or CNBC, you've likely seen Cordle give his take. Cordle has agreed with his former employer not to specifically discuss it by name so as to avoid any legal scraps with the company.

That hardly stops Cordle from pitching zingers at his old industry. "There's just way too many competitors right now," he says. As for the legacy U.S. airlines, his dire outlook: "They're dinosaurs. They have company culture disadvantages. When you have unions that want to go back to a bygone era of compensations, you're battling uphill, and that's what they have. Their labor is old and disgruntled. You can't provide good service when you have angry grandmas serving meals. Banks and investors keep bailing them out, but it's better to put them out of their misery at some point."

And then, for punctuation, he reiterates, "They're just dinosaurs."

Cordle's firm did an exhaustive study on the airlines and oil prices in late 2008. His work predicts which airlines would survive past $8-per-gallon gasoline. Cordle fully expects his study to be relevant; oil, he says, is bound to reach those heights within three or four years. For half of the current airline seats to fall out of the sky, as Cordle predicts will happen with $8 gas, it will take more than airline belt cinching. It will take brand extinctions.

The first big airline to permanently punch out will be US Airways. The company, a crude amalgamation of Arizona-based America West and Northeast favorite US Airways, has awkward hubs in Charlotte, Philadelphia, and Phoenix. "US Airways is already in a slow liquidation right now," says Cordle.

At the time of this writing, US Airways was still flying full bore. But by the time you read this, the airline could already be filing for Chapter 11 bankruptcy protection for the third time since 2002. US Airways has been playing with other people's money for half a decade now. They paid off government loans from 2002 with different debt they raised from yet more outside financiers. Charlotte, Philadelphia, Phoenix, and Las Vegas will see their travel options dwindle with the disappearance of US Airways. Southwest

Airlines, a player in all those cities, will undoubtedly swoop in and ramp up their flights in the absence of US Airways. But Southwest won't replace the seats on a one-to-one basis. Not even close. Travelers will immediately pay more to fly in these markets.

The next airline carcass will be that of United Airlines. A drastic stretch of mismanagement by the company's executives will squander what is arguably the best set of hub airports and routes in North America. United's hubs evenly split the lower forty-eight states in a straight line down their center, starting in Washington, to Chicago, to Denver, and then to San Francisco, which is one of United's gateways to its profitable Asian routes. Despite these built-in advantages, United couldn't avoid a comically long stint in Chapter 11 that began in December 2002 and didn't end until February 2006. In an industry that regularly enriches bankruptcy lawyers, United's was the largest and longest Chapter 11 stretch ever.

For every $10 a barrel of oil increases, United loses $500 to $600 million. United's executives have called for consolidation in the airline industry, but Continental, after entertaining prospects of a merger with United in early 2008, rejected United, deciding to stand pat and alone. United has already grounded 100 planes in the desert, knowing it must contract to survive. The industry will indeed contract, and part of the contraction will be the whole of United. United's capitulation will offer spoils to whomever can claim them. Some of its Washington DC routes will be snatched by Southwest. But United's real plums—its Asian routes out of San Francisco and Chicago's O'Hare—will go to a different suitor.

Delta and Northwest announced in April 2008 that they would merge and operate wholly as Delta Air Lines. Together they fly and together they will fall. The 2008 merger created the largest airline in the world with a curious set of hubs: Atlanta, Cincinnati, New York (JFK), and Salt Lake City for Delta, and Detroit, Minneapolis, Memphis, and Tokyo for Northwest. Delta was hardly in high health before the merger, having filed for Chapter 11 in 2005, emerging in 2007. Northwest, too, exited bankruptcy in 2007. Mushed all together, the airline has nearly $20 billion of debt and almost zero free cash flow. It's awfully hard to pay down a gargantuan pile of debt if you're not making money. Delta, even in a leaner, meaner form with some Upper Midwest hubs, will be permanently torpedoed by $8 gasoline.

That leaves two legacy airlines, American and Continental. American, somewhat amazingly, has been the lone major U.S. carrier to avoid bankruptcy in the modern era. But American, too, carries a bag of debt around its neck. American's IOUs top $10 billion and their susceptibility to ills brought on by high oil prices may be the most pronounced in the industry. American flies a fleet of inefficient jets, including 300 jet fuel–guzzling MD-80s. That's half of their fleet. While not going on a plane-buying spree has been a major factor in keeping American out of Chapter 11, its outdated planes will be a decided disadvantage in a future of gas prices of $8 and up.

American lost more than a billion dollars a quarter with gas at $4. With oil rising past $200 a barrel and gas pushing $8 a gallon, American will crumble. There will be nobody willing to extend American the financing it would need to complete a Chapter 11 process. The airline will wither and die in bankruptcy, waiting for a lender that will never emerge. American's domestic network will disappear. Dallas will suffer the most, as American represents the lion's share of that city's flights. Saint Louis, already a downsized hub for American, will also face huge reductions in service not likely to be recovered. Southwest and JetBlue will split American's appealing domestic routes out of Chicago, New York, and Los Angeles. American's hub in Miami, its portal to its lucrative and extensive Latin American network, will be scavenged by Continental, which will cherry-pick the best South and Central American routes and become the dominant U.S. presence in those places.

Continental, Cordle says, has the legacy airlines' best chance of making it past gas at $8 a gallon. "Their employee morale is No. 1, their management team is the best in the business, and they know how to maximize value," Cordle explains.

Continental has debt, but only $5 billion, about half as much as most of its U.S. competitors. And its Latin American network makes more money than American's even though it's only half the size. Continental's European network, about the same size as American's, makes twice as much money. Continental's Pacific network is quite profitable, too, though it's small compared to United's and Northwest's. Continental, having gone through a Chapter 11 reorganization in both the 1980s and the 1990s, has long had an eye toward prudent and lean operations. This is an airliner that has been operating with more caution, thrift, and financial shrewdness than its legacy competitors for more than fifteen years.

Much of that acumen is thanks to Gordon Bethune, a former Boeing executive who came to Continental in 1994 as the carrier teetered toward a third and likely fatal bankruptcy. Bethune steered the airline away from insolvency and then toward excellence. Continental once ranked near the bottom of every imaginable customer satisfaction category. Bethune's focus on customer fulfillment led the airline to snare more J. D. Power & Associates awards than any other airline on the globe. Bethune and his lieutenants also optimized Continental's route structure, getting rid of unprofitable routes and destinations, focusing on its Newark and Houston hubs. Bethune radically overhauled the airline's fleet with a bevy of new Boeing planes that he negotiated bargain prices for. Bethune, who retired in 2004, achieved legendary status on Wall Street and in the halls of business schools around the nation with his dazzling turnaround of Continental. His aura and his values will persevere at Continental.

The Future of the U.S. Airlines Will Look
Something Like This

With $8 gasoline, the American domestic network will contract to
50% of its current size. Midsize towns with decent air service currently, like Grand Rapids, Michigan, and Dayton, Ohio, will lose
most of their flights. A coast-to-coast ticket will cost closer to $1,000
than $200. Southwest and JetBlue will become the dominant do-
mestic airlines in an age of $8 gasoline. Their elegant and lean op-
erations will allow them to persevere through high oil costs. The
lack of competition from giant money-losing airlines will allow Jet-
Blue and Southwest to charge the premiums they will need to turn
a profit at $8 gasoline.

Regional jets, those of the thirty-seat variety, will disappear.
There will no longer be twenty-five flights from Chicago to Cleveland a day. There will be two. And they will be on big planes.
Flights of that length—350 miles or so—will be the shortest commercial flights available. If you want to fly from New York to Boston or from Chicago to Indianapolis or from Seattle to Portland,
you'd better own a plane, because those kinds of short-hop commercial flights just won't exist. Technology such as video phones
and satellite teleconferencing will further hasten the death of the
short-hop business trip. Planes burn an inordinate amount of fuel
just getting up to cruising altitude, so shorter flights cost more per
mile. Few people will pay $750 for a 200-mile flight, so major air
service between cities in the same regions will cease.

The lack of regional flights may open a niche market for very
small players with ten- to twenty-person jets making one or two
hauls a day at $900 a pop between places such as New York and
Boston. But the big boys—Southwest and JetBlue—won't do it. As
the price of gas increases, the radius of available flights will stretch
out longer and longer. At $12 gas, trips less than 500 miles will be
done by car, by bus, or by rail.

Continental will survive at $8, barely. The sole legacy carrier will shrink its domestic network, leaving JetBlue and Southwest to compete for those U.S. scraps. Continental will focus on becoming the lone American carrier of international consequence. It will open international hubs, as was mentioned above, in Miami, as well as in San Francisco, Los Angeles, and Chicago, in addition to its existing New York–area hub in Newark. Continental will resurrect American and United flights to London, Paris, Brussels, and other major European cities. Continental, thankfully for consumers, will not have an exclusive grip on international flights out of North America.

Some foreign carriers will persevere through the storm and will keep competition for international flights honest. Carriers you can expect to survive: Lufthansa, British Airways, Air France–KLM, and Japan's All Nippon Airways. Many flagship foreign carriers are better financially positioned than U.S. carriers to survive higher oil prices. Many of them have been profitable at $4 gas prices, whereas all of the American legacy carriers have lost money. Foreign carriers tend to face less competition at home. None of them face five or six giant competitors for domestic traffic, as do the U.S. carriers. And international flights, which tend to be far more profitable, comprise a higher percentage of foreign carriers' business than they do for U.S. carriers, who spend a lot of their money and energy schlepping people to and from places like Baltimore and Dallas for $300.

Some countries, such as Belgium, the Netherlands, Switzerland, Austria, Ireland, and Italy, will lose their national carriers altogether as foreign airlines take over the transatlantic business—Continental, Air France, British Airways, and Lufthansa. The same thing can be expected on the Pacific Rim, where Korean Air, China Eastern, Asiana, and Thai Airways will all disappear.

A standard coach ticket for a U.S.-European flight will cost $2,000 on the cheap end with sustained gas prices of $8 a gallon.

Taking the family across the pond for a swing through Paris, London, and Rome will no longer be palatable for even upper-middle-class families. As gasoline prices march up from $8, transatlantic flights will become, more and more, a province of the elite and the rich. A trip to Europe will be a once-a-decade treat for people who sacrifice and save. The only good news here is that Europe's extensive electric train network will keep traveling about the continent somewhat affordable. But getting across the Atlantic will be half the cost of any vacation. As gas increases from $8, the airlines' capacity will continue to shrink. More planes will be grounded and more second-tier cities will see their air connections obliterated.

Airline terminals that once stretched like monolithic petals from a giant airport stem will be closed. Airports now are far too big for a future of higher oil prices. Giant airports in Denver, Dallas, Detroit, Atlanta, and Houston will shut down more than half of their gates. Metros with more than one big airport, such as New York (JFK, LaGuardia, and Newark), Chicago (O'Hare and Midway), and San Francisco (SFO, Oakland, and San Jose) will consolidate their traffic into one field. Parking at airports will no longer be ridiculous. The hinterland lots, the ones farthest out from the airport, will be closed. The erstwhile short-term lots will be all that we need for our small cars.

As the price of gas increases and the traditional airlines head to the graveyard, we'll see all manner of gimmicky startups and odd innovations in the air. One we should all expect: flying by the pound. The idea has already been satirically floated by ads in the Philadelphia *Inquirer* and the Philadelphia *Daily News* that pushed a fictional airline, Derrie-Air, and told readers that, "The more you weigh, the more you pay." The papers' owner, Philadelphia Media Holdings, and Gyro Ad Agency put the ads together as a publicity prank. Most people had a nice chuckle at it. But somewhere, some entrepreneur's brain is cranking through the possibility of operating an airline this way. Obviously, larger people would avoid a *real*

Derrie-Air's planes, but that would be the point. When it comes to fuel economy, it's all about shaving weight. If Derrie-Air could fill its planes with the skinnier folk around, it would be operating with an acute advantage. Politically correct pandering, obviously, won't matter to a future Derrie-Air and it won't matter to the svelte people who fly it. Who can afford to be so sensitive? All this idea needs is $8 gasoline, a little capital, and a few cheap airplanes, which will hardly be tough to find. Just ask a man named Potter in the Mojave Desert.

The Crashing Impact of a Venerable Business Collapsing

The U.S. airline business is a big one. When half of it vanishes, it will leave a crater. Southwest, JetBlue, Continental, and perhaps another low-cost carrier will pick up some of the slack and a few of the wandering employees, but this will be an economic conflagration left to burn itself out. Factoring out the parts and routes that will be sustained by the survivors, losing the airlines mentioned above will amount to this: 2,800 planes grounded, 200,000 jobs lost, 13,000 flights eliminated, and $67 billion of revenue gone. It will get worse, too, as the price of gasoline increases from $8.

Where do the pilots go? The flight attendants? The baggage crews? The mechanics? They'll need to pick new careers. A lucky few pilots will be able to continue to fly for a living, but most of them won't. There's no shiny side to this nickel; it's all dirty. Jets need oil. There's simply no other way to get them aloft. People will change their lives and cut flying out as the price of tickets doubles, triples, and keeps soaring. The aviation industry, along with its giant pool of employees, faces an unshakable destiny of being radically deflated. The above figures apply to job losses only at the airlines. Thousands more jobs will be lost throughout the structure that supports our flight network: jobs at airports, maintenance shops, plane caterers, rental car companies, travel agencies, aircraft leasing companies, and even airport peripheral players such as taxi and shuttle drivers.

The economic damage will be deep and pronounced. This will be the beginning of the destruction of a major piston in our economy. A giant herd of people will have been set loose without jobs and without hope of employment elsewhere in their industry.

Cheap Used Planes and Expensive Fuel Means Trouble for Airbus and Boeing

When airlines start dropping flights and capacity, even before more than half of them are herded to Chapter 11 and extinction, the world's secondary market will be choking on airplanes. Potter expects plenty of cheap carriers to pop up to fill the voids left by fallen behemoths, for the simple reason that running an airline, suddenly, will have low start-up costs. "You'll be able to pick up a 737 with plenty of life left on it for, what, seven hundred thousand bucks?" he says, incredulously, of an airplane that lists at $50 million. "That's pennies. Get the cheap plane, throw some fuel in it, slap on a safety certificate, and away you go."

But the price of fuel won't stop rising at $8, and the planes picked up by these new whirlybird airline operators will soon find their way back to the secondary market, as their operations collapse under the cost of jet fuel. Dealers like Potter may even get to sell the same plane two or three times. And when the big trees start coming down, the old airlines with the fanciest tricked-out planes will unload their birds on the market. Premium planes like 777s and late model 737s will be floating around for dimes on the dollar. These are planes that, right now, airlines have to get in line to order. They're hot. The wait times for 777s and 787s stretch past six years.

So what happens to the businesses of Airbus and Boeing when the secondary market gets sloshed with hordes of newer aircraft?

Clearly, the two companies will lose giant swaths of their commercial airliner businesses. Both companies will have to concentrate on next-generation crafts that have superiorly efficient fuel and maintenance costs.

Eventually, either Boeing or Airbus will give up the fight to sell commercial airliners. There just will not be enough business in the world to sustain two big commercial jet makers. Boeing, with its defense contracts, and its satellite and missile businesses, may find itself leaving the jetliner game to Airbus, which, because of the subsidies it receives from European governments, may be able to survive more easily in a trampled commercial airline market. On the surface, that scenario seems plausible. But that plot outline ignores Boeing's current and considerable advantage in constructing the first plane designed for the age of oil scarcity.

Boeing's Big Bet on the World's Shriveling Oil Supplies

There's a palpable din of determination as workers scurry about the space, fetching tools, scaling towering and complex scaffolding, and examining plans with careful eyes. These craftsmen aren't erecting a building. They're inside a building that's fully built. It's the largest building, in fact, in the world, with 472 million cubic feet of airy space, nine times the size of the Sears Tower. The sprawling structure is just a couple of log lengths from Possession Sound, a back bay of Washington State's Pacific inlet, Puget Sound.

It's here, about forty-five minutes north of Seattle, where Boeing puts together its greatest airplanes, its 747s, 767s, and 777s. Boeing recently started putting out a different type of airplane here: the 787. This plane is a large part of the Chicago company's resurgence. Workers in this building, the best in the world at what they do, know they're contributing to something special, something different, something that will redefine the rules of aviation.

Scaffolding hangs over wings and travels along fuselages,

mimicking the form of the planes in a delicate spider web of trusses, braces, and suspensions. Workers tread planks along the scaffolding, checking the plane's wiring installations and fasteners. The inside of the plane is striking for its vastness. It's a raw display of skeletal fuselage construction, the bony steel and titanium members still exposed, sections of insulation blankets stuffed in between them. Still void of all its comfy passenger innards, an observer can truly appreciate the volume of a widebody plane. It's like stuffing two three-bedroom homes onto a set of wings and wheels.

Pat Shanahan, who heads up the 787 program, beams like a rock star as he talks about the construction and points at the form of what many think to be the greatest passenger plane ever designed. Shanahan's crews had recently hit their stride after countless setbacks in assembling the plane, from labor strife to supplier ineptness. "If you would have come here six months ago, it was all long faces, real frustration," Shanahan says. "Now they are really motivated. They can see the light. These guys are pumped."

The workers may be almost as pumped as Boeing's customers, who have lined up for a chance to snag one of these planes for $150 million. For the 787, which, as of this writing, has never carried a paying passenger, Boeing has already amassed a ridiculous 900 orders. Some perspective: In Boeing's lineup, the 787 replaces the 767, a successful plane by any standard and the most popular transatlantic jetliner of all time. Boeing has been selling the 767 for more than twenty-five years. The company just sold its 1,000th 767 three years ago. "Boeing has managed to create the iPod of planes," says industry analyst Ronald Epstein. "Everybody feels like they have to have one."

I was one of the lucky few allowed on the first walk-through of the 787 put on by Boeing for the world press in 2008. The global excitement garnered by this plane became demonstrably clear when I saw the diversity of the journalists covering the event. North Americans may have been in the minority. The media of nearly every major country in Europe had at least two representatives there. And many Asian countries—Thailand, Singapore, South Korea, Japan, and Taiwan—had even more than that. This plane, perhaps more than any other in history, is a big deal.

What possibly can make an airplane so desired by the world? Simple: It burns less gas. The 787 uses 20% less fuel, in fact, than a comparable aluminum-skinned aircraft. The 787 is the first of its kind in that it's a large, commercial airliner whose fuselage is made not out of metal punctuated by rivets, but out of carbon fiber and epoxy in what's called composite. The carbon laminate composite construction is homogenous. The carbon fiber, which is soaked in the epoxy, gets wrapped around a mold and baked at high temperatures and pressures, creating a one-piece fuselage section. If the same section were made out of aluminum, it would require 1,500 separate sheets of the metal and 50,000 fasteners. The composite construction is complemented by titanium, a strong, lightweight, and expensive metal that makes up 15% of the plane.

The 787 represents the largest step forward in commercial planes since perhaps Boeing's 747, the jumbo jet that launched the modern widebody era. The 787's tolerances are so tight and its composite construction, which doesn't corrode, requires so little maintenance that, overall, it should cost airline companies 35% less to operate than a comparable aluminum plane. The 787, by any measure, is an awesome spectacle of engineering.

Airlines across the world know this. They know the kinds of advantages a 787 affords, which explains why they're scrambling, hoping, praying to get an order filled. But the 787 cannot save air travel as we know it. Having a dozen of these planes in a fleet will not blunt the catastrophic effects of $8 gasoline. Nor will any other innovation on the current horizon. Restoring air travel to the affordability levels we now know will challenge us for decades. The economics are stark. The airlines' collapse will come sooner than most think, as gas prices of $8 are not far away.

Other $8 Effects: Families Will Concentrate in One Region

When it costs $1,000, at least, to cross the country by plane, more than business meetings will be affected. Distant relatives will be, in essence, more distant. Right now, it's easy for young people and families to move wherever their careers or fancies take them. A young family with roots in Cincinnati can move to Phoenix with few worries. They can get back to see the brood for Thanksgiving, Christmas, and usually one or two times during the year. And they can count on winter visits from their sun-seeking Midwestern relatives, too. Those who dearly miss their relatives always have that next holiday to look forward to. "Well, we'll see Grams and Gramps in two months," they say. That attitude can go a long way toward keeping families tight.

It won't be so simple in the future. Moving to the other side of the country will mean *staying* on the other side of the country. It gets harder to give the nod to a cross-country relocation when you'll see Mom and Dad only once a year, if that. In this way, the future of high-cost air travel will lead to more people sticking to the regions whence they came. Video calls supply a nice medium to keep in touch with close relatives, but they're hardly a replacement for the bonds imparted by physical touch. Fewer relatives will move far away. The integrity of family, insofar as it's defined as simply being together, will be one of the winners in the future of gas prices of $8 and up. You'll see more of Aunt Sis and your cousin Lil, and children will enjoy their grandparents even more than they already do.

Other $8 Effects: Most College-Bound Teenagers Will See Their School Choices Shrink

One of the negatives of widening the country by increasing airfares will be a reversal of geographic diversification on our nation's campuses. A sharp student from Chicago, who, in the past, might have considered attending Berkeley or Virginia along with regional picks like Illinois, Michigan, and Northwestern, will no longer be able to give those distant schools serious thought. They won't get home for the holidays and they can't expect their parents, who ultimately bear much of the college burden, to visit. Obviously, the rich will be immune to this effect. A well-heeled teen genius from San Francisco will go to Princeton, if that's what her heart wants, Newark airfare be damned. Nonelite private schools will be harmed the most, as they depend on big tuitions from a high percentage of students who don't come from the same state. Coupled with the declining number of children in future generations, middling private colleges face an unknown future. Several dozen across the country will undoubtedly shutter their classrooms for good. Those schools without generous endowments to cushion them—again, these are usually the more marginal schools—will likely be first to go.

But state schools that depend on out-of-state students will be hurt as well, including the University of Vermont, which draws 65% of its students from out of state, and the University of North Dakota, whose ranks are 48% nonnative. Giant public schools anchored in states with smaller populations that depend on out-of-state students for more than a quarter of their body will have to shrink, too. The University of Iowa, for instance, with 34% non-Iowans, will contract, as will the University of Oregon, with 28% of its students coming from outside its state borders. This regional mind-set for colleges will mark the end of an incredible era where capable students could attend college in just about any part of the country they might choose.

Other $8 Effects: Resort Townies Will Live Lonelier Lives

The last twenty years have seen an explosion of destination resorts in the United States and around the world. New towns have sprouted up where once there was only a dirt strip. Towns that were once small and rural are now cosmopolitan and the playgrounds of millionaires. Jackson, Wyoming, not too long ago, was a tacky hotel stop-off for Yellowstone tourists. In the last fifteen years, the town and the nearby ski resort, Jackson Hole Mountain Resort, have changed immeasurably. The town now boasts a dozen restaurants of culinary note. On the south side of the ski resort's lower slopes, in what was once scrub brush and ponderosa pine less than a decade ago, there is now a Four Seasons Hotel and spa. Rooms there during the ski season can run more than $2,500 a night.

Jackson has become a magnet for wealth. Homes that were worth $150,000 in 1999 are now worth north of $1 million. The cheapest real estate in town consists of ratty one-bedroom apartments built in the hideous fashion of 1970s tract construction. Those hovels sell for $500,000 each. If you're not rich, owning your home in Jackson is next to impossible (if you didn't buy it ten years ago). A local backcountry skiing guide, Jim "Woody" Woodmencey, likes to say, "My children won't be able to live here unless I give them my house."

Jackson's situation is not anomalous to other towns that have staked their future to the resort industry. Aspen, with its average home price of more than $4 million, will always be exhibit No. 1. But similar explosions have taken place in Crested Butte, Colorado; Park City, Utah; Vail, Colorado; Tahoe City, California; and Telluride, Colorado. It's not that long-time residents have gotten rich off tourists and are bidding up the local real estate. The tech industry and Wall Street have fueled a growth in the number of Americans who can afford to own a pricey second home. So when prices in Jackson spike, it's the result of a dot.com prodigy bidding against a New York banker for a $12-million, 10,000-square-foot house that will barely get used. Locals call these structures ten-two-twos, meaning 10,000 square feet that will be used by two people for two weeks a year.

This phenomenon has been fueled by two things: an increase in the number of very wealthy Americans and cheap gasoline. What makes Jackson Hole and Aspen and Vail so attractive to the jet set, above the fact that they're inherently attractive places, is that airlines fly there. Jackson would be a downright remote place if not for a strip of concrete in front of the Tetons that, in the winter, allows jets as big as 757s from United, American, and Delta to land there from Chicago, Denver, and Dallas. The Vail-Eagle Airport in Colorado sports the same types of flights and planes. In most of these cases, the resorts guarantee the seats to the airlines coming in—that is, Jackson Hole Mountain Resort or Vail Resort guarantees American Airlines that it will snare at least $300 in revenue per seat it flies to the resort's airport. If the airlines fail to reach that revenue mark, the resort makes up the difference. It's rare that they have to. The flights keep skiers coming to Jackson Hole and, in turn, ensure the real estate stays hot and the Four Seasons stays open.

In a world of $8 gasoline, however, guaranteeing those flights will be a risky play, as the airlines will likely demand $800 a seat or more. People who ski at Vail, Aspen, and Jackson Hole are undoubtedly, on average, wealthier than most Americans. But they're not all so wealthy that they'll put up $1,000 per flight per family member for five days of skiing twice a year. The people who spend the most money at the resorts are the people who have flown in from the East Coast, the Midwest, or the West Coast. Denver-area locals do not keep the high-end eateries and ski shops of Vail open. Of course, there are plenty of uberrich folk who fly into Jackson on their own jets and won't be overtly affected by higher airline ticket prices. But the majority of people skiing Jackson Hole's slopes and roasting marshmallows outside the Four Seasons flew there on an American Airlines or a United flight. The reordering of the airlines will slam the resort world in the gut. Resort operations will shrink and their surrounding real estate will wilt as the cost of visiting second homes becomes an obstacle even to the wealthy.

Ski resort towns illustrate the point here well, but the same can be said for any destination resorts that depend on airborne buses to haul in customers, be it Cabo San Lucas, the Bahamas, Cancun, or Hawaii. On the positive side, it will be easier for true locals to own a house in these places because the pressure of out-side money on the real estate market will be far less acute. The job markets in these places, however, will suffer as the No. 1 area in-dustry, tourism, contracts to a more modest footprint.

We can't talk about resorts and ignore Disney World, which was mentioned earlier in the chapter. Many people went to Disney World as young children and had what was then the time of their lives. But alas, in a world of $8 gas, ruptured airline networks, and exorbitant ticket prices, who will travel to Disney World, outside of Florida day-trippers? What will Disney do at $8? It's a perplexing question.

But in the end, as gas prices climb past $10 and higher, Disney World will undoubtedly be closed, economics having the final, de-cisive say on the matter. Disney will persevere as a company; geo-graphical distances don't strain its cartoons, DVDs, and movies. Snow White won't disappear. But her human likeness, surrounded by all of her dwarves and her Disney cohorts in a warm, tropical setting punctuated by a castle belonging to Cinderella, will be gone forever. Those of us that saw the place will recount its splendor in vivid detail, either conjured or remembered, for our grandkids, who will undoubtedly gawp in awe and not a small amount of envy.

Other $8 Effects: The Desert Temple Built for Games of Chance Will Go Bust

Las Vegas: What will become of this carnival of excess in the desert once people can't hop there for $300? Almost nobody, save a few L.A. gambling junkies, drives to Vegas. And the five-hour drive from Southern California won't be too appealing, either, when filling the tank costs $150. Who will fuel Vegas's decadence, the fountains, the lights, the felt-topped tables, and the free cocktails?

Las Vegas has become, during the last fifteen years, a place where the highest of rollers can hang in absurd luxury and also a place where Joe Normal can revel in his own levels of perceived opulence. That will change. The strip, after years of advancing like an unstoppable sand-eating virus, will shrink. The periphery hotels and casinos will be gone. Only the newest, most ridiculous resorts will survive. Conventions will still be held in Las Vegas, but not at the rate with which they are now. Companies will not be able to afford $1,000 plane tickets for fifty employees. Conventions, in the manner we're now used to, in fact, will be greatly impacted. Associations and groups that may have held annual conventions may switch to holding their gatherings every two or three years.

Las Vegas will persevere, but at a size of less than half its current largesse. Of the twenty-five largest hotels in the world, all of which have more than 2,500 rooms, nineteen of them are in Las Vegas. Half of these bloated gambling cathedrals, with sustained gas prices of more than $8, will be gone. The winners will be the newest, cleanest, and most luxurious of the resorts. Nobody will want to stay at Circus Circus when rooms can be affordably had at the MGM Grand. Circus Circus will be torn down and it won't be rebuilt. The Flamingo, a presence and Hollywood magnet for more than fifty years, will fall, too. The Imperial Palace will also come down and so, too, will the newer Excalibur and the iconic, off-strip Las Vegas Hilton.

In a true harbinger that the Vegas boom times have come to a close, the hotel-casino that, more than any other, is the godfather of today's Las Vegas, will shut its doors. The Mirage, when it opened in 1989, was a wonder of engineering, construction, and vanity. Its fountains and its exploding volcano put the rest of Vegas into an awestruck stupor. But the Mirage's reign as casino ubersupremo didn't last long. Its extravagance and technological wizardry has since been passed more than a dozen times by newer casinos in Vegas's lineup such as the Bellagio, the Luxor, and the newest Wynn creation. When the Mirage succumbs to the demolition man's dynamite—and it will—its rubble will join the wreckage of half of the strip, never to rise again.

CHAPTER 10

The Car Diminished but Reborn

Our Vehicular Romance

It was one of those bizarre Chicago days that come along at least a couple of times a year when the weather belies the date. Sometimes that can be good and sometimes that can be bad. In this case, it was good. It was also a day where I was sharply struck, again, by America's love and fascination with its vehicles. The leaves were still clinging to many of the branches in Evanston on this early November day, and the temperature had settled in at a marvelous 72 degrees. It was sunny. It smelled like fall and it felt like fall, but there was no foreboding nip of winter involved. I was sitting on the small deck at the back of our house, enjoying the sunshine and getting some editing done. Our house has no backyard, and our deck sits almost right next to the alley.

I often look up from my papers when a car goes slowly rumbling by, sometimes to wave, sometimes to stare, but always to peek out of curiosity. I looked up this time to see an old Ford Aerostar van going by. I recognized the car and the driver. He wears a thick gray beard and I've never seen him without a bandana wrapped around his head. I don't know his name, but I have a sense of what he does. He's a kind of antiques bounty hunter, always finding things for my neighbor two doors down who works as an antiques reseller and appraiser. I think the Aerostar owner might be a horse racing man, too; his license plate reads THER OFF. I gave him a wave as he rumbled by, doubtlessly after depositing something with my neighbor, and he waved back. He continued down the alley for about two more houses until he suddenly pulled sharply to the left and parked the Aerostar. He got out of the van almost excitedly to have a look at an old 1960s Ford Mustang that one of my neighbors keeps next to her garage. Usually the car is covered, but it wasn't on this day.

The bounty hunter is clearly enthused. He ogles the car from the left side, then the right. Then he's peering in the windows, scoping the interior. Soon he's wriggling along on the concrete to get a look at the chassis. I was getting little editing done at this point; I found the bounty hunter's car explorations far more interesting than my own work. I tried to keep my spying inconspicuous. But that got harder when he popped open his van's tailgate and started busting out tools. What was this guy doing? He disappeared out of my view toward the front of the car for several minutes, but I could hear clinking and clanking. He was working on something. Then he reemerged at his van and pulled out what looked to be a very delicate dust brush—probably something he used on antiques. Clearly, he held this car in the same kind of esteem he would a Victorian chest of drawers. He took the brush and used it to flick off the few dozen maple leaves that had collected on the Mustang's hood and windows. All the leaves removed, he stood back and inhaled the grandeur of the Ford, which was painted a glinty metallic gray blue.

Something clearly wasn't perfect to him. He dove back into his truck and came back with a shining cloth and proceeded to clean the car's chrome flourishings. He had been thoroughly engrossed in spiffing the car up for at least twenty minutes when the vehicle's owner showed up. She had probably seen him through her back window and wondered why an old hippie was detailing her car. If there was ever any tension in this meeting, it didn't last for more than half a second. I couldn't hear what they were saying, but the man proved to be a gregarious chatterbox, likely confessing that he was so taken with the Mustang that he had to give it a proper polish. Right now. Soon the two were laughing and deep in conversation. She stood and talked while he kept on with his rag, shining up the car. It went on this way for another twenty minutes. My wife came home, gave me a kiss, and went inside. Normally, I would follow her in to talk about her day and my day, but I stayed there, on the deck, engrossed in this chance encounter that I had nothing to do with.

Eventually, the bounty hunter got that car as shiny as one could without an electric buffer. He stood back, admired the car's form, and shared another five minutes of friendly conversation with the Mustang's owner. He finally put all his tools away and drove off in his rusty Aerostar, but not before leaving with a smile on his face. The Mustang's owner, too, beamed as she turned back toward her house. Unbeknownst to both of them, I shared their smiles and laughed to myself. What more proof does one need to see that our love of cars is real? It's a true force that long ago gripped America's consciousness.

It will require a mammoth amount of determination to change how and what we drive in this country. People won't give up their SUVs and their sports cars without a reason so compelling they can no longer deny its fundamental honesty. Ten-dollar gasoline will be a crescendo. It will tear down bulwarks to progress and technology. It will change how we think about travel. And most of all, $10 gas will be the powerful force that nudges Americans away from their deep relationships with the automobile—relationships like the one I witnessed in my alley—and toward a future of pragmatism and economy. Most people know change is coming; they may bury their acknowledgment deep in their psyche, but they know. And some people, in fact, have been preparing for $10 gas for a long time.

A Peek at the Future of Vehicles, Well Browned

My pants are brown, my shirt is brown, my shoes are brown. My socks: brown. I'm riding jumpseat in a giant truck rumbling through the early morning scurryings of Manhattan's Soho neighborhood. It's a beautiful October day. The only people treading the worn concrete at this time of the morning are people who live and work in Soho; the throngs of tourists who will descend here later are still watching CNN in their hotel rooms or are trying to figure out why New York delis insist on jamming coffee in the bag with the bagel.

As we rumble down Prince Street, toward Sixth Avenue, we turn sharply left on West Broadway and my side of the truck swings widely through the intersection. My door is open to the morning air. Corner pedestrians, coffee cups in their hands, give me nods as I swing by. I'm quite enjoying myself. Why aren't car rides this much fun? We have no trouble finding a parking space, as most of West Broadway is free and clear. We sidle up to the curb in front of a Lacoste store, which, in most places, would be one of the more upmarket shops around, but in Soho it's part of the proletariat.

We stop short of the curb to give notice, with a polite shout, to a city worker near the street who is emptying a sidewalk garbage can. He didn't hear the truck pull up. He laughs and shoots us a wave—he knows well Rene Lindain, who is driving the truck. Rene and I hop out, take a look around the neighborhood as the morning sun plays off the windows of millionaires' lofts above, and walk toward the back of the truck, a UPS truck. I am working for the ubiquitous shipping company on this day.

Rene drives this Soho route every day. He has learned to be

particularly vigilant when it comes to signaling his presence to pedestrians or street workers such as the man who is emptying out the trash can. Rene has developed a wrist reflex that lets him bump the horn ever so slightly—loud enough to be heard but abbreviated enough not to be mistaken for a malicious blare, of which New York has plenty. All UPS drivers face a rigorous safety course before they can ply the streets in the famous brown bubble truck, but Rene faces extra challenges, and not merely because he operates his truck in the densest city in America, but also because he drives a truck that runs about town almost silently. It's Big Brown on stealth. This truck is no hybrid—it's pure electric. This truck derives its propulsion purely from the electrons of its three giant batteries mounted underneath the cab and cargo area.

The truck's nighttime home is the UPS hub in Southwest Manhattan on Houston and Greenwich streets. In the morning, the 150 trucks that operate out of this facility line up perpendicularly to a giant loading dock, where workers pack the truck's shelves according to the order of the driver's routes. At 7:30 a.m., this distribution center boils in regimented chaos. People and boxes fly everywhere, most of them wearing brown, be it the sharp uniform or the drab homogeny of cardboard. Rene's truck and another one next to it look exactly the same as the diesel trucks they're aligned with, save for a note in gold lettering below the UPS logo on the side of the truck: ZERO EMISSION ELECTRIC VEHICLE. And there's one other difference—burly cords extend from a close-by column at the building's edge to beneath the trucks' hoods. The trucks are gassing up—on electricity—for the day.

On the road, the truck rides as bumpy and jerky as any other brown UPS beast, but without the rattling diesel knock, of course. Most UPS drivers have to shift gears and work a clutch in their trucks. No such worries with the electric drivetrain. Rene drives like he's at home in the Smart Car he just bought; he hits the gas (the battery) and goes. And whereas most UPS trucks operate with a hand brake, this truck has a brake pedal. All in all, it amounts to a powerful golf cart with a ton of cargo space. Even the truck's shifting mechanism resembles that of a fairway-navigating golf cart. It's simply a two-inch lever mounted against the steel dash with three settings: forward, neutral, and reverse. The truck's acceleration is far better than that of its diesel counterparts. At a red light, we pull up alongside a U.S. Postal Service diesel truck piloted by a driver named Lynne; Rene knows him and exchanges some flippant repartee. When the light turns green, the Postal Service truck putt-putt-putts slowly away from its stop whereas our electric truck takes off like a shot, not limited by the foibles of a combustion engine.

We've got the truck empty of its deliveries by 2 p.m.; it will be time for pickups soon. Rene has been working this neighborhood for seventeen years and his popularity with the locals is evident. He draws shouts from models, directors, artists, and actors from across the street, hugs in doorways. My favorite part of the day, easily, has been the time we spent driving. Whooshing along, pulled by the electric motor, the sliding doors open to the Manhattan traffic.

This real-life day of work I spent at UPS reflects the company's continuing rehearsal for the future. That's why the company takes the time and spends the money to operate an expensive vehicle like this on the streets of New York. When the dust settles at $10 a gallon gas, UPS will be one of the winners thanks to its prescient preparations. The electric truck's strengths play perfectly to the stop-start rhythm of Manhattan driving. UPS has been testing two electric trucks on Manhattan routes for more than four years. The trucks work beautifully—they actually require less upkeep and maintenance than the standard UPS package truck—and they fit seamlessly into the system of the Houston Street distribution center. The electric trucks pull a full load; there's nothing trial-like about their routes.

UPS's business relies upon the free and affordable flow of oil.

The company is acutely aware of its dependence. That's exactly why UPS has so intensely studied using trucks that run on things other than gasoline. UPS counts these electric trucks as part of its fleet of 1,600 alternate fuel vehicles—the largest private fleet of its kind in the world. Many of those trucks run on propane or natural gas, which, obviously, will face some of the same scarcity issues as gasoline. But UPS also operates hybrid electric vehicles and recently added an exciting new kind of truck that gets double the mileage of a conventional diesel truck by pairing a gasoline engine with pressurized hydraulic tanks that power the crankshaft. In 2008, UPS purchased 500 electric hybrid trucks to add to its fleet. That's a tiny chunk of the 90,000 vehicles it has on the road worldwide (68,000 in the United States), but UPS is setting itself up for the oil swoon and the escalating price of gas.

UPS spent $2.1 billion on fuel in 2005. That amount doubled in 2008. Freezing its business model as gas rises to $10 per gallon is not an option for UPS. Naturally, UPS will increase its prices with the rising cost of fuel, as will its competitors at FedEx and the U.S. Postal Service. But the sharpest companies, such as UPS, are the ones that don't let changing circumstances dictate their destiny. They grab change by the throat and squeeze out nickels that nobody else thought to even look for. UPS is, after all, a company that in 2007 largely eliminated left-hand turns on its drivers' routes by using mapping software, saving 28.5 million miles and 3 million gallons of gasoline. By leveraging technology, UPS will mitigate gasoline's body blow and will be ready to step off the petroleum escalator the moment it becomes economically possible.

UPS has been heavily experimenting with electric trucks in the cities of Europe, where gasoline can cost three times as much as it does in the United States. UPS has an electric truck operating in central London right now—the part of London with the $16 entrance toll. The fee, however, is waived for electric vehicles as part of the UK's program to nudge companies toward alternative energies. Couple that with the gasoline savings and the electric vehicles begin to make a fiscal case for themselves. And that's what this is all about: the fiscal case. "When gas approaches six and eight dollars a gallon, we'll certainly be expediting the examination of our fleets and how we can move away from gasoline," says Robert Hall, the director of maintenance and automotive engineering at UPS. "At ten dollars, you can bet there will be real change."

A typical UPS package truck costs $50,000. A hybrid version can run close to $100,000, and a straight electric can run even more than that. The first reason for the price differentials is the simple fact that the alternative trucks are packed with more expensive electronics, from the lithium-ion batteries to the CPUs that control the electronic drive systems. The second and more powerful reason is that the hybrid and electric trucks simply have no scale in their manufacturing bases, unlike the diesel trucks that UPS and other companies order thousands of every year, allowing their suppliers to capture the efficiencies and value of massive scale. As demand creeps up, says Hall, so will production, which will bring the price of these technologically advanced trucks down. All that will be happening, of course, as the price of gasoline continues its upward drift. So there will be enormous pressure and advantages for companies to examine trucks propelled by alternatives to gasoline.

UPS also has been calmly instituting change among the giant airplane fleet of 580 heavy jets that it operates—enough planes to make it the ninth largest airline in the world. Most of UPS's flying time is during the wee hours of the night, when it's shuttling packages to and fro to meet the coming day's delivery schedule. After 10 p.m., UPS has Louisville's airport, its hub, almost to itself. Because of that, air traffic control allows UPS pilots to use continuous descent patterns when landing, saving the company millions of gallons of jet fuel. Normally, a plane approaches an airport at a high elevation and gets approved by air traffic control to move to incrementally lower elevations. A plane would commonly go from 35,000 feet to 30,000 feet and then stay there until it gets approval to move down to 25,000 feet, and so on. With a sky full of traffic, controllers need this measure of safety. It makes keeping track of planes easier, but the constant plateau-like pattern of descending, leveling, and descending chugs a lot of jet fuel. When gasoline costs $10, all major airports of the world will have planes descend continuously, rather than in stepped formations as our skies will be far roomier with the decrease in airline flights that will commence at $8 gas.

UPS doesn't actually see $10 gasoline as a bad thing. "We think, at that point, e-commerce will become even more prominent, which could further augment our position as a middleman," says Norman Black, UPS's head of investor relations. "People won't want to get in their cars and pay for gas to shop at bricks-and-mortar stores. High fuel prices could generate future opportunities that we've never dreamed of."

High fuel prices would enable UPS to enact plans it's been role-playing with for years. Many will be set into motion by $6 and $8 gas. When we reach $10, UPS will have become firmly committed to converting much of its fleet to using propulsion sources outside of the pure combustion engine we're all hooked on now. Rene's electric package truck that floats around Soho as an unnoticed novelty will become the norm.

Gas prices of $10 a gallon may seem far away, but if you look at the fundamentals of the world's supplies and the certainty of rising demands, it's a number we will almost definitely see within the next ten years. When we get to $10, companies and consumers alike will fully realize that the rudiments of driving will have changed forever. UPS's smartly laid plans will reap benefits for the Atlanta behemoth. They've proven that electric trucks can replace their diesel trucks and that customers and the company's performance won't suffer. The only thing missing is the financial piece. When gas station marquees start rolling out double-digit dollar numbers and hang a $ in front of a 1 in front of a 0, the time will have arrived for the electric trucks of UPS and for our own cars powered by plugs.

Plug-In Hybrids Will Form the Bridge We Need to an Electric Car World

We will be weaned into full electric cardom by plug-in hybrid cars, which operate similarly to current hybrids such as the Toyota Prius and Honda Insight, except that they carry bigger batteries and offer owners the option of plugging into the wall every night—an option we will all take. The plug-in hybrid, after a nightly recharge in the garage, will typically be able to travel 30 to 40 miles at moderate speeds on pure battery power. When the battery's juice runs low, the hybrid's gasoline engine kicks in and recharges the battery as the car continues to drive. For people who drive less than 30 miles a day, this will mean they'll have very infrequent visits to the gas station. But their car will still be able to hit the road for a long-distance trip of 400 miles if need be, because of the gasoline engine.

Plug-in hybrids, in some form or another, will be on the roads by 2010. But they won't come cheaply. GM's Chevy Volt, Detroit's highly anticipated plug-in dynamo, will run more than $40,000. It's hard to justify that kind of cost when gas is $6 or less. But as Nissan, Toyota, Honda, and Ford get their own plug-in entrants into the derby, prices will come down. These cars will never be as cheap as a straight gasoline vehicle, however, because they carry expensive batteries and electronic systems in addition to their gasoline engines. But as the price of gasoline moves upward from $6, the value and utility of plug-in hybrids will increase and they will appear in more and more garages. Plug-in hybrids, along with some funky competitors that are bound to pop up, will help sustain us on our journey toward an all-electric future.

By the way, semi-tractor trailer trucks, those of the highway-driving variety, are simply too big to be powered by batteries. Their numbers will most certainly be trimmed by gas prices topping the $10 mark. Shipping's cost will become prohibitively expensive for some items. Moving across the country will become an even more vexing and expensive chore than ever before. Many people, instead of schlepping their things in a U-Haul from Virginia to San Diego and shelling out $3,000 for gasoline plus the cost of the rental truck, will be better off simply selling almost all their things in Virginia and then restocking on the attires of living once they get to San Diego. This will be a sad reality for some people who cling sentimentally to their stuff, but for others, it will be liberating. Cut your wires and go. Each new destination of life would carry with it a new tranche of furnishings and surroundings.

Strange, Newfangled Competitors to the All-Electric Car Will Emerge

I am again riding in a UPS package truck during the month of October. But this day isn't so warm. It's rather cold. It's cold for Atlanta, anyway, at 47 degrees. Atlanta's streets are full of people wearing a wide variation of bombproof jackets built to withstand a Hudson Bay January. Lots of fluffy down jackets with faux-fur-lined hoods and hats, gloves, and scarves. I assume these people won't be moving to Chicago. On the UPS truck, I still ride in the passenger jump seat with the door open. Chilly or not, riding with the door open is not a perk I'm willing to relinquish. We're zipping about the downtown with no mission in particular; this is not a truck currently making deliveries, although it's perfectly capable. As we pass the outside of Atlanta's Centennial Olympic Park dedicated to the 1996 games, we rumble through a right turn onto Marietta Street and accelerate. Only thing is, there's no sound. No engine, no whoosh, nothing. And this truck has no batteries.

What it does have is what UPS and the EPA call a hydraulic hybrid drivetrain. The EPA developed the technology that stores energy in compressed tanks of hydraulic fluid that are five-foot-long cylinders about twelve inches in diameter. The tanks act like a kind of battery that squirrels away energy by compressing their fluid to very high pressures. When the truck moves forward, the tanks release their pressure and turn the axels, propelling the truck. When the brakes get slammed, almost all the energy that the truck has going forward gets quickly compressed into the hydraulic tank system. Electric hybrids do the same thing—they capture energy from braking and return some of it to the onboard battery. But batteries themselves are not well suited to take massive doses of energy like this all at once; they're only able to absorb electrons at a trickle, as if they were being charged from a wall socket.

UPS has been testing a couple of these trucks on routes in southeast Michigan. "When the drivers started using this, they kept thinking the truck was stalled, but it wasn't," laughs John Kargul, director of technology transfer at the EPA. The hydraulic tanks often operate in utter silence. Hydraulic hybrids carry the added benefit of being easier to repair and maintain than a battery-powered car. "Today's car mechanics, they understand this stuff, hydraulics. It's metal, it's bearings. They look at this and say, 'I understand this. I can work on this.' Hydraulics are old technology," Kargul says.

During the gasoline crisis of the early 1980s, truck manufacturers experimented with hydraulic hybrids but could not make the system any more efficient than a normal gasoline truck. One reason was because their accumulators, which were made of steel, had to be incredibly heavy to handle the requisite pressures of the hydraulic fluid. Back then, researchers also didn't have access to the cheap and small computing power that's now used to regulate the diesel engine, which runs about half the time the truck is on; in the 1980s, that was all manually controlled and inefficient. With the modern improvements in materials weight and automated technology, the new hydraulic truck gets 18 mpg, compared to the standard UPS truck, which gets 10 mpg. The EPA estimates that when the hydraulic technology is honed and UPS is able to order several thousand of the hybrid trucks at once, the hybrid will cost about $7,000 more than a normal package truck. That's a cost that will be recouped, typically, within two years if gas prices are $5 or higher. UPS's hydraulic hybrid could form the company's bridge from a fleet based on gasoline combustion to one based on lithium-ion battery recharging. The hydraulic hybrid, because of the size of the tanks required, is too bulky to operate in normal family sedans. But it will prove to be an important technology in trucks and large vehicles of the exact type that UPS drives.

Other fresh technologies will seize on the panic for a gasoline alternative. We'll be desperate. Many forms of propulsion will get their fifteen seconds. One of them sure to pop up is air power. A Frenchman, Guy Negre, has created a car that runs on compressed air. If that concept doesn't capture the public's imagination, there isn't much that could. Negre's Motor Development International has test air cars zipping around the French Riviera near the company's offices outside Nice. They come in bright colors, can go 70 mph, and have a range of 125 miles on flat roads. The motor simply uses a steady, powerful gush of compressed air to push its two pistons up and down. Exhaust from the engine consists of harmless atmospheric air, cold enough to serve as air-conditioning on a hot day.

Negre, a sixty-seven-year-old mechanical engineer, worked on Renault's F1 racing-design crew in the 1980s and 1990s and pioneered the use of magnesium in pistons, a major breakthrough in racing. During his tinkering in the 1980s, Negre became fixated on a green car. In 1991 he founded MDI with $36,000 in venture money, not enough to build a factory, but as a resourceful engineer, Negre found a way to patch some test models together over the years.

The absence of combustion allows Negre to use a lean aluminum engine casing. MDI's engine weighs 80 pounds, a third the weight of the dinky engine in a Toyota Corolla. The fuel is air compressed to 4,350 pounds per square inch, or 300 times the pressure of the air you breathe. Negre insists that despite the enormous pressure, the tank, in a collision, would split down its sides, harmlessly expelling the air in a giant *phoomp*.

Negre, who speaks some English but isn't utterly fluent, likes to say that, "The future of cars is air." That's an excitable engineer for you. Using air as an energy storage medium is clever, clean, and cheap. Air car's limited range would require plenty of fill-ups at compressed-air service stations, except those don't exist. But, of course, they could be built. Drivers could fill up at home by plugging in the car's onboard compressor, which would take four hours. Again, that's not a deal breaker and it's similar to an electric car's recharge time. The air car weighs only 1,873 pounds (unfueled) and might not meet the safety regulations of the United States but Negre says he can upgrade the safety features: "If we want to be in the U.S., we will have to pass, so that's what we plan on doing," he declares.

MDI plans to license the product to manufacturers in attractive markets. Negre presumes that these franchisees will buy parts, assemble them, and sell cars directly to the public from a small showroom on the site of the factory. A U.S. company called Zero Pollution Motors has purchased a license from MDI to build an air car factory in the States. Shiva Vencat, chief executive of Zero Pollution Motors in New Paltz, New York, wants to roll out the U.S. car in 2010 for $18,000. "I honestly think that if you have a car out there with an equivalent of a hundred miles per gallon that's only eighteen thousand dollars, you're going to have more than two percent market share, but we want to be conservative," Vencat says, by which he means that his sales goal of 300,000 a year will be easily achieved.

Vencat is dreaming, most likely. There will be a place for air cars in our future as niche players. There may even be tens of thousands on our roads, but we will not become a nation of air car drivers. Cars propelled with air have serious user drawbacks when compared with the frontrunner of the future, vehicles powered by lithium-ion batteries. The air car, as designed now, uses a small propane heater to raise the pressure of the air in its tanks as it dissipates. Warmer air requires more volume, which drives up the pressure and lets the car go farther on a charge of air.

But even with this fossil fuel appendage, the air car cannot run even a skeletal version of the niceties that Americans have come to expect in their cars, such as heat, stereos, power windows, locks, etc., let alone the extravagant fixtures of recent times such as DVD players and video game systems. Air power is good at moving small, light vehicles. But put any real weight on an air-powered chassis and your range gets cut precipitously. Air cars could fill a need for families who need a cheap vehicle for use in and around the neighborhood. Their main car could then be a battery-powered sedan or station wagon, offering the safety, speed, and comforts similar to the cars we have today.

Ultimately, our needs and the realities of energy scarcity will push us toward becoming a nation of electric car drivers. The only thing we have in relative abundance is energy from our power plants—our trump card is our electric grid. Batteries allow us to play this card with aplomb.

A Hydrogen-Powered Solution Is Not in the Offing Anytime Soon

As the gasoline cost crisis continues unfolding, we'll likely see hydrogen raised again as the clean, guiltless solution to our energy problems. GM has spent more than $1 billion chasing this idea, but their chase will likely end with their dreams trampled.[1] The idea of a hydrogen-based transportation system amounts to one of the bigger hoodwinks perpetrated on Americans since smoking's health claims in the 1950s. I will not waste much time undressing hydrogen, because it doesn't take more than a sentence or two. Hydrogen, as an energy source, works beautifully. Hydrogen fuel cells operate cleanly, quietly, and efficiently. They work by separating electrons from hydrogen atoms and forcing them through a circuit, where they do work such as turn a motor or light a bulb. The electrons return to the fuel cell to bond with the leftover hydrogen ions and oxygen, forming the fuel cell's harmless exhaust: water vapor.

Aside from the fact that fuel cells cost a fortune, the ultimate problem with hydrogen is, simply, where we get it. There are no hydrogen mines. There are no vast stores of this simplest of elements sitting beneath our feet. And we can't pull it from the air or water without using massive amounts of energy. So where does almost all the hydrogen we use come from? Natural gas or, even worse, oil. Industry strips natural gas, CH_4, of its hydrogen, leaving behind carbon that forms CO_2 and ends up in our atmosphere. So, in essence, unless there is an unforeseen breakthrough in getting hydrogen from a source such as seawater, our hydrogen stores amount to the stores of our fossil fuels. Hydrogen doesn't sound like a solution because, as of now, it's not.

Electric Cars Will Eventually Rule Our Thinning Traffic, 100 Years After Some Thought

Mankind has been toying with electric cars for more than 150 years. Long before we ever built a carburetor to mix gasoline and air in a combustion engine, we were propelling crude four-wheeled platforms on the power of a lead-acid battery. In 1834, New Hampshire blacksmith Thomas Davenport, the inventor of the electromagnetic motor, built a carriage that ran on juice supplied by a charged rail. That moment was lost to history for decades, however, as the steam engine proved to be more industrious and less temperamental for the heady times of railroads.

However, in the early years of the twentieth century, there were dozens of companies turning out electric cars. In 1897, Philadelphia's Electric Carriage & Wagon Company manufactured a fleet of electric taxis for New York. It did seem, for a time, that we would become a nation of electric vehicle users. It took the genius of Henry Ford in 1908 to fork us decisively in a different direction when he introduced his gas-powered Model T at half the cost of electric cars. And the Model T would only continue to get cheaper as Ford honed his assembly line proficiency.

It will turn out that what Ford really did was delay us, by more than 100 years, from realizing our transportation destiny: electric cars powered by batteries. The idea is simple enough. The cars plug into the wall and charge up at night. Cars will also charge up during the day at workplaces where parking slots are so equipped. Batteries aren't perfect. But they're the best and most affordable of the options we will be given in a world where oil scarcity becomes more acute by the day.

Filling up a large battery that can propel an average sedan about 100 miles would cost less than $5 at current electricity prices—a steep discount compared with gasoline. Once we've handled the enormous burden of paying for our electric car network, our driven miles should cost considerably less. Our fuel would be kilowatts delivered to our car batteries from our electric utilities. That fuel will be a bargain compared to gasoline. Even when using a modern hybrid car, such as a Toyota Prius, which gets close to 50 miles per gallon, the power generated by the Prius from gasoline costs 40 cents per kilowatt-hour, at gas prices of $4 a gallon. Power from the electrical outlet runs, in most places, less than 20 cents a kilowatt-hour, and off-peak power (at night) can cost half that. The longer we delay migrating from a gasoline-based transportation world to an electric one, the worse our pain will be. And the pain, says Shai Agassi, will be bad.

The Man Who May Have Cracked Battery-Powered Cars' Most Vexing Problems

Agassi heads up Better Place, a company he founded to solve the logistical riddles facing electric cars in a world and infrastructure built for gasoline. "We don't have a choice," Agassi says. "We either do this, or we suffer the catastrophic failures of economic ruin and global warming."

A native Israeli, Agassi comes to the transportation world from an unlikely place. Agassi and his father founded a software company in the 1990s that SAP, the German business software giant, bought for $400 million in 2001. Agassi then joined SAP, where he was president of products and recognized as a likely candidate to ascend to the CEO pulpit. But in the fall of 2007, Agassi chucked his future at SAP to start Better Place. He had been seized by a cause. When he talks, Agassi likes to pause for suspense's sake before he's about to make a weighty point. He enjoys torpedoing conventional wisdom and often sets up his bombs with the statement: "Let me send your mind reeling a bit." He sees things one way, his way. But in the past, he's been right more often than not. A highly placed SAP executive told me that, "Agassi can sound downright arrogant sometimes, but he's the best salesman I've ever seen." It's true that Agassi's persuasive talents and intellect have won him scores of influential fans. Better Place has raised more than $200 million of capital and its goals are nothing short of world-changing.

It's plain that Agassi isn't an ordinary CEO pushing an ordinary corporate agenda. He works for an idea and a clutch of values, not numbers in an annual report. All idealism aside, however, Better Place is still a company, and one that plans on making money. It's just that for Better Place, making money also means, in Agassi's eyes, saving Western society from the coming resources scourge should we continue down our current path. For a nation switching from gasoline cars to electric cars, all manner of challenges exist. It's not quite as simple as buying the car, driving home, and plugging it into the garage wall. Well, it might be close to that simple for consumers and car owners, but the back-story here lies in the enormous complexities of making electric cars possible for a large swath of the population. It's complicated because our local utility lines can't handle a third of the homes on a normal block plugging in their cars all at once, let alone most of the homes. Transformers would explode. Local grids would melt down. It's complicated because batteries take a long time to recharge. It's complicated because batteries can cost more than $10,000 per car.

So how do we make the electric car transition without spending $1 trillion to rework the national power grid? That's where Better Place comes in. They want to be the Exxon Mobil of the electric car world. Where Exxon drills for oil and ships gasoline to our network of service stations, Better Place wants to be our arbiter of electrons. Better Place wants to facilitate our current, balkanized electric grid to become the equivalent of our vast network of gas stations. Better Place isn't in this to sell cars—anybody can sell cars—they want to solve the big, seemingly intractable problems facing electric cars and, in the process, become the lithium-ion version of Exxon.

Better Place wants people to buy electric cars without the batteries. They equate batteries and their power to gasoline. We don't buy our cars now with a long-term down payment on the gasoline our vehicle will use throughout the next ten years, so, Better Place asks, why should we do the same for a battery? People will buy cars like they buy cell phones, Agassi says, and then it's up to Better Place—the wireless carrier—to keep the cars running at an affordable rate, based on how much electricity one uses. What Agassi is building here isn't wholly dissimilar from the software firms he's built most of his professional life. Specially designed software allows people to overcome barriers that previously made accomplishing certain tasks difficult. Software takes what was once incredibly complex and makes it simple. Like what a word processor does for writing page upon page of grammatically correct prose or what a spreadsheet does for keeping track of formulas and numbers or what tax software does for once-stymied filers. Agassi is used to fixing problems of high complexity, so he's a natural to crack some of the cumbersome problems that, without software, would doom a world of electric cars.

There are three main problems, as were mentioned, facing a potential tide of electric cars sweeping our vehicle markets. It may not be Agassi who ultimately solves all these conundrums, but somebody will have to lead what will be a giant unraveling of our electrical grid's weaknesses and electric cars' drawbacks. Agassi, at this point, is the only guy with a plan and with more than two nickels devoted toward the cause. The first problem that needs to be cracked is the sheer cost of electric cars' batteries. Under Better Place's plan, that problem is mitigated by having electric car users pay a monthly battery subscription fee—that's my wording, not theirs—that will run less, they say, than the monthly cost of gasoline at $4 a gallon. Drivers won't own the batteries. Better Place will.

This basically amortizes the price of battery power storage across the whole life of the vehicle—a cost structure drivers are already used to from buying gasoline. Dealing with batteries this way also keeps car owners from having to deal with cell replacement and disposal costs when their car reaches ten years of age or so. Replacing a battery can run more than $10,000—it would be like having to bear the cost of rebuilding your transmission five times, all at once.

The second problem that Better Place seeks to solve: the simple fact that you just can't get very far on a battery—100 miles at the most, probably less. Better Place's solution is as simple as the problem. Just as we now pull up to a gas station to refill when we're about to go empty, we will pull into a Better Place depot when our battery is near exhaustion and we have more driving to do. There's no way to charge a battery of the size cars use in less than a few hours, but that doesn't mean a different, fully charged battery can't be swapped in. A Better Place station will swap out a dying battery in less than five minutes, allowing the driver to continue along her day with an interruption of the same curt magnitude as filling up at the gas pump.

The third major problem that Better Place's plan addresses—and this is a dilemma that might be slightly arcane to most people but nonetheless just as knotty as the first two—is the fact that much of our local electrical grid isn't ready for several people on one block to simultaneously plug in their electric cars overnight. We might have the spare juice in our power plants, but the local lines can't carry the required amperage all at once. "There's nothing else in your house that gets plugged in for six hours and draws thirty amps and 220 volts," says Mike Lindheim, an electrical engineer with Better Place. "There's simply nothing else that pulls that much power. And imagine if you had a whole lot of people doing that," he says. If three or four people on a small block all plugged in their cars all at once, the local transformer would likely explode. The replacement of our local electrical infrastructure will happen eventually, but it will take several decades and hundreds of billions of dollars.

Better Place has the interim solution. All electric cars would carry an onboard computer that would constantly communicate with the Better Place network, transmitting where the car was, how much juice it had left, whether it was plugged in, etc. When a driver wants to travel to point A and thinks the distance might be a bit far for his car's current charge, he tells the car's onboard GPS where he is going and the computer lets him know if he can make it. If he doesn't have the power required and he doesn't want to wait to charge up, the computer communicates with Better Place and tells the driver what battery service station is closest to his route; it then alerts the battery stop that the driver will be coming in for a fresh cell in about fifteen minutes. To the driver, it equates to nothing more than a stop at the gas station.

Similarly, the onboard computer would know when the car gets plugged into the garage outlet and it would communicate that fact to Better Place's network, which would also know if there were already three other cars on the same block plugged in. Better Place would then communicate with all the plugged-in cars, determining which of them had the lowest charges and should be refilled first. To keep the local grid's transformers from being overwhelmed, Better Place's computers would alternate the cars' charging patterns during the night, ensuring that all four cars have fully charged batteries by morning. So you may plug your car in when you get home, but that won't necessarily mean it's charging at that moment. The cars require only four hours to reach a full charge, and most cars, when they get plugged in for the night, won't have empty batteries; many will be half full or more, requiring only one or two hours of charge, leaving plenty of hours in the night to get the whole block fueled up.

All these solutions would be run by Better Place's proprietary software, using methods of coding and algorithms that Agassi's programmers are already familiar with. The charging infrastructure we need to start switching to electric cars is already here, Agassi says, it just needs somebody—a powerful network of computers—to manage cars' charging patterns. Better Place is already sitting down with some of the country's major utilities to discuss putting together a comprehensive mapping survey of the electric capacities that are on the ground in every major city and neighborhood. With this information in hand and digitized, Better Place could then smoothly slip new electric car owners into the network.

But getting that network in the first place, Agassi says, will take more than the raw forces of capitalism. "We have a car industry that's self-regulating right now, and it's not working," he explains. "There is no incentive for any car company to change from what they're doing now—their products' planning and life cycles are too long. They simply won't change. The only way they will change is if they're forced to."

Agassi may sound like he's preaching government interference. He is. Better Place, at this point in its nascent life, doesn't pitch its network to consumers, it pitches to heads of state. Agassi's sales skills have already proved themselves three times in a span of less than twelve months when he landed deals with the Israeli, Danish, and Australian governments. In Israel, the 78% tax levied on vehicles will be cut to 10% for Better Place's electric cars. That's a powerful consumer incentive. In Denmark, there will be zero tax on the cars. In Australia, the government is fronting a $500 million fund to encourage carmakers to make their electric vehicles on Australian soil.

France's Renault will be making the electric cars for Better Place's operations in Israel and Denmark. The vehicles will debut in both countries in 2011, by the end of which Agassi hopes to have 100,000 vehicles operating on the Better Place grid. The standard sedan that Renault will offer for the program will be priced between $20,000 and $25,000. Not a cheap vehicle. But that number isn't a bank buster to the point of relegating the car to novelty or luxury status. It's a concept that will undoubtedly be embraced by many once the price of gas reaches $10. It won't be a choice that everybody gets, however; it will be a choice limited to those who can afford the capital cost of a new car that costs more than $20,000, perhaps more than $25,000. It's a price that will exclude a large chunk of car buyers, and certainly people who buy used cars.

Agassi says that we can't afford to wait until gas costs $10 per gallon to embrace electric cars. By that time, he says, we will have boxed ourselves into a very tight corner. With electricity and batteries, "We can build Saudi Arabia instead of fighting over Saudi Arabia," Agassi argues. "None of our society's future scenarios are good ones unless we disconnect the car from gasoline." Agassi isn't

totally wrong. The longer we wait, the harder these changes will be
to institute, but his sound bites are also driven by his strident mission to make Better Place one of the biggest companies in the
world. His declarations have to be weighed with his own ambitions. The good thing about Better Place for all of us is that it's
enacting a live trial on two different stages—Israel and Denmark—
that we get to sit back and watch during the coming years. Whether
or not it's Agassi and Better Place that takes the United States and,
ultimately, the world, forward into the era of mainstream electric
vehicles, we'll undoubtedly take away innumerable lessons from
Better Place's current work. Work that will help them or somebody else put electric cars into wide circulation when gas prices
reach $10 per gallon.

The Future of Cars Will Be Electric, but It Won't Be a Smooth Ride

Converting our personal transportation platform from one based
on gasoline to one powered by electricity is one of the most im-
perative measures we will take in shaping a sustainable future for
our country and for global civilization as a whole. This will not be
an easy transition. Car ownership rates, at $10 gas, will plummet.
Many people will end up forfeiting their cars altogether, as the
price of gas squeezes them out of their old Accords, Camrys, and
Tauruses and the high price of electric cars, which will all be new
as there will be no used car market, keeps them from getting into
a battery car.

Traffic flows on major arteries will ebb and the side effects
that began to take hold at $6 gas—fewer crash deaths, less pollu-
tion, less obesity—will be firing in full force at $10 gas. Road usage
fees will become widespread. The model of taxing everybody to
maintain our roads worked fine when everybody used the roads.
But that model will be subverted as people become excluded from

the road grid by the high cost of gas and the high costs of electric cars when that market is still small. The road burden will be shifted onto those who actually use the road, putting driving, unfortunately, further out of reach for those in lower income brackets. Highways will be all about tolls. Some city spurs and local interstate stretches will be closed as the demand for open highway decreases.

Gasoline cars will persist past $10 gas, but their role will decrease with every dollar we move upward. People will keep their gas car on the side of the house, as a spare vehicle that can be used in a pinch or for longer journeys. This will mark the end of a 75-year period where we let the car define our society, our fabric, our identity. Vehicles, so long a statement of purpose, style, and preference, will become utilitarian, like a horse. As long as it drives and isn't too uncomfortable, it'll work. Unplug, drive to work, plug it back in. As part of society loses its ability to stay affordably mobile on an independent basis, public transportation and the densities it enables will move to the fore, their forces becoming potent and indelible at $12 per gallon.

The carmakers we know will adjust or die, if they're not already dead. Surely this field of personal transportation will be led by at least one or two intrepid and visionary startup companies, companies that could end up being the largest incubated startups of all time, eclipsing the likes of Google, Microsoft, and the rest of the nascent Internet-era icons. Perhaps Better Place will rule them all. Americans will see their plugs as the new pump. The total revamping of our vehicle fleet will take decades, but we will look back at $10 gasoline as being the spark that sent our civilization in new, exciting directions.

Bicycle lanes, already more than a novel curiosity in many U.S. cities, will become a point of emphasis. The best bike lane and path networks in America will become lures for families and others looking to save money and change the way their lives work.

This story won't unfold neatly and calmly. These things rarely do. People will be desperate and money will fly toward all manner of car propulsion technology. For a family driving a modest amount, say 15,000 miles a year on two cars, and driving vehicles that do well on overall fuel economy, say 30 mpg, their annual fuel costs would be $10,000. That's not an amount that Americans are prepared for and it cannot persevere. We will change our lives. We will change how we drive, how much we drive, and where we drive. We will change the places in which we live. There will be some sense of panic in the marketplace. People will yell: What are we supposed to do now? The public will want quick and easy solutions. But unfortunately, there won't be any. The riotous nature of our transportation crisis will get companies and people looking in all directions for a savior technology. Many variations of energy, some familiar, some not, will be touted by their attached lobbyists. But know this: There will be no magic formula; there will be no mad scientist cracking some secret resource open as our replacement fuel. It will be society's job to change. Our tools are on the table; we must use and hone what we've been given with prudence.

Extinction Will Come for Gasoline-Slurping Big Boy Toys

As innovations are born, old ones will die. The superfluous gadgetry of the gasoline world—that which exists purely for recreation—will be first to go. The debate over snowmobiles in Yellowstone will become moot as most of their manufacturers will capitulate to the intense pressures of ever-steepening gasoline prices. The number of people willing to pay $200 just for the gasoline needed for a day of fun on the back of a motorized snow sled will be too few to keep the business thriving. Snowmobiles will become machines relegated to duties of emergency need rather than duties of recreation. Backcountry skiers, snowshoers, and cross-country buffs will revel in the purity of a quiet woods.

Snowmobiles will be only one of many carcasses left in $10 gas's wake. Jet skis and wave runners will disappear, too. Sailors of the world will rejoice as their job of navigating densely popular lakes and harbors will grow much easier. We won't miss jet skis' 12,000 annual accidents in the United States, dozens of which result in deaths. The giant fleet of motorboats, speedboats, and ski boats that crowd our waters will be thinned to a tiny convoy. Sailboats, canoes, kayaks, and rowboats will rule the waves.

All-terrain vehicles and dirt bikes, the kinds that tear up the woods with their gasoline whine and their spiky tires, will be relegated to antique status. Mountain bikers, hikers, and trail runners will rejoice. Many people will have their hobbies stolen from them by the rising price of gas. It will no longer be possible for a family to enjoy a powerboat in the summer. The thrill of shoving the throttles fully forward and getting pushed back into the cabin seat as the July sun warms the spray coming over the windshield—that feeling is one borne purely of cheap oil, so enjoy it while you might. Ultimately, these sacrifices—powerboats, jet skis, snowmobiles— will be small. People will get along without their 400-horsepower pickup truck that drags their 300-horsepower bass boat from lake to lake. They will still be able to stalk largemouth bass, but they'll do it from a small boat propelled by a paddle or a stealthy electric trolling motor. It's fitting that the hobbies that so brazenly incinerate our natural resources will be the ones to disappear. We will still enjoy our forests, snowfields, and lakes, and arguably, to an even greater degree. These places will, in the end, benefit greatly from the removal of gasoline's chemical and noise pollutions.

The Rise of Ecofriendly Plastic Will Be Swift, Thanks to $10 Gas

The product capitulations at $10 won't stop with gasoline toys. This is the point where we will begin to see new kinds of products stepping to the fore of our lives, replacing petroleum-based substances that we have leaned on for fifty years. The gross, unsustainable habits formed by our society in the 1950s won't give way easily, but $10 gas will prove to be the onset of permanent decay for our plastic society. Already, we're seeing companies bent on improving their public relations and, increasingly, their bottom lines, turn to conservation for a way to curb their use of plastics and oil derivatives. Whole Foods will pay you a dime for every grocery bag you bring in and reuse. Most grocers these days give you the option of recycled paper bags over petroleum-derived plastic ones; that was not common just five years ago. IKEA, by charging five cents for each plastic bag, encourages customers to get their stuff out of the cavernous Swedish store without using disposable plastics. IKEA figures customers will use 50% fewer bags, saving 35 million of them a year from landfills and keeping more IKEA earnings out of the hands of oil refineries.

Plastics, however, aren't going away. Their utility has enabled us to raise our standards of living and has brought new levels of comfort to lower classes of people all over the world. Plastics are durable, lightweight, strong, and easy to color. Plastic can be supple. It can be tough. Plastic wire insulation, cases, and circuit board supports allow our computers to be small and powerful. Polyvinyl chloride pipes have allowed us to safely—and incredibly cheaply—move sewage and waste away from people and into treatment facilities. Our astronauts wear seven-layer insulated suits made from polymers, and their helmets are polycarbonate down to the transparent visors. We've explored the bottom of the ocean with lenses and electronics that owe their integrity to thick layers of clear acrylic. In 1960, the bathyscaphe Trieste reached a depth of 35,797 feet—seven miles—in the Challenger Deep section of the Mariana Trench. Jacques Piccard and Don Walsh peered out at a slimy ocean floor teeming with small flounder and sole through a thick plate of plastic Plexiglas, the only transparent substance that can withstand the Challenger Deep pressure of 16,000 pounds per square inch.[2]

Plastic is the most amazing substance man has ever contrived. But it's also one of the most damaging. Plastics derived from petroleum biodegrade so slowly that many of them will be hanging around eons from now. One thousand years from now, your ashes will have been sucked up by a nutrient-seeking oak tree, which will be cut down for firewood and burned again. Your ash will then manifest in yet another organic life-form perhaps two continents away. You might be in a stalk of wheat in Mongolia, but your old whiffle ball bat, the thick yellow one with the handle that you wrapped duct tape around, will still be jammed in a rock formation near your old house. Plastics made from oil are, and will continue to be, a testament to the stubborn presence, good or bad, of man on earth.

But as oil creeps up and up in price, some things, like plastic shopping bags, will be left to history. In some cases, such as shopping bags, the replacements might be as simple as a canvas tote bag that we keep at home, hanging on a hook in our mudroom. In other cases, we will see replacements step up and in for petroleum-based plastics. The most interesting of these replacements will be plastics themselves, but they won't be made from oil, they'll be made by, of all things, bacteria.

Plastics from the Prairie and the Leaf Rather Than the Depths and the Drill

On the rolling Iowa prairie, on the east side of the state near the Mississippi River, rises a cacophony of steel vats the size of silos. From the steel cylinders travels a silver pipeline raised on I-beams painted stark white. Seven giant cranes fill the horizon, like a slice of Shanghai economic bluster embedded in the Midwest cornbelt. Corn that comes here, and it doesn't come from far away, won't be turned into ethanol. It will be turned into wonderful, pliable, strong, and biodegradable plastic. A lot of it: This plant will soon crank out 110 million pounds per year. And that number could quadruple within a few years, say the plant's joint owners, Archer Daniels Midland, the Illinois corn and chemical giant, and Metabolix, a Boston firm that has pioneered plastics made from grain-based sugars.

The plant began making plastic in early 2009 using principles developed by Dr. Oliver Peoples. While a research scientist at MIT in the early 1990s, Peoples and two other researchers started wondering if they could use modern genetic tools to make biobased plastics. The benefits were obvious: If he figured out what genetic switches to throw, Peoples could control many characteristics of plastics, including its ability to biodegrade, its hardness, its malleability, and its opaqueness. Here's how it works, in a simplified nugget: The engineered organism (bacteria), which is housed in large metal tanks, eats a feedstock of sugar and starch derived from corn, sugar beets, or switch grass. The organism gorges and swells, becoming 80% plastic by weight. The plastic can then be easily extracted from the tank and compacted into the standard nodules, the tiny ball-like form of commoditized plastic, ready to be melted and formed.

Peoples, after figuring out the science, was convinced that he had a hot concept on his hands, so in 1992, while still at MIT, he founded Metabolix. "We decided it was time for the world to change how it makes these chemicals," Peoples says.

The world's oil supply was in the middle of a rutty glut that would run longer than a decade, however, so Peoples's timing wasn't fabulous. And the concern over plastics' environmental detriments wasn't the shrill whistle we hear now. "It turned out that not too many people were interested in making plastic like this," Peoples recalls.

Times have changed. Metabolix went public in November 2006 and has, at times, had a market value of more than $500 million. The good times have coincided with increasing oil prices. Bioplastics are currently favored for uses where their biodegrading characteristics can be best taken advantage of. Because the plastics—by genetically altering the bugs that create them—can be made to break down incredibly quickly in soil (from as little as a month to more than a year), they're excellent candidates for applications that demand environmentally sensitive solutions.

Metabolix's plastic, Mirel, is now used in pots, compost bags, and materials that are to be used near water. "You know that famous island of plastic junk in the Pacific, the one that never goes away and grows every week?" says Metabolix CEO Rick Eno. He is talking about the North Pacific Subtropical Gyre, also known as the Great Pacific Garbage Patch.[3] It's a place in the middle of the vast Pacific where much of our ocean-bound plastic ends up. A consistent high-pressure zone keeps prevailing winds from penetrating the area, keeping the water there in a constant swirl, and keeping all plastic debris that enters from floating off. The area stretches across 1,000 miles of sea and has more than 3 million tons of floating plastic trash, blown to the ocean from landfills, jettisoned off boats, and just straight dumped onto beaches. "Well, our plastic wouldn't stay there," he says. "It would just degrade. Our stuff will disappear in soil, home compost, wetlands, even the ocean—it doesn't have to become permanent waste and a stress on the environment."

Mirel is slowly becoming popular in food packaging such as bottles and caps for things that have definite shelf lives. "The benefit is obvious there," Eno says. Target plans to make a gift card out of the stuff that will biodegrade within six weeks in soil. (A nice side benefit for Target: It gets unredeemed gift card liabilities off the books by way of disintegration!) Hotels are starting to make their keycards, which are disposed of by the millions every month around the country, out of the biodegradable plastic. Metabolix is planning to make printer parts and ink cartridges for businesses interested in cutting their carbon footprint. And they are pursuing cosmetics makers who would be able to mold Mirel into fashionable lipstick containers while being able to tout their green sensibilities. Eno calls rising environmental awareness and the burgeoning price and scarcity of oil as "a kind of perfect storm for our product."

Niche products are nice and there's no doubt that bioplastics are making big strides in the material world. But their so-called perfect storm has yet to arrive. When gas is near $4 a gallon, a pound of conventional plastic polypropylene or polyethylene goes for around $1.20 a pound. That price basically piggybacks, more or less, on the price of oil. When the price of oil doubles, the price of polypropylene will spike as well. A pound of Mirel made with bacteria and sugar goes for $2.50 a pound, double or so that of the conventional poly plastics. This market will get really interesting when the price of gasoline goes to $10 a gallon. At that point, the price of plain old polypropylene will have equalized with the price of bioplastics. Mirel and its contemporaries will no longer be a novelty product espoused by those holier-than-thou enviro greenmeisters. It will be a true competitor to plastic made with oil. And because it can be made as hard, as soft, or as durable as needed, its use isn't limited to short-term applications. It can be used in just about any application short of permanent pipes.

Imagine all that plastic in our landfills—the millions and millions of tons—disappearing within a few short years instead of dozens of centuries. That's the reality of bioplastics, yet another wonder hovering just out of the mainstream, waiting for rising gas prices to unlock their latent potential.

CHAPTER $12

Urban Revolution and
Suburban Decay

I was standing on the Union Square platform at 14th Street with my good friend Tom Pennington, thinking about the spidery, amazing network of the New York subway system. Tom and I graduated college together, both as civil engineering majors. Career-wise, we've gone in different directions. Tom is now one of a handful of American civil engineers who specialize in tunneling. He works for Parsons Brinkerhoff, a company that's designed several of the few new and large tunneling projects in America, including some of the new Manhattan subway tunnels. Tom has been a part of the engineering squad on the designs and has spent months of his life poring over their details. He has an intuitive handle on how much work these things—these subways—entail, and how much money they cost. We weren't on a fact-finding mission or anything like that this night. We were simply two friends waiting for a train. But as I stood there, I turned to Tom and motioned at the four lanes of track, their platforms, their tunnels, and their support beams. "So how much would it cost to build New York's entire subway system right now, from scratch, like it wasn't even here?"

Tom considered this for a very brief moment and almost

shuddered. Then he scoffed out loud and just shook his head. "I don't think it could happen," he said. "It just couldn't."

In our current world, with our current attachment to individualized transportation, Tom is right—the New York City subway system, built anew, couldn't happen. But the world of $12 gas will be much different. In that world, subway systems will romp across our cities and course beneath our homes, rerouting America toward an urban ideal.

Listen to the Rock—It Holds Lessons for Our Future

Long-time civil engineer Edward Kennedy is trundling down eighteen flights of stairs that descend into the earth on Manhattan's Upper East Side at Second Avenue and Sixty-Third Street. The stairs start at a nondescript brick structure with a padlocked metal door. The thousands of daily passing pedestrians don't give the battered door a second thought, but what sits beyond its threshold is a foyer to one of man's engineering coups.

The stairs are narrow, steep, and concrete. Their rise-to-tread ratio wouldn't pass a home inspection. Kennedy takes each stair steadily and solidly, not too fast, but not in a doddering way, either. The concrete walls show the plywood grain that once held them firm in a form. The landing numbers are painted on the wall in black. Kennedy is a civil engineer who specializes in piercing tranches of the earth's rock with tunnels. He is also a storyteller. He likes to pause at every third landing or so to relive an old tunnel tale or some piece of geotechnical lore. "The rock talks to you," Kennedy says. "And you better listen."

We stop at a landing about two-thirds of the way to the bottom. There is a door here and Kennedy motions at it. "This isn't our spot, but let me show you something."

We slip through the door and walk another twenty feet, where we meet a dirty metal railing. "Okay. Wait a second," Kennedy says. "I hear one coming. Yep, here it is."

New York's F train goes tearing by, only five feet from where we stand, its packed-on passengers oblivious to us, the observers. "Not many people get to see the subway from in here." Kennedy smiles. He leads the way back to the stairs, where he continues down the abrupt flights to the final landing.

We're now 140 feet below the Manhattan streetscape. Kennedy unlocks a final door that leads us into what looks like a giant cave. Except this cave has walls that are so smooth they look like poured concrete, as if we've found our way into the middle of a giant pipe. But the walls aren't concrete. They're 100% pure granite. Examined closely, the walls show a tiny corrugated pattern, as if a cheese grater had shaved their sides. Of course, we're not in a cave. It's a tunnel. A granite tunnel. It's twenty-two feet in diameter and has a rickety-looking train track running down its center. Two giant, inflatable ducts traverse the upper reaches of the tunnel, carrying air from the surface southward down the tunnel. "Now we wait for the man train," Kennedy says. "Should be here soon."

The rumble of the man train becomes audible about two minutes later, but it doesn't show up for another seven minutes. It's loud and it's slow. It's nothing more than a diesel-powered engine cab that drags—or pushes, depending on the direction—a banged-up metal passenger car about fifteen feet long. Passengers hoist themselves through a small entrance door and have a seat on one of the benches that runs up and down either side of the car. This is not a subway car; it's a mining car. It gets workers to and from the head of the tunnel. The car's windows are simply large rectangular holes in the sheet metal covered with wire grating. The little train, when it's moving, is so loud that passengers can barely hear each other's shouts.

The train passes mile after mile of smooth granite periodically broken up by rock bolts, whose ends stick out of the stone like giant pinheads. Workers anchor the bolts far into the rock when they encounter a section of granite with minor flaws that could cause a granite chunk or two to come crashing down. Street names have been etched onto the walls of the tunnel. We go by Sixtieth Street, then Fifty-Eighth, then Fifty-Sixth. One worker's spray paint scrawl asks, "How much further?" Soon we're in the Forties and the man train stops in a mire of muck. The tracks have disappeared underwater at this point. Groundwater and, of course, water from the East and Hudson rivers, is always looking for a way into New York's tunnels. New York City Transit employs 753 pumps that flush out 13 million gallons of water every day.[1] Without the pumps, the whole tunnel network could fill with water in thirty-six hours. It's sufficient to say that an unfinished tunnel is no place for wing tips; it's rubber boots all the way.

This tunnel is being dug so that Long Island commuter trains can finally go from Queens to Grand Central Station, which is on Manhattan's East Side. Currently, trains from Long Island only go to Penn Station, which is on the West Side of the island, causing East Side–bound commuters to spend thirty to forty minutes per day going from one side of town to the other. The project will increase the Long Island to Manhattan rail capacity by 50%, and will eliminate two lanes of traffic on the East River bridges and tunnel during rush hour. Penn Station commuters will benefit from less congestion as their station ceases handling passengers heading to the East Side.

Kennedy tromps through the tunnel's muck, stopping to chat with workers, who remove their dust respirators to talk. One of them takes the lead and brings us toward a machine that's pure science fiction, except it's real. You can't walk around the tunnel boring machine, because it *is* the tunnel. Where it goes, be it through granite or schist, tunnel follows. The machine is 400 feet long. It bores forward by gripping the sides of the tunnel and propelling itself into the rock ahead, applying 3 million pounds of pressure through forty-nine steel cutting disks that bring the granite crumbling down. The wrecked rock is carried from the front of the machine to the back by a conveyor belt that runs through the center of the beast. The machine averages a little more than fifty feet of progress per day. Each twelve inches of tunnel progress creates twenty-five cubic yards of crushed rock. The boring is done with the accuracy of a dentist, guided by lasers and satellites.

Tunneling this way, with this machine that came from Italy, beats how things were done 100 years ago when most of New York's subways were dug. Then it was all done by legions of workers, called sandhogs, who used drills, dynamite, and picks to make New York's coursing underground train system the envy of much of the world. The tunnel being dug now is a project of gall and grandeur—to burrow eight miles through solid granite beneath one of the world's densest cities that's already noodled with underground passageways. This tunnel has been bored beneath the Waldorf-Astoria hotel and Mies van der Rohe's Seagram Building with nary a peep from Park Avenue tenants. But construction of this scale in the current world—especially that of tunnel building—carries with it an exorbitant price tag. This tunnel will cost $7.2 billion.

New York Realizes the Value of What It Has and It Wants More

It may seem odd that New York, the town with, by far, more trains, tunnels, and mass transit than any other city in America, would be spending so much money to extend what it already has just a little farther. How can New York justify that kind of spending when it *already* has so much? If New York can spend $7 billion for one set of commuter train tubes, why can't other cities—places like Atlanta, Dallas, Phoenix, and Denver—put up a fraction of that to build better systems for themselves? The simple answer is because there is no demand. Of course, that's not completely true. There exist pockets of people in every city who clamor for more mass transit, more funding, etc., but they are a very small minority. Most Americans are quite content with a two-car garage, two cars to go in it, and driving to most everywhere.

People in Dallas or Atlanta might say: "All of that so commuters won't have to cross town? What a waste." These cities won't spend that much on building new rail or extending their current systems. But New Yorkers know the value of infrastructure. And that $7 billion tunnel project is only part of the New York story. Railroads are spending another $7 billion for new tunnels from New Jersey to Manhattan on the West Side and the city has started construction on the now mythic Second Avenue subway line. A Second Avenue subway has been talked about for almost ninety years, when a need for an additional line on Manhattan's East Side first became apparent. In 1929, the plans had been made and contracts were to be doled out starting in 1930. The public was aghast and amazed at the $89 million price tag. But then came October 1929, Wall Street's catastrophe, and the Great Depression. In 1939, the project was dug back up and pegged at a cost of $249 million. Subway construction got shelved, however, by World War II. In 1951, the public approved a bond issue for $500 million to cover the Second Avenue subway's construction, but almost all that money was diverted into improvements for the current system. Money popped back up in 1972 and construction began. But that movement was halted in 1975 when the city's financial straits turned calamitous. The project got pushed again to the fore in 2007 and crews are digging again. The price this time around could reach $20 billion.

That's $20 billion for a subway line that people in New York now get along without. How can this cost be justified? Because the Metropolitan Transportation Authority knows that as soon as trains are running on the Second Avenue tracks, the subway cars will be full. The line closest to what will be the new subway is the Lexington Avenue subway, the only choice there is for the East Side, which has seen residential development explode during the last decade. The Lexington Avenue line carries more passengers by itself in a day—1.3 million—than any other U.S. city's entire train system outside of Chicago's.

During the 1990s, no city in America—not Phoenix or Las Vegas, Denver or San Diego—added more people than New York did.[2] New York's population increased by 685,714 to 8,008,278—more than double the second largest increase in the United States, which belonged to Phoenix at 337,642 people added. Nobody noticed because New York is built to handle it. New York's density, at 26,403 people per square mile, is prolific. Among large U.S. cities, its No. 1 ranking is a noncontest. Its density measures 46% higher than second-place San Francisco's and is double third-place Chicago's. Consider the densities of our newer cities: Dallas and Houston at about 3,400 people per square mile, Phoenix at 2,800, or Denver at 3,600. New York's density is more than seven times all these places.

In the case of the Second Avenue subway, New York's density begets the infrastructure. That pattern will be repeated in more and more parts of the country as people crowd the cities looking for freedom from their excessive energy addictions and their associated financial burdens. Households, crippled by the cost of $12 gas, will pick up and move to places where they can walk, bike, and get along with one car or no car. Families simply won't be able to afford living in the far-out suburbs. Those places' viabilities depend on cheap energy. When cheap energy disappears, so, too, will much of exurbia's population. People will mass into gentrifying neighborhoods of increasing density across the country. Our cities, swelling with new residents, will need mass transit infrastructure—subways, trolleys, and light rail—to relieve the pressure. It may seem hard to imagine this kind of thing happening in cities such as

Los Angeles, San Diego, Miami, and Atlanta, but it will. The day will arrive when energy scarcity pushes the rest of the country to act more like New York.

More than 1.6 million people live on the island of Manhattan, which is a scant 23 square miles, giving it a ridiculous 70,000 people per square mile. The only reason Manhattan works, the only reason this place can be functional, is because of the mass transit infrastructure that so brilliantly underpins the whole island. As our cities swell with people seeking relief from a future of high energy costs, mass transit, on a colossal scale, will be needed to keep our cities functional. As gas prices increase from $8 to $10 to $12 per gallon, the value of mass transit infrastructure will only increase, and more and more of our cities and their populations will think and want to behave as New Yorkers have been doing for decades. Taxes supporting new mass transit projects, taxes that would be outrageously unpopular in our current times, will pass with ease and the next great tale of the American demographic novel will unfold.

It's important to realize, too, that electric cars, though they will be swinging to popularity, can't and won't stop our assimilation into cities. Getting an electric car will be possible, but they won't be cheap and they won't be plentiful; and our thorough changeover to electric cars will take decades. In the meantime, many people will be looking to drive less or not at all. This movement will give rise to a massive shift of population as our fringe suburbs lose their value and our inner cities reinvent themselves again. When gas reaches $12 a gallon, Americans will feel themselves in a limbo of sorts—the nascent stage of electric vehicles' slow takeover and gasoline prices so high that driving to the supermarket becomes an exercise of coasting through stop signs in neutral to save every precious drop of fuel. The only thing real, the only thing proven to save us money and time and to stand the perseverance of market swings and real estate undulations, will be our cities' great neighborhoods and the infrastructure that supports them.

Trains will overflow. New subway cars will be bought, and manufacturing will revive on the back of this movement as the demand for light rail, urban electric trains, and buses spikes to levels unseen. The American dream of one-acre lots, four bedrooms, three cars, and a suburb full of sparkling big box stores will be shaken. The dream of America won't fail, but it will change. To many people already, New York is the American dream. That way of living, in dense, efficient, and elegant blocks, will spread across the country, from one city to the next, from Atlanta to Saint Louis to Minneapolis to Denver. No city will reach New York's level of compression; that's something that's been developing for more than 200 years. But the densification of our cities is academic. It's only a question of when energy prices and gas prices soar past $10 to $12.

Projects like the $7 billion tunnel connecting Long Island to Grand Central Station will no longer be the once-every-two-decades exception. Endeavors of this ilk will pop up in city after city, as people demand progress and mass transit that's desirable to ride, not merely sufficient. People's reluctance to pay for such things in the form of taxes, fares, or tolls has always been a hurdle rarely cleared outside New York and a few other cities on a very few number of projects. Americans will drop these protests as energy costs vacuum more and more of their paychecks. On a macro scale, there is one path to mitigating our runaway energy use: density.

The Modern City, from Scratch and for Real

The world's great cities, its metropolises of consequence, are dwelling sites that have existed for, most often, centuries. Paris, London, New York, Tokyo, Chicago, Moscow, San Francisco—these places have been hoarding their culture, their generations, and their joy of life for, in all cases, more than 150 years and, in most cases, at least twice that long. Great cities, with the conveniences and efficiencies of density, do not crop up overnight. When small cities grew into big ones during the twentieth century, they did so without a plan and without a nod toward mass transit and density. They grew helter skelter. They grew wherever asphalt and home builders took them. They grew into sprawling nests of chaos that can't be well negotiated by car, rail, or bike. Our newer metropolitan areas simply conformed to the easy excesses of cheap oil. Atlanta, Houston, Dallas, Phoenix—these places weren't born purely out of bad planning. They were born out of cheap oil.

New York's grand density and its ability to function so well, with so many people working and living so close together, came from a vision and a plan hatched before the gilded era of the automobile. By the time the car had truly arrived, New York's momentum was such that it wouldn't surrender many jobs or citizens to outliers of easy suburban expansion and newfangled development. There is a value, people realized, of being so close to so many. Your financier is a fifteen-minute subway ride downtown. Your advertising firm is a five-minute walk cross-town. And access to cutting-edge culture and a pliable client base is merely out the door, on the street.

Cities today are living with their foibles and strengths in full view. Houston will not morph into New York. Its residents could certainly benefit from a dense, centralized downtown and urban plan, but tearing up what's already there is, for now, cost prohibitive. So Houston makes do. But knowing what we know now—how would we build a brand-new city? If we could do Houston all over again, from scratch, what would we build? With a giant pot of money and a willing and ready population champing to live, work, and play in our city—what would we build?

This is an intriguing question that can be rolled for all its details in our universities' urban planning classes. But the world—the real world—has an answer for us. It's called New Songdo City. Its twenty high-rise towers are rising from a muddy expanse stamped by the rolling paths of giant dump trucks, backhoes, and bulldozers.

This place is a 1,500-acre plot steeped in the finer points of planning legends such as Daniel Burnham and Frederick Law Olmsted. This will be a city. A city from scratch. Nothing like this has been done since Brazil threw up Brasilia fifty years ago, the capital city that has evolved to be unremarkable compared with Rio de Janeiro or São Paulo. South Korea's New Songdo City will be smaller than Brasilia, but the cerebral efforts behind its cohesive, dense, and sustainable plan are exhaustive and even more carefully crafted. Whereas Dubai has been an unbridled orgy in arbitrary excess, buildings and roads sprouting wherever money lands, New Songdo City has been planned in the meticulous tradition of Pierre-Charles L'Enfant's 1791 scheme for Washington DC.

Songdo won't be done until 2015, at the earliest. By then, 65,000 people will live there and 300,000 will work there. Songdo will be, quite literally, a city that rose from nothing. South Koreans value their land, but with 48 million people living inside an area roughly the size of Indiana, there aren't many spare acres. And there's absolutely zero open real estate anywhere near Seoul, the dynamic capital city that has helped South Korea ascend to become an economic power. Seoul's surging metro area, which holds about half the country's population, has nowhere left to go. Mountains pen Seoul off to its east and south. To the west, it's sea. To the north, a malevolent and dangerous dictatorship. The government picked the path of least resistance and, in what began a continuing list of engineering feats in Songdo, dumped 110 million cubic yards of mountain rubble into the Yellow Sea, creating Songdo's 1,500 acres 40 miles southwest of Seoul.

The government wanted a city built here that would impress the world, a place that can become the business capital of Northeast Asia. But it also wanted it to be a zenith for culture, design, and lifestyle. For that tall task, the government picked an American developer, Gale International, to put Songdo together. Gale pitched the government on a plan of dense high-rises stacked around a lush 100-acre central park. The city would be supported by two subway stops taking riders to Seoul and central Incheon. At first, the government balked, not used to relegating any of their precious land to green space. "The topography of the peninsula is extremely rocky," says John Hynes, "and so, too, is the path to business deals."

Hynes is Gale's CEO and comes from Boston, a city not unfamiliar with density and quality of life. It's No. 4 in the United States, with 12,000 people per square mile and that number would likely be higher except the city is so old that most of its buildings simply aren't very tall. Hynes didn't get into the real estate business to build the world's most advanced city, but "Now that we're here, we've realized the opportunity we have." Hynes defines the cliché of a Boston Brahmin. His grandfather was the city's mayor and his father was a popular television news anchor. He graduated from Harvard, where he cocaptained the school's hockey team. His hockey roots show through in the intensity he's brought to the Songdo project, an intensity that helped him persuade the Koreans to stick with Gale's plan for a large central park. "The park in the middle of Songdo all goes back to synergies," Hynes says. "You have this enormous human pressure of the skyscrapers, the offices, and the residential towers. The park acts like a kind of release valve."

Gale overlaid their Songdo plan on maps of Paris, New York, and Washington. They showed the government evidence of higher land values and happier homeowners with this sliver of parkland. The government, wanting a grand slam, acceded. It's not hard to see where Gale and its designers drew inspiration: The firm's headquarters, on the forty-fourth floor of a building on New York's Fifth Avenue at Fifty-Seventh Street, have a full and stunning view of Central Park's 843 acres. "They're happy because it makes a better city and we're happy because, in the end, the park will make all of this dense residential development worth quite a bit more," Hynes explains.

When it's finished, Songdo will be the most energy- and resource-efficient city in the world. Because it's all brand new, Gale and its designers were able to leverage all manner of modern advantages, from recycled materials to advanced insulation techniques (Korea's climate is cold, like the Upper Midwest) to synchronizing pedestrian-laden elevators with nearby crosswalk signals. Songdo's design pays special reverence to water conservation. "In America, we tend to forget that water is such a finite resource," says Ashok Raiji, one of the project's principal engineers from the British firm Arup. "Korea's level of water stress is equal to that of Libya."

All of Songdo's buildings recycle their used sink, shower, and bathtub water for use in toilets and irrigation. This type of technology, called graywater, has been used before in conservation-minded projects, but it's never been installed on a city-wide basis until Songdo. "It's a lot of extra work," Raiji says, "but it's something that in this climate, with their resources, should be done to guard against a future of lessening water supplies and higher energy costs."

Songdo will use gearless elevator systems from Otis that will use 75% less energy than standard ones; its elevators have flat polyurethane-coated steel belts that require no lubrication. Otis will debut its ReGen drive, which draws energy from a fully loaded descending elevator or a lightly loaded ascending car and converts it to electricity, like a hybrid car converts braking energy. The concrete in Songdo's buildings utilizes 40% less portland cement than normal concrete, resulting in a mix with a 40% smaller carbon footprint and even more strength (14,000 pounds per square inch). This sounds a bit arcane and immaterial to the wider issues regarding energy, but it's not. Our use of concrete in the future will become more judicious and will utilize better, more efficient methods to make the stuff. The industry that makes portland cement, be it in China, the United States, or Europe, is a notorious energy gulper.

The creation of cement contributes 5% to 7% of man's greenhouse gases. In a future of high-energy costs with gasoline topping $12 a gallon, we will all shift toward greener concretes as energy preservation takes the fore. Songdo, again, is merely ahead of the curve here.

Gale's headquarters in Songdo will be an ecowonder. Its outer walls will be made of glass and will react to the moving sun differently according to season; in the winter, the glass, controlled electronically, will let as much warming light through as possible; during summer, scalding heat will be turned away. Every major façade of the building will, in addition to the roof, hold photovoltaic cells that help heat, cool, and electrify the building. The roof, where it isn't hosting solar cells, will be flat and green with insulating vegetation and a passive system that traps rainwater for use in irrigation and cooling. The inside climate control will be a hyperefficient system of underfloor airflow. Hot or cold air will seep through the cracks in the floor upward, greatly increasing heating efficiencies and operating in a passive, cheaper, and more effective way than forced air traveling through ducts to only one or two given spots in a room. Kenneth Drucker, an architect at HOK, is the firm's lead designer on Songdo, where his firm has been charged with designing several blocks of buildings. "I've never seen an undertaking like this," he says. "It's incredible how much can be accomplished so quickly when so many minds come together. This truly is a testament to sustainable design."

Songdo's interconnectedness, from the way its apartments are wired to the way traffic signals work, will be a glimpse into our future of higher energy costs, too. As the price of gasoline scoots upward, and other energies with it, we will utilize technology more and more to wean ourselves away from energy usage and toward efficiency. Computers will link everything in Songdo. A person who left the oven on at home will be able to shut it off from their BlackBerry. Sensors built into floors will recognize when a person falls and doesn't get up, alerting an ambulance. A person eating breakfast in a Songdo apartment's kitchen will be able to monitor trains and walk signals below from an easy touch screen included with every condo, enabling them to make a perfectly timed exit from the house, walking up to the subway platform just as the train arrives. Thermostats and climate controls will be easily toggled remotely, allowing residents to turn on the heat when they're five minutes from home or to turn it down when they've left it cranked up.

Intricate, sustainable, and very dense—Songdo will have 27,700 people per square mile, about equal with New York—the city represents a model for our future, a future that will be closer with every dollar gasoline and energy prices inevitably climb. The city will cost nearly $40 billion to erect; it's the largest private real estate deal ever forged. Including the government's infrastructure being built, the total cost could top $60 billion. Luckily for Gale, South Koreans have responded to this newfangled idea of a city. In its first public sale of apartments in 2006, the application line stretched for two miles. Gale received 170,000 qualified offers for 2,200 units. The units sold out in one day for $1 billion.

The whole process of meting out Songdo's land and its development was treated like a religious rite in South Korea. Plans were worked, altered, and reworked to find the perfect balance for business, residential, and efficiency requirements. That's what happens when a country runs out of land. This place will constantly be cited in the future for its daring advances and urban experimentation. Our future, an urban one, will reflect many of the lessons gleaned from Songdo. Building on this scale with this kind of rapidity, of course, simply isn't possible in most cases. Our transformation from a civilization orbiting suburban sprawl to one concentrating in pockets of urban elegance will be slow, but relentless.

The Tide of Gasoline Prices Will Shift
Americans from the Burbs to the Cities

If Songdo shows how we might construct a new urban city from
nothing, how will our existing urban footprints, from central cities
all the way out to the exurbs, change in a world of $12 gasoline?
The planners and architects of Kohn Pedersen Fox have gnawed
on this question in more than one way, and they have some answers. KPF is the New York architecture and planning firm that
planned Songdo, from the location of the South Korean city's vanguard sixty-five-story tower to the grandeur of its central park. William Pedersen cofounded KPF in 1976 and has helped the firm
grow into one of the most influential design firms on the planet,
with more than 400 architects and offices in New York, London,
and Hong Kong. Pedersen, by any measurement, has attained a
high level of success. His demeanor and friendliness don't betray
that fact, nor do his youthful spirit and countenance betray his age
of seventy years. From three feet away, he looks to be in the prime
of his early fifties. Pedersen's silver hair is as thick as carpet. His
face carries the light ruddiness of experience, but not weariness.
Pedersen still designs with the vigor of a newly christened associate,
but he started his career almost fifty years ago, when architecture
was still enveloped in Mies van der Rohe's thoughts on simplicity.
Pedersen currently lives in a Manhattan apartment. He walks or
rides his bike across Central Park every day to work. "It's a beautiful
arrangement," he says. "Here we have this intense density but we
can all make the park a daily part of our lives, and it helps open up
our minds, keeps us instilled with a sense of openness."

When it comes to the future of Americans and their dwellings
in a future of higher energy costs, Pedersen sees a country that will
slowly churn toward a future of urban synergies and density and
away from single-family homes on half-acre lots thirty miles outside central cities. Propelling the trend will be the simple fact that

the suburbs just won't be affordable for most of the people who now live there. Leaving the energy-intensive living of the burbs won't be something that everybody welcomes, of course. "Fundamentally, Americans look so much differently upon urbanism than Asians do. I think you can trace it back to the Jeffersonian ideal, the agrarian ideal," he explains. "This idea that you can live on your own land and be totally independent if you need to be. The idea that you can support yourself."

If civilization is to march forward, however, a couple of acres simply won't be an accessible or realistic part of most Americans' lives, nor, with high energy costs, will a huge house and a huge yard be a desirable way to live. It will be an entrapment, an entrapment to giant utility bills and the attachment to a dwelling unit that will, with time, become a kind of pariah. A single-family home of 3,000 square feet, which is large but not ridiculously so, is what many families currently aspire to. Many of the McMansions dotting the exurbs of America are, in fact, quite a bit larger than 3,000 square feet; houses 30% to 50% bigger than that have become commonplace in upper-middle-class America. The average size of a U.S. single-family home has ballooned to 2,479 square feet.[3] That's 41% bigger than the U.S. home of 1978 and twice as large as an average 1960s house. About 60% of the increase since 1978 has come since 1995, roughly coinciding with a deep rut for energy prices. When low energy prices made it possible, Americans gorged on living space. With an overheated housing market and easy credit coupling with cheap natural gas, heating oil, and gasoline, why not go big?

But there is nothing that can save these bloated testaments to the American largesse of the last ten years. Put simply, these homes will be doomed by two swords, not one. The first blade to draw their blood will be the one of transportation. As we drive less and mass transit marches to the fore of American life, the farthest of the far burbs will lose relevance. Their real estate values will crash.

It won't be a sudden crash. It will be an unrelenting lilt toward the red, a bend toward insolvency for those who fail to see the future as it unfolds in front of them. This won't be the asking price depression of the subprime crisis. That calamity came out of assets simply being overvalued; the effects of the subprime dip will eventually fade away. But when rising energy prices render an exurb less valuable, that change will be permanent. During and after the subprime crash, people still wanted to live in these places. When gas hits $12, nobody will want to live in these places, and it will only get worse as gasoline prices continue to climb over time.

Exurb homeowners, buried in the minutiae and banalities of everyday life, will look up after years, perhaps even a decade, and realize, through the thick cloak of denial they've wrapped themselves in, that their home equity is gone, their house is worth less than they paid and their neighborhood has eroded to a collection of half-filled, rapidly decaying stick boxes.

Anybody wanting to live in these places has to drive everywhere and drive far. Work is miles away, the grocery store is miles away, and the kids' schools are miles away. These places, such as Cary, Illinois, which is forty miles outside Chicago's downtown, or Rosenberg, Texas, thirty-five miles outside of Houston, or Pike County, Pennsylvania, ninety miles from New York, will lose their luster as the middle class loses its cheap gasoline and, with it, its cheap transportation. Exurb homeowners accepted long drives and commutes as an avenue to getting the huge house and lot they wanted. That was when cheap gas seemed a certainty rather than a fleeting perk. Rising gas prices, during the summer of 2008, brought economic pain to these places. In the future, their hurt will continue. "It's going to be very painful for a lot of people who are trapped with few alternatives," says Pedersen. "You establish your lifestyle based on certain conditions, and when those conditions change, you can be left in a bad position."

Electric cars, which will infiltrate the market as fast as they might, won't be enough to save suburbia. Their cost—at $25,000 with almost no used market as there won't be old models floating around—will be prohibitive for families accustomed to driving three cars: one for Dad, one for Mom, and one for the kids. Picking up a five-year-old Pontiac for $5,000 won't be an option any longer, with gas at $12. So these families will simply dump these homes and move to where they can walk, train, and bike. These people will power the urban renaissance and hasten exurbia's decline.

The second blade that will deflate America's outer ring suburbs will be, in many ways, the same blade as the first, but it will come in a different form. Where gasoline prices chopped off easy and cheap transportation to these far-flung hamlets of quick-set concrete and aluminum fascia, natural gas and heating oil prices will cripple them from within, straining home budgets that, in many cases, were stretching to own these pads of magnificent square footage in the first place.

Heating a 3,000-square-foot house during a cold winter month in the Northeast or the Midwest might have cost little more than $300 when energy prices were low in the late 1990s. Obviously, things have changed. Even with the global recession stamping out demand and energy prices at six-year lows, heating that same house now during an especially wicked February could easily reach $1,000 a month or more. Those kinds of numbers are intimidating, but not backbreaking. The straw will pile up, though, as energy prices, spurred by a recovering global appetite and shrinking reserves, climb to two, three, and four times their current levels. When gasoline prices touch $12 per gallon, the cost of keeping that house cozy in February will have reached scorching heights of $2,000 to $3,000. This is not a sustainable burden. The costs of cooling that house, though not as necessary as heating—we can all live in 90-degree heat, it's just not pleasant—will have increased a similar percentage.

As energy prices go up, the 3,000-square-foot house won't

r. There will always be people who can afford to live however they might want. Large single-family homes will persevere
within city limits and first-ring suburbs. That's the good stock,
where, because of mass transit and walkable destinations, people
will want to live. What will slowly erode: the stock of large, cheap
single-family homes at the edges of metropolitan areas. These
homes, typically, are newer and were built in tract fashion during
the last 20 to 30 years. Architecture snobs detest them, but the fact
remains that most of America likes them and they will not enjoy
giving them up. It won't be easy to descramble Americans' hard-
wired suburban sensibilities. Most people *want* 3,000 square feet.
They want big cars, big stores, and lots of stuff. These attitudes
need renovation, a renovation that will come at the hands of high
energy prices.

Nothing motivates people to change their lives like fiscal
incentives—and these incentives won't be passive. Like a tape-
worm attached to people's paychecks, they will eat away at exur-
bians' disposable incomes until these people become convinced,
household by household, that energy's salad days aren't returning.
Only then will they dump their tract house, be it at a loss or through
default, and head in toward the central city, where the jobs will be,
where the mass transit will be, where energy efficiencies can be
fully leveraged. The city's density, once abhorred by so many, will
again be a lure. Cities such as Milwaukee, Boston, Minneapolis,
New York, Chicago, Philadelphia, Pittsburgh, and Cleveland will
reclaim heirs to families lost decades ago to burgeoning, far-off
suburbs that will now lurch toward their decaying demise.

What will happen to these towns, these amalgamations of
mass-produced housing, cheap sheetrock, and vinyl siding? Bill
Pedersen, whose design career has encompassed many such places'
ascensions, says it succinctly: "Well, they're not very well built, so
they'll probably just take care of themselves," he chuckles. "They'll
just fall down."

Our Cities Will Regroup, Renew, and Grow Denser

As people leave the suburbs because they can't afford 3,000 square feet, four exterior walls, and two SUVs, our cities will swell with newcomers. They'll be bursting with the added population, and in order to continue functioning as cities of order, peace, and livability, our metropolises will have to change to accommodate their new densities. The good thing about added densities in cities is that the advantages to living in urban settings can stack up higher and higher as the degree of density increases (within limits, of course). This assumes good design, however. Unfortunately, not all of our cities were designed with density in mind. In fact, many of our cities weren't designed at all. They just expanded willy-nilly, a patchwork of twisting asphalt and slapdash housing wherever developers could make a buck. The general rule of thumb in America: The newer the city, the worse the planning.

It's not easy to reorder a city according to density. It's expensive. But we'll have the stiff wind of energy prices driving us toward efficiencies that only cities can provide. Our urban transformation will take decades, but it will reach an unstoppable critical mass at $12. "The price of energy," says Pedersen, "will demand urbanism. It's going to change the characterization of American cities tremendously."

Some of our cities, such as Chicago, New York, San Francisco, and Seattle, have already experienced wide-sweeping renaissances. But others, such as Saint Louis, Detroit, Cleveland, and Pittsburgh, have not. They have, in fact, atrophied from their insides out. But their time will come. And what has happened in places such as Brooklyn and Seattle's Capitol Hill and Chicago's near West Side will spread farther throughout these cities, lifting neighborhoods out of decades of perpetual blight, crime, and indifference.

Cities without a central density pattern will slowly develop them. Cities sprawling across land with no purpose will get regimentation.

Our cities' cores will sprout with tall buildings that house a mix of offices and apartments. Transit stops will seek out clusters of high-rises, making it easy for those who work and live in them to hop on a train and head home, to work, or to play. The inner ring around our dense downtowns will be a cluster of condo buildings as high as twenty stories and multileveled commercial development, maintaining a high level of density without the high costs of the skyscraper construction downtown. A little ways out from this ring will be a mix of small, existing single-family homes and attached townhomes, dotted by intermittent parks and neighborhood stores.

Cities such as Detroit, Saint Louis, Pittsburgh, and Cleveland will see their stocks rise the fastest. These are the cities with existing downtown infrastructure that's terribly underused. Buildings of thirty or forty stories wait in these cities to be seized by someone with vision, someone with the drive to make them great again. These grand old buildings will revisit their glory days as they'll transform from half-vacant, sleepy office outposts back to the bustling centers of culture and commerce they were seventy years ago. "The great thing about tall buildings is that they tend to get reused rather than razed. Almost all of them are built well, and almost all of them are still around," says Paul Katz, an architect and principal at KPF. "It's a lot easier, and a lot cheaper, to reclaim that space than to build new."

Our revitalized urban landscapes will embrace the tentacles of expanding train networks and local marketplaces. Smaller, more local stores will put an end to the bloated model of supermarket that has steadily enlarged with American homes and Americans themselves during the past fifty years. Our cities, infused with money and surging populations, won't become urban homogenizations in the mold of exurb tract housing, however. Our new dwellings, thrown up where space demands or current deteriorated housing allows, will be a mishmash of modest, tightly spaced single-family homes, high-rises, and townhomes.

KPF's Pedersen has firsthand experience in all three of the main American housing mediums: a single-family home in Minnesota, where he grew up; later in a Brooklyn brownstone; and now in a high-rise apartment on Manhattan's Upper West Side.

Pedersen sees most Americans' futures intertwining with all three, but with an emphasis on high-rises and townhomes that are akin to the old brownstone model of living. This mix will make for dense neighborhoods, with dozens of families on each block. These places would require grade and middle schools to be built at close intervals, meaning children would never be more than a half mile from their classroom, an easy ten-minute walk. Larger high schools would be within a mile of every home. Small strips of marketplace shops would dot neighborhoods, keeping most households within a short walk of a loaf of bread.

Socially, this would be a giant upgrade for families used to schlepping all about exurbia to accomplish the mundane missions of life: grocery runs, school dropoffs, and work commutes. These neighborhoods will cluster along new or renovated railways that carry people into the central city. As the railways draw closer to the city, tight town house developments will give way to condo developments attractive to singles and young couples. Nearer downtown, the buildings will grow higher and denser still. It won't be anomalous to the densification order many of our cities exhibit right now, except that many of our newer cities, such as Atlanta, Phoenix, or Houston, give way to sprawl very quickly after the central city, underutilizing urban land that will grow all the more valuable as energy's price increases. The densification of our cities will occur one project at a time, grouped about existing transit lines.

In a world of $12 gasoline, these projects will be waiting like gnashing piranhas for the next train line to be built, the next station to be added, or the next subway tunnel to be dug. There will be a shortage of desirable, walkable, and dense developments near city cores when gas reaches $12. Developers will rush to fill the void, but these projects will need the infrastructure of improved mass transit to be the true bastions of quality urban life that people will be seeking. Governments will have to build on a massive scale. "To have density, you need infrastructure, and the only infrastructure we've built here since World War II has been the interstate highway system," says KPF's Katz. "And that highway system, of course, has led to sprawl."

The expressways will ultimately prove useful, however, as they offer municipalities unmolested right of ways radiating out of central cities—easements that can be used by governments to locate train lines. Building trains aboveground on existing open corridors costs far less than building elevated train platforms and a mere fraction of the expense that burrowing subway tunnels entails. It's inevitable, says Katz, that portions of many of our inner-city interstate corridors will eventually be used for mass transit, starting with dedicated, high-speed bus lanes and then, later, permanent train lines. Because there will be so many fewer people regularly driving and so few cars on the road, cities will be able to commandeer lanes from highways and install trains on them. There will be little need for twelve-lane stretches of monster roads burrowing through cities in a future of $12 gas. Towns like Atlanta, Houston, Los Angeles, and Dallas will take some of those lanes and send train spurs firing out of them at all angles, mirroring the current highway designs. Outer ring train networks will connect close-in suburbs and densifying neighborhoods to one another.

The cost of our cities' transformations will be incalculable. For that reason, this is something that will not take a mere five years. It will persist for decades, a steady melting of the far-out suburban landscape and a solidification of our urban cores. The suburban melt will fill up the sponges that comprise our cities, sponges that have, in many cases, gone hard. But their infrastructure remains, their avenues remain, their many pores for people, civilization, and culture remain; all it takes is money. "The mod-

ern city was on the right track until the emergence of the automobile," Katz says.

We can reclaim our place on that vector. The money that's
needed to reinvigorate our urban cores is money that, right now,
most Americans do not wish to part with. We cannot raise taxes for
mass transit infrastructure because, in most cities' cases, save New
York and a few others, the majority of the populations do not want it.
Twelve-dollar gas will more than change their minds and lubricate
the wheels of urban renewal with a gusto America has never seen.

Subways: The Ultimate Expression of Urbanism

Subway tubes will puncture the ground beneath cities' central
cores, alleviating pressure on the dense grid above. They will elegantly whisk people from one side of town to another, all out of
sight. Subways, in places of the greatest density, are the best things
that can be built for cities. They avoid the clutter and confusion of
surface or elevated trains and let buildings and development morph
as they will, unaffected by the harsh dividing barricades that urban
train lines can be. Subways are the ultimate in mass transport, but
they're also, of course, the most expensive, which is why when cities install new trains these days, they opt for some form of on-grade
light rail or elevated system (save New York). But subways, as
evinced by New York's venerable but highly functional system, are
the best mass transit investment a city can make. "You only build a
tunnel through rock once," says Edward Kennedy, the civil engineer on Manhattan's East Side Access project. "They don't take
much maintenance; they're just granite tubes. It's the project that
keeps on giving."

Elevated trains, on the other hand, require constant maintenance and need to be virtually rebuilt in their entirety every 75 to
100 years, which Chicagoans are now finding out. Elevated train-
ways' foundation footings erode and destabilize the steel trusswork,

which itself corrodes and requires constant painting and overhauling. This work often requires lines to be shut down for months or even years. Chicago shut down its 100-year-old elevated Green Line for two years in the 1990s to replace 1,700 footings and install 7,500 tons of new structural steel, slathering it with 73,000 gallons of paint.[4]

Had the Green Line been a subway, no such project would have been needed. With subways' benefits laid out for society's perusal, cities other than New York will begin to bore tunnels beneath their streets as mass transit becomes a top priority for tax-paying citizens. Subway construction will roar to life in Miami, Houston, Charlotte, and Denver. Underground construction will churn anew in Atlanta and Los Angeles. Chicago's train system will expand and incorporate long-neglected neighborhoods with subway spurs and loops. Dallas and Houston will bore through Texas bedrock to raise their systems from anemic to comprehensive. Boston's and Philadelphia's systems will update, expand, and refresh.

Urban families will shed their automobiles, opting for one car instead of three. Freedom from automobile, gasoline, and insurance bills will free up families' capital for other things, such as higher housing costs and mass transit fares. Families will revel in the freedom of an ultimately easier lifestyle. "Not having to use an automobile is a tremendous boon to one's life, I think," Pedersen says. "I don't want to wish for the price of gas to go up, but I think that there are a lot of advantages to having that happen. Tighter cities make for better communities."

America's Zoning Laws, for So Long a Lever for Sprawl, Will Be Trashed

As the suburban model decays, America's zoning and building codes will be rewritten. Their homogenous nature and their pedantic enforcement have played no small role in America's aimless sprawl.

Minimum setbacks, lot size requirements, and Byzantine building codes, much of them excessive, have spawned what can only be called enforced sprawl. The bureaucracy of our building regulations has kept creative minds out of the planning field and kept density, even where it's warranted and would be desired by most residents, out of most towns. It's hard to develop a block of attached townhomes centered around a village green when the locality has zoned the area strictly for large, single-family homes with maximum heights and minimum setbacks. "The zoning laws that have really pushed most of our development since World War II are already changing," says Mary Ann Lazarus, the sustainable design director for HOK, a global design firm with twenty-nine offices on four continents. "And the price of fuel will quicken those changes."

Many of America's finest buildings and developments were erected more than 100 years ago, when building codes were nonexistent or laxly enforced. Those buildings were made hardier than anything going up today. The designs of Daniel Burnham and Louis Sullivan answered to nobody but their creators; that was enforcement enough.

Changing zoning laws, in a future of higher energy prices, will allow the return of more than densely packed buildings. The neighborhood store, the corner bakery, the butcher shop—these places will return to our urban neighborhoods. Older American cities and inner-ring suburbs are pocked with buildings that, at one time, were clearly storefronts of some sort. Either by the owner's choosing or by zoning law requirements, most of these little outposts have been converted to single-family homes or ground-level apartments, window blinds awkwardly shading the giant glass storefronts that abut the sidewalk. As urbanites ditch their cars for a lifestyle centered on pedestrian shopping trips, small local stores will once again be ensconced within our residential neighborhoods, not just in dedicated strip malls.

Zoning laws, like everything else, will yield and reform around the realities of $12 gasoline. Bureaucratic obstacles will be no match for the financial and demographic necessities that densification will represent. Every day that passes, the United States consumes another 20 million barrels of oil and our suburban society grows closer to extinction. Minivan lovers will learn to love the city. They will learn to love density and the freedom that reliable and widespread mass transportation can provide. Places like Denver, Dallas, and Atlanta will move from being mere regional hubs to world-class cities as people, culture, and commerce crowd in. Engineers like Edward Kennedy, the tunneling guru, will be busy as their projects won't be exclusive to New York anymore. The entire country, in fact, will live more and more like New York does every day.

CHAPTER 14

The Fate of Small Towns, U.S. Manufacturing Renaissance, and Our Material World

Small Towns' Revenge on the Big Box, Enabled by $14 Gasoline

The flagpole is smartly attached to the side of the building, but it bears no flag. Its crusty ropes clatter against the steel pole in the December wind, sending cold pings across the empty patch of parking lot. The asphalt has the composition of a raisin; its wrinkles, blemishes, and cracks erupt with the consistency of parched desert. There's not a smooth swath of pavement anywhere. Brown grass and dead weeds, some of them three feet high, gush from the asphalt fissures, their roots having found sustenance somewhere below the barren blacktop.

The building's trademark gray and steel blue paint job has recently been washed away with a thick layer of mundane taupe. Perhaps the realtor people think this measure will cleanse the site of its former life, its stigma, and provoke some interest in the rotting cinderblock corpse. Trash wanders against the building's walls and loiters nearly everywhere in the parking lot. Nobody, it seems, cleans this place up now. A Burger King franchise, positioned 100 yards from the front of the building, has gone out of business, robbed of the steady customer flow that used to come through on trips to this concrete box. The stoplight on the main road has been recalibrated to flash red for outcoming parking lot traffic—of which there is almost none now—while just blinking a mild yellow for the main road. No reason to stop traffic for an empty building.

Someone has egged the glass façade of the place. A couple dozen eggs found their marks near the entrance, their crusty entrails streaking all the way down the building. Half of the handicap parking signs in the lot have been stolen, making for interesting ornaments, no doubt, on a few adolescent bedroom walls. The old garden department of the store has turned into an empty chain-linked prison, secured by rusting yellow chains and padlocks that may never meet their keys again. The chain-link garden center sits fifty feet from a mobile home park. Do the residents here prefer things now, lonesome and quiet, or before, bustling, noisy, and imposing?

The backside of the hulking building has been festooned with graffiti that lacks the edge of true urban defacement. One spray paint caricature features an old man saying simply, "Smoke herb." The giant black pads affixed to the trucking docks lilt off the building, gone hard and rigid out of disuse, waiting for the next round of merchandise-packing big rigs—trucks that will never come. There is a small chain-link barricade, 10 feet square, surrounding one of the rear doors. This fence has plastic windbreakers woven through its grid. Somebody has piled scavenged wood across the tops of the fence sections for a makeshift roof. The fence's gates are locked with more of the yellow chains, but somebody, probably the lumberjack who made the roof, has bent the lower halves of the gate apart, allowing a squatting person to crawl through. The ground inside the hut is scattered with tattered clothing, used condoms, and random detritus. It smells like urine.

The whole property, just outside downtown Coshocton, Ohio, oozes a vacant loneliness. Smokestacks belonging to a Smurfit-Stone box-making plant lord over the town, which is home to about 12,000 people. But whereas the plant, with its foul odors and plumes of smoke and steam, is a cauldron of activity, this building, with its unclaimed flagpole and its hives of garbage, is an empty retail tenement. The structure is a testament to small-town decay. The building seems so new, but it's clearly unused and uncared for.

It's called a ghost box. It's what those in anti-Wal-Mart circles call a store that the Arkansas company has abandoned. There are more than a few of these. In fact, more than 200 of these vacated carcasses pepper America's exurbs and small-town fringes. Just a few years ago, Wal-Mart had 350 of these stores rolling around their balance sheet. It's taken an intense effort during the last three years by the company's real estate arm to carve that number down. Wal-Mart has ditched a total of about 1,000 stores during the last ten years, leaving some of them after little more than a decade. The company deserts a site usually to move into a bigger structure that's often, but not always, constructed within several miles of the original store. In the case of Coshocton, Wal-Mart opened a behemoth store a few miles outside town, on a highway entrance ramp. A typical Wal-Mart retrenchment will create a 120,000-square-foot ghost box on one side of town so the retailer can open a 200,000-square-foot Supercenter that includes a grocery store on the other side of town.

Getting rid of the ghost boxes once they've been abandoned falls to a segment of the company called Wal-Mart Realty, which employs 500 people and whose main purpose is to dump used Wal-Mart properties.[1] In a future of $14 gas, these people will be busy. Almost every one of Wal-Mart's giant stores will be relegated to serving a different purpose when gas prices reach $14. The force that brought globalization to every American's closet will have been laid to waste by gas prices soaring past $14. Wal-Mart will die. Ghost boxes will dot the exurbian and rural landscape from coast to coast. At $14, the framework upon which Wal-Mart has spread cheap Chinese junk around the country will fall apart. Supply chains that go from node to node to node across oceans and continents won't survive except for products of the utmost importance. Cheap spatulas and ballpoint pens won't qualify.

There will be two things stemming from high gasoline prices that contribute to the obsolescence of big box stores that, in most cases, are located on the fringes of towns and suburbs rather than city cores. One, obviously, is that people will not be carelessly gallivanting about town in their cars anymore. Electric cars will exist, yes, but cars and roads will not be the glue of society any longer. People will walk or travel to stores less than two miles from their home, not the five to ten miles people now schlep to make a visit to Wal-Mart, Meijer, or Target.

The second big banana, and the biggest reason for Wal-Mart's demise—at least Wal-Mart as we know it now—will be the outrageous cost of maintaining the retailer's vast distribution and product network. Wal-Mart's model works because of cheap gasoline. The company is able to leverage cheap labor in China to make many of its wares because of the low cost of getting those products back to the United States aboard giant cargo ships. Wal-Mart by itself is China's eighth-largest trading partner. Once the boodle gets to a West Coast port, it's moved by rail and by truck to Wal-Mart's 140 distribution centers. This task requires Wal-Mart's fleet of 7,200 semi-tractor trailer trucks, which fan out the goods to Wal-Mart's 4,000 U.S. stores. Without gasoline at affordable prices, goods from China don't float in at mass quantities, choking a main Wal-Mart advantage. Flinging the goods around the country, from port to distribution center to store, will become prohibitively expensive.

Consider some of Wal-Mart's incredibly cheap wooden furniture. The wood comes from Russian timber in vast Siberian forests, which migrant laborers and loggers fell with clattering chainsaws. The wood gets stacked on giant semitrucks that haul the trunks to a mill, where it's cut into long, flat pieces. The freshly cut lumber then gets loaded on a train and travels more than 1,000 miles to factories in China, where laborers earning cents on the hour fashion the Siberian lumber into shelves, desks, and chairs. These goods, in turn, get stacked on pallets and shoved back onto railroad cars, where they head hundreds of miles to one of China's giant ports.

The newly minted furniture gets stuffed into containers and gains lodging on a trans-Pacific cargo ship, arriving in a place like Long Beach or Seattle a week later. The furniture then finds its way onto trains belonging to Union Pacific or Burlington Northern, and heads out across the American West, across the Rockies, to a dropoff point in Nebraska. From there, it's back onto a semi-truck for a ride to one of Wal-Mart's main distribution centers. At the distribution center, a veritable international airport of cheap stuff, the Russian-wood, Chinese-built furniture gets transferred to a Wal-Mart truck that makes its way to a secondary Wal-Mart distribution center. From there, the junk is finally brought to a Wal-Mart store, where employees set up the kitchen table for $69 and the computer desk for $59. It's an awesomely complex model and one that works only with cheap petroleum.

The sound of Wal-Mart falling will be one that all of us hear. Wal-Mart is the largest company on the planet. It tallies nearly $400 billion in sales annually. It employs 2.1 million people. When Wal-Mart winces, the whole world knows. Wal-Mart has about 6,000 global suppliers; more than 80% of them are in China. China's manufacturing sector will be in chaos. The makers of the cheapest stuff, the commodity junk, such as pens, inexpensive clothes, and housewares, will be hardest hit. Only the United States can inhale that much junk. Companies will be wrecked, supply chains will be decimated, jobs will be lost. Small towns will lose their anchors, the store that supplied nearly everything to everybody. But some small towns will climb out of their hole. They will revel in their new-found identity, shedding the homogenization that Wal-Mart spread.

Retailers such as Home Depot, Lowe's, Target, and K-Mart will contribute their colossal structures to the ghost box count as well. In the United States, 10,000 ghost boxes will serve as giant rotting gravestones for the era of mass globalization and merchandising. They will surround our condensing towns and cities like ancient tin-walled ramparts, forged for battles long since passed.

The Future of Small Towns in a $14-per-Gallon World, Sans Wal-Mart

Nowhere has Wal-Mart's power been more pungent than in America's small towns. Wal-Mart, in effect, has co-opted America's rural centers as its own captive customer base. Whether a rural consumer is buying a chicken leg, a mop, or a hammer, they're probably doing it at Wal-Mart. Wal-Mart's effect on small-town life in America has been well chronicled. It's not a flattering tale. Kenneth Stone, an economist at the University of Iowa, has made his name documenting the change that Wal-Mart brings to rural communities. His studies that detail the destruction of Iowa's Main Streets proved to be a keystone for many of the controversies that surround Wal-Mart's business plan. Wal-Mart first invaded Iowa in 1982. It marched across the state during the next ten years. According to Stone, Iowa lost 2,200 of its retail stores from 1983 to 1993. That includes 37% of the state's grocery stores, 43% of its men's apparel stores, and 33% of its hardware stores.

Wal-Mart, in effect, turned these towns inside out. Most small towns once had central business districts surrounded by homes built within five to six blocks. This kind of town design, simple as it is, manifested during a time when the car was not king. Automobiles may have existed, but we hadn't yet wrapped our lives around their shiny chrome accoutrements. There was always a core to the town, a heart, from which homes radiated. Wal-Mart transplanted that heart into a tin-roofed warehouse several miles from town, where real estate was cheapest and zoning nonexistent. Two things happened. First, people shopped at Wal-Mart instead of Main Street, which choked Main Street's revenue and caused most of its stores to disappear. Second, the town's development sprawled toward Wal-Mart, creating a thick slice of splurb between the old, centralized town and the out-in-the-boonies Wal-Mart. But it's difficult to blame people for shopping at Wal-Mart instead of Main Street when Wal-Mart's prices were more than 20% cheaper, on average, than those of the town's other stores.

This massive store of foodstuffs, trinkets, furniture, and household staples under one 200,000-square-foot roof will prove to be an idea that worked only during a span of three or four decades. But a company that wields as much control as Wal-Mart does won't just topple without a fight. Wal-Mart has already begun experimenting with different business models—it has a sector of stores called Neighborhood Markets, which are around 40,000 square feet—a quarter the size of a normal Wal-Mart—and can be nuzzled into walkable communities without demanding a huge pad of real estate. Some of the new Wal-Marts will be as small as 15,000 square feet and will be called Marketside Stores. Wal-Mart isn't blind to the future, but they're not convinced of it either. As small towns reconsolidate around a central core, Wal-Mart may find a way to be a part of it. Perhaps they run small stores on the town square or right on Main Street, which is how many Wal-Marts originally operated during the 1960s when Sam Walton began building his empire. It wasn't until the 1970s that Wal-Mart began pursuing a widespread plan of freestanding colossi outside of towns. "They're talking about twelve-thousand-square-foot stores on one hand and a NAFTA superhighway for their trucks that cuts a swath through America from Mexico to Canada on the other, so they're hedging their bets, they're not sure which way this is going to go," says Al Norman, who runs Sprawlbusters, an organization that helps towns deal with issues of sprawl and local retail woes related to Wal-Mart.

If Wal-Mart wants to survive in small towns, it will have to try and do so on the localities' terms, not its own. Wal-Mart made people hike far outside of town to shop its shelves; in the future, it will be Wal-Mart chasing people back toward the center of town. To avoid rural extinction, Wal-Marts will have to offer local goods, and negotiate with local growers, builders, and resellers to stock its shelves. It won't be able to bring in pallets of junk from China, be it plastic spoons, rubber balls, or cheap furniture. Stuff—the goods and wares we live our lives with—will again have value. The disposable armoire and the $50 kitchen table will be a thing of the past. This will be a positive change for our lives, our footprints, and our planet.

Urban areas that Wal-Mart has penetrated will be affected the least by the demise of giant stores, as local stores, located more frequently in cities, will pick up the slack. The suburban ideal, where everyone gets a half-acre and a modestly built frame house, will end. That way of life will not be sustainable for the huge swath of the population that now lives it, as was discussed in Chapter $12. Following that trend, it's easy to dismiss small towns' futures as doomed. But small towns will survive. In some cases, they will thrive. Small-town life will not be for everyone, but some will seek it out and prefer it to the urban and fast-paced life of the city. And for the first time in decades, small-town life will resemble the kind of existence that we've associated with rural towns for so long, even though life in these places, for decades, hasn't been anything but a homogenized, standardized, and watered-down version of suburbia.

Goods in these places come from Wal-Mart and stores of its ilk. Organic foods and products that differentiate themselves from the standard are easier to find in cities, not in small towns. People living in these places, be they in the South, the Midwest, or the Northeast, have faced commercialism of the lowest common denominator. What they get to buy is determined purely by national companies that can extend their low-price platforms into every nook of America thanks to low fuel prices. The high price of gas, however, will end the stranglehold of banal products and big-box blight on small-town America.

The Small-Town Stampede Back to Main Street

Stores will return to the downtowns of yore as small towns' populations, stretched across a wide landscape toward highways and big-box stores, return to the small-town infrastructures that their grandparents and great-grandparents built. They'll return to modest homes and close-by neighbors, they'll return closer to rail stations and post offices, they'll return closer to the businesses of life. No longer will these businesses be spread out like a commerce smorgasbord smeared across dozens of miles of minimall strips and highway outposts. They will return to Main Street, whence they came.

People who live in these towns will also work in these towns. They will be doctors, teachers, mechanics, shopkeepers, plumbers, carpenters, family lawyers, police officers, firemen; their work will be in town, for townspeople. Their functions will be clear, not unlike they were two or three generations ago. The publicized tales of America's so-called supercommuters, people who drive more than two hours to work and again home every day, will fade into a past that won't return. People will no longer think they can have a life in the country and a job in the city. It's never been a pragmatic approach to life, but it's been one that's possible with cheap, quickly built housing and oil priced so low that it will, in the future, have seemed just about free.

The economic engines that kept small towns roiling with prosperity in the past—labor-intensive farming in the Midwest, cotton in the South, tobacco in the Carolinas, mining in the foothills of the West—have been fading away for decades and their demise will continue in the future. The change has led us from being a country where 36% of our population lived rurally in 1950 to one where only 20% of our people live rurally now.[2] Our small towns have shriveled not because people prefer exurbs and sprawl—as that's where most of these transplants ended up—but because jobs in these small towns disappeared. And as the exurbs drew nearer to rural life, so did their job opportunities and their homogenizing force. With cheap gasoline, it's never been a question of affording to drive to a job at the edge of metropolitan sprawl for rural people; it's just been a question of tolerance for the amount of time it saps.

Voids left from industries such as mining will be filled by high-earning telecommuters. Small-town folk who do not contribute to the town's welfare in their daily job will support the town by earning wages gleaned from companies and business outside the town. They will be consultants, writers, graphic artists, and accountants. They will depend on the Internet to see and hear their clients, not a jet plane or a two-hour commute. These people, the Internet-enabled telecommuters who prefer the coziness of small-town life, will be the new source of outside capital. They will be to small towns what mining and tobacco once were. They will transfer the wealth of the greater outside world to the streets of small towns, all through the portal of technology. Their earnings will be spent in town and will, in most cases, stay in town, enabling the surviving small towns to be lively, cultured places unto themselves.

Goods will come into these towns from the outside, but they won't stream in with the volume of the bountiful Wal-Mart pallets that once flooded small-town America. Shipping merchandise will be expensive, and there's no way that small towns will be able to avoid shouldering the cost of getting goods to their towns. Prices of commodity-like merchandise in small towns will simply be more expensive than those in urban areas. But the difference won't be crippling. The people who don't like it or can't afford it will simply leave small towns for an urban life. The people left behind will be those who have small-town values ensconced in their hearts. Closely knit neighbors, generational legacies, and town loyalty will be the marks of the folks who live in these places.

And because getting things to town will cost more, people in small towns will value what they have. They will fix things rather than rush out for a plastic replacement. Every small town will have a thriving secondhand store that perhaps doubles as a repair shop for all manner of goods: furniture, electronics, and the bric-a-brac of modern life. People with repairing, technical, and handyman skills will be valued in small towns. No reason to buy a new water heater with its included shipping costs when Bob from down the block can fix it for $100. The vacuum cleaner will get fixed, not replaced. The handy people in small towns will be busy and they will contribute to a community that will live in a far more sustainable way than contemporary small towns, where a cheap replacement for just about anything is never more than thirty miles away at Wal-Mart.

Small towns that prosper in a future of high gas prices will be the ones that are able to grow food locally. Produce will be fiercely local, as further described in Chapter $16. A town that calls for every staple to be shipped in from afar will likely not survive. There will be plenty of small towns that simply do not make the transition from a satellite living on cheap oil to a town that's half self-sustaining and populated by people who not only prefer a small-town life, but also are stringently loyal to their small town and are willing to sacrifice for their neighbors, their town, and their way of life. The hamlets that don't survive, like the Wal-Marts who fall ahead of them, will be home only to ghosts, gusts, and a reclaiming Mother Nature.

The Small Towns That Survive Will Have the Robust Structure of Their Pasts

Small towns likely to thrive in a future of high gasoline prices are ones that already have venerable downtown infrastructures sitting in place, with existing railroad connections and river frontage. Many small towns' infrastructures, their grand main streets and their brick and stone downtown buildings, have been all but abandoned. Their windows are empty, their heat is turned off, and their values hover at next to nothing. But if they're still there, largely intact, they can and will be used again. Main Streets will swing back to life as small towns again congregate closer to the old center of town.

Towns with intact downtowns, city halls, and other buildings of consequence will have an edge over towns that may have razed sections of their old Main Streets or let them fall to decay. "The skeleton of a good building can last centuries," Paul Katz, the KPF architect, says. "We can just reuse them right where they sit."

It's easy and cheap to rehabilitate a sturdy brick building, especially compared with building from scratch. That gap between a spruce-up renovation and building anew will grow even larger in a future of higher energy costs, as materials will cost more to make, ship, and shape. Four walls, a foundation, and a roof will always be worth something, and their value will only grow when they're located in newly relevant centers of towns and the corresponding cost of building new has grown exponentially.

Small-town sprawl will freeze in its place, its outer reaches withering, decaying, and dying. People will reinvent century-old buildings and turn around homes that looked doomed. New home construction in small towns, when it happens, will be similar to the town house movement in cities. Shared walls will carry large energy bonuses for everybody, not just city dwellers. The hearts of small towns will be minicities unto themselves, with townhomes and apartments ramping up local density and enabling a vibrant downtown packed with commerce. People in small towns will want to walk to shops, to schools, and if they're going somewhere farther—perhaps to the city ninety minutes away—to the train station.

The railroads will again assume the role that was stolen by interstates in small towns: the role of long-haul kingpin for both passengers and freight. A small town's lifeblood will no longer chug along asphalt byways, but it will hum on steel tracks. The small towns that survive in a world of high energy costs will be the ones positioned advantageously on major railroad lines. Small towns with direct lines into rail hubs such as Chicago, Omaha, Kansas City, and Philadelphia will prosper. Regular passenger rail service will revive. And freight, so cheaply delivered on rails even now in a world of cheap gas, will grow even cheaper compared with trucks. The average American freight train can deliver 436 tons[3] of cargo one mile on one gallon of gas, more than four times the 105 tons that semitrucks can deliver one mile on a gallon. That gap won't narrow—and its significance will only grow with time. The 300% advantage rail now holds will be exacerbated as gas goes from $3 a gallon to $6 per gallon to $12 per gallon. A rail renaissance will grow more expansive with every dollar gasoline climbs. Towns strategically positioned on the best rail lines will reap the benefits.

What this means simply is that our oldest small towns, the ones with fine old buildings, magnificent Main Streets (even if empty), and of course, mainline rail service (which, usually, was the reason for their original prosperity) will be the winners in a future of $14 gas.

These railway towns, the ones with quaint downtowns and built-in natural splendor, will often reap the added advantage of tourism. Just as some small towns of today have made their Main Streets sparkle with tourists' money, so will some small towns in

the future. But being on a backcountry road, no matter how winding and attractive, will no longer cut it. City-borne travelers will
want to hop on the rails and ride, not drive, to their favorite bed-
and-breakfast.

Towns that have the advantage of being on major waterways,
in addition to a railroad, will be at a double advantage. The only
method to ship cargo that's cheaper than rail is by water. A river
barge can move 576 tons of freight one mile on a gallon of gas.
That's an impressive statistic that won't escape the MBA types of
the future. Where barge traffic can be used to ship all manner of
materials, it will be used. Small towns positioned on rivers that
once teemed with freight will find themselves again perched on
the edges of a lucrative commercial portal.

Small-town life will remain very attractive to a large set of
people. Consumerist knickknacks will cost more in small towns,
but the core lures to small-town neighborhoods will be fully rein-
vigorated with the advent of high energy costs: closeness, trust,
convenience, and familiarity. Small towns will draw people who
want to know exactly where their food comes from. Their bread
will come not from an interstate-borne truck, but from the baker on
Main Street and wheat from nearby fields. Tomatoes won't come
from a farm thousands of miles away in Mexico, but from a hothouse visible from the east side of town. The organic movement,
out of one part preference and one part necessity, will give theme
and meaning to a small town's cuisine.

Crime in small towns, never an overriding problem to be
sure, will become even sparser, as anonymous acts of vandalism
or theft become harder to commit and harder to stomach for
would-be perpetrators. As small towns condense and realign into
walkable, bikable, and tighter communities, the roots of random
crime will be further extinguished. More people in less space
mean more witnesses, more friends, and a more even sense of
community.

The American Manufacturing Renaissance Must Defeat the Container Ship

In 1956, a cargo ship in Newark harbor took on fifty-eight giant metal boxes, each of them about forty feet long, eight feet wide, and eight feet high. The ship, an aging rusty hulk called the *Ideal-X*, made its way to Houston five days later. Without any ceremony whatsoever, the fifty-eight metal boxes were transferred to fifty-eight trucks waiting at the port and the semis rumbled off to destinations throughout the Southwest. Nobody besides the port workers noticed the exchange. And nobody cared. But that shipping swap marked the beginning of the container age that changed the shipping industry and global commerce forever.[4] Shipping containers allowed space on cargo ships to be easily sold and sorted. Ships went from cluttered bins of assorted cargoes to neat file cabinets of goods, easily packed and loaded and unloaded.

It took shipping containers decades to fully revolutionize trade. Old established ports weren't equipped to handle the boxes in bulk, so containers remained an outlier until ports constructed in the 1970s, 1980s, and 1990s were built with the express purpose of leveraging this prescient way of shipping, packing, and sorting. The shipping container, with its neat rows and orderly delineations, allowed myriad medium-sized companies to easily charter their way onto the holds of the world's largest oceangoing ships at affordable rates. It also saved a giant chunk of labor costs at the ports themselves because ships' cargoes didn't have to be disseminated, sorted, and routed at the ports, other than the containers themselves. In 1959, a study determined that 60% to 75% of the cost of shipping internationally across oceans came from what took place inside the shipping yards themselves: getting the cargo, which was packed into the ship like a traveler packs a jumbled steamer box, sorted and arranged for its next mode of shipping.[5] Before the shipping container fully arrived, international trade simply didn't make much sense.

As the efficiencies of the metal box bubbled to the fore, business for container ships surged. Business for old, union-fortified ports, built for the precontainer economy, withered and shrank as new ports, built expressly for these efficient boxes, usurped them. New York, Liverpool, and Newark faded in shipping relevance as the new powers of Seattle, Hong Kong, and Long Beach moved to become the vanguard, their operations built around a forty-foot metal box.

The container ships themselves are wonders of brute mass. They can be 1,100 feet long and 140 feet across and their cargo consists of 100% containers. Above deck, they're stacked in rows of as many as eighteen across and seven deep with more rows stacked eight deep below deck. A common container ship may carry 3,000 of these boxes and 100,000 tons of total cargo. Each container gets stuffed with 40 tons of goods. Despite the massive scale of the cargo, the containers, and the ship itself, it only takes a crew of twenty to get one of these floating bastions of raw capitalism from one side of the world to another. When the ships sidle up to dock, enormous spider cranes immediately go to work, 200 feet high and weighing more than 20 million pounds. The crane booms sweep out for 110 feet, easily long enough to reach across the massive ships and wider than the Panama canal.

The shipping container has effectively taken over world commerce. It has enabled colossal volumes of goods to be transported from country to country, from continent to continent, with minimal labor costs. The container has made factories in southern China relevant to a gidget maker in Omaha. Though it took decades to fully commandeer world trade, the container is now thoroughly ensconced in all markets of global consequence. The sorting mechanism of the container has enabled the United States to import four times the variety of goods that it did thirty years ago. During the last fifteen years, many of our country's last strongholds of manufacturing have been dismantled and shut down as companies turned to cheap and easy labor in places such as China, Taiwan, and Vietnam. The current lanes of international business, however long, have been traced into the globe like a worn path through the woods.

The paradigm of sending our cash abroad for cheap stuff has been thoroughly chiseled into our economy. As noted, it's the model that makes Wal-Mart go. It's the model that stuffs our closets full of junk. Unseating that model will not come easy; the world's giant economies have been built around this container mechanism and our complex systems that transport it. Six-dollar gas won't bring manufacturers paddling back for North American shores. Nor will $8 gas or even $10 gas. It will take more. Cataclysmic change will be necessary. That cataclysm is coming, not in the form of trade wars, tariffs, or taxes, but in the form of $14 gasoline. The world's markets and their complexities will come untangled as, suddenly, the physical distance from manufacturer to customer becomes as relevant as a worker's wage.

In 2000, when gas was hovering around $1.50 per gallon in much of the nation, shipping a forty-foot container from Shanghai to New York cost $3,300. In 2005, with gas near $2.50, shipping the same container the same route cost $5,100.[6] During the spring of 2008, with gas at $3.50, sending the container from China to the East Coast took $8,350. When gas approaches $5, getting the metal box to New York will run $10,000; when gas approaches $8 per gallon, the ocean freight for a container will run $15,000. That equates to sticking a 15% tariff onto goods coming in from China, says Jeff Rubin, chief economist and strategist for CIBC World Markets in Toronto. "Globalization is reversible," Rubin likes to say.

And he's right. It's simply a question of gas prices. A tariff of 15% takes a large hack out of the margins of companies sourcing their goods from overseas. For the biggest-margin items, and those would be the things that are a step up in complexity from a ballpoint pen—stuff like power tools, consumer electronics, cell phones, etc.—it will take more than a 15% tariff to overpower the leverage of cheap Chinese labor. The system of build-it-there, sell-it-here is deeply ingrained. As the incumbent way of doing things, the China model holds the built-in advantage of having few capital costs beyond maintenance, whereas moving manufacturing back to North America entails not only reorganizing shipping routes, but also building factory lines anew, training a different fleet of workers, who, of course, make a lot more money than their counterparts in Guangzhou.

But when that tariff goes past 25%, expect a massive defection of manufacturers from Asia back to their corporate home of North America. That tariff is coming in the form of $14 gasoline. At that point, profit margins will have been thoroughly erased by the cost of container ships' fuel. It takes about 13,000 tons of fuel to get a container ship carrying 5,000 of the metal boxes from Shanghai to an East Coast port. But when gas is $4 a gallon, that fuel runs about $550 a ton, meaning that ship spends about $7.2 million just on fuel. When gas approaches $14, the fuel will cost that same ship nearly $30 million. Plenty of manufacturers will begin relocating at least some of their lines to North America before gas reaches $14, but that price will mark a wholesale flush of manufacturing from Asia back to North America. Anybody who is going to move will move.

But not everybody will move. The Chinese and other Asian economies have become giant consumer markets in their own right. Their heft, as the years go on, will only grow, allowing them to absorb more and more of what's made on their own shores. But manufacturers focused on the American market will look back toward the United States, toward Mexico, and toward Canada.

America Returns to the Roots of Its Prosperity: Manufacturing

Small towns across America will see their fortunes buoyed as manufacturing returns home. Towns like Dewitt, Nebraska, which lost its Irwin Tools plant to China in 2008, or Whitmire, South Carolina, which lost sock maker Renfro to China the same year, or Paonia, Colorado, which lost its Chaco Sandals factory to China, also in 2008, will get an injection of jobs, capital, and pride. Towns on major rail lines will stand the best chance of snaring returning factories, as companies will prefer rail to get mass quantities of raw materials in and thousands of boxes of the finished goods out.

Al Norman, the Sprawlbusters founder, laughingly recalls a sign he used to see from a commuter train in New Jersey several decades ago. "It said, 'Trenton makes, the world takes,'" he remembers. The billboard referred to Trenton's key position as a manufacturing center. "Trenton is now in Shenzhen, China," he explains, "but it will move again, back to where it always should have been: home sweet home."

New York Times columnist Thomas Friedman has sold a lot of books proclaiming, simply, that *The World Is Flat*. The earth's massive curvature, however, will reassert itself in an era of $14 gasoline. Untangling globalism's far-reaching relationships will take years. Ports will go unused. Shipping lanes will grow sparse. Trade deficits will shrink. *Made in China* won't be the ubiquitous moniker marking our goods that it is now.

We'll be left with major ports, ships, and an international infrastructure built around a fading container economy. Some of these ports will go quiet with the same quickness they became bustling. The port of Shenzhen, a city in southern China, was mostly rice paddies fifteen years ago; now the port is the third busiest in the world. Containers will pile up around the globe with nowhere to go, clogging railway hubs, harbors, and distribution centers. Millions of these corrugated containers, having been relegated to dinosaur status, sitting idly by in ports like Long Beach and Seattle, will turn into tomorrow's scrap metal, destined for I-beams, car doors, and food cans. We won't abandon international trade, but the whimsical nature with which we now ship goods to and fro will fade into history. If we import something from China, we'll have a damned good reason.

A resurgent manufacturing sector for the American economy will have two edges. The first edge, the obvious one, will be positive: more jobs, more employment stability, less money going abroad, and theoretically, more tax revenues for the government. The second edge, depending on one's outlook, can be considered negative or positive: less cheap stuff. Americans love cheap stuff. We love being able to swing down to the grocery store and pick up a can opener for $2. We love getting twenty clothes hangers for $3. We love going to Home Depot or Lowe's and getting a set of ten screwdrivers for $7 or a set of three adjustable wrenches for $5. Before China moved in, stuff simply cost us more money. By the same token, though, we used to buy less stuff. Now, if we lose a pair of pliers or a kitchen tool, we give a cursory look around the house before we just go buy another of whatever we've lost. Inevitably, the old item shows up and we're left with two. China has enabled us, through cheap transportation and cheap oil, to become a true disposable society.

Will our quality of life truly suffer with less Chinese junk? Maybe just a little. And there's little doubt that Americans in the lower middle class will be most affected; Wal-Mart and China have grown the specter of things that people with low incomes can afford. But it's also true that blue-collar America stands to benefit most with the return of manufacturing to U.S. shores. Their work base has steadily eroded during the past twenty-five years, helping create a larger and larger schism between the upper class (the people who, in more cases than not, are able to capture the earnings of globalism) and the middle class, who, simply, have less-well-paying jobs.

Cheap stuff is part of the reason Americans lust for 4,000-square-foot homes with three-car garages: people need all that room for all their stuff. We will have less room in the future as our housing units shrink and condense. That evolution alone—the shrinking of our homes—would have pressured much of the disposable inventory of Wal-Mart toward extinction. Incessant packaging, boxes galore, plastic doodads, knickknacks, and detritus—it seems as if half the junk coming out of China accessorizes or packages the original junk they were making. The combined pressures of expensive shipping and the shrinking American house will mean that we will actually want and value the stuff we choose to keep.

Gas Prices of $14 Will Be Good for the Earth

Globalization's decline will lead us toward lives of closets less packed, garbage cans half full, and landfills that fill up slower and slower. Globalization's lessening role in our everyday lives will be another way, among many, that we lessen our impact on the earth. Humans have never been able curb their behavior on a massive, societal basis strictly for altruistic environmental purposes—unless such changes are mandated by government. The financial cost of our garbage, in this current world, is not a burden of consequence in our lives. But it will become one.

We will generate less waste in a future of high gasoline prices, as our economy adopts ways to trim back on garbage collection as its costs spiral upward. We use an inordinate amount of energy to throw stuff out. Our society burns gasoline to get giant garbage trucks down every street, alley, and neighborhood in the country and then out to landfills often dozens of miles from where the truck picked up its trash.

There are more than twice as many garbage trucks, 179,000,

in the United States as there are urban transit buses. These refuse-hauling monsters get an average of 2.8 miles per gallon.[7] Garbage trucks move at an average speed of 10 mph, an incredibly inefficient pace for a combustion engine, but one that's necessary because of the garbage truck's duties. The average garbage truck guzzles 8,600 gallons of diesel fuel a year, a gluttonous total. All the U.S. garbage trucks together use 1.5 billion gallons of fuel, about 4% of all the diesel used in the United States, and accounting for billions of dollars of fuel money sent overseas.

In the future, the costs of the fuel our garbage trucks burn, just like all energy costs, will be brought into tighter focus, and they will be reduced to the point of man's ingenuity to do so. In a future of $14 gas, packaging will be minimal, garbage cans will be smaller, and throwing something out will no longer be the flip decision it now is. We won't be fighting for the earth when we cut back on garbage production, we'll be fighting for dollars. It will be all the same, however, to a thankful planet.

The Materials That Make Our Material World

All materials, be they plastic, wood, or metal, will cost more in a world of high gasoline prices. Transporting raw materials—ore, oil, logs, coal, sugar—borne on rail, road, or ship, takes gasoline. So as gas prices increase, so, too, will the price of just about all raw materials. Substances that are based on petroleum—asphalt, plastic, synthetic rubber—face a doubly steep ramp: Not only will the gas needed to transport them be more expensive, but so, too, will their feedstock.

Materials made from petroleum make up many of the staples of our homes, roads, and belongings. Luckily there are alternatives to most of these materials already in circulation, alternatives that, because of the rising price of oil, will become competitive in markets where oil-based materials once ruled. The breadth of products that come directly from petroleum is massive. Everything from milk jugs to laundry detergent to masking tape to perfume to mascara to hand lotion to sunscreen to the insulation in a sleeping bag to the cushions in your couch to the case of your computer to the eraser on your pencil to the ink in your pen. The list goes on forever. Some of these things will continue being made of petroleum-derived plastics or liquids; they'll just cost more. If a ballpoint pen costs us $1.50 instead of 50 cents, it won't cripple the economy. Instead, we'll just be less cavalier about buying and trashing these things that were once utterly disposable. There are some things, however, big things, that will change.

When a homeowner gets the grim word from a contractor or an inspector that it's time to replace the roof, there's most often only one candidate for the new roofing material: asphalt shingles. Oil-based roofing materials are wonderful at doing one thing, being cheap. Their cost, compared with their upscale competitors of aluminum, galvanized steel, copper, slate, and cedar, is minuscule. Asphalt shingles aren't free, but they're close. When you pay somebody $5,000 to reroof your home, most of that cost is in labor. A comparable metal roof, whose benefits go far beyond its superior looks, can run four times as much. Sure, a metal roof might last seventy-five years, but most of us aren't concerned about what will be happening in seventy-five years.

In a future of $14 gas, asphalt roofing won't cost as much as metal, but the gap will have narrowed severely. A premium of 50% for a metal roof won't seem obnoxious to consumers who want to avoid replacing their asphalt shingles in another ten or twelve years. Buy the metal roof once, and you're done. In addition, metal roofs weigh only 20% of what a bulky asphalt roof weighs, putting less stress on walls, trusses, and joists. And as disposing of waste becomes more expensive, getting rid of an old asphalt roof will become quite pricey.

When it comes to roofing, waste will be paramount. Asphalt

roofing generates copious amounts of waste. Most every time a new asphalt roof gets put on, an old one gets pulled off. Every year, 20 billion pounds of asphalt shingles get dumped in U.S. landfills.[8] Just one year of that waste, lined up in 40,000-pound Dumpsters, would stretch from New York to Los Angeles, back to New York, and then, still more, all the way to Chicago. Getting rid of a Dumpster full of roofing might run only about $500 for a homeowner now. When gas is $14, that cost will be nearer to $3,000.

Metal roofs that can be affixed directly on top of existing and failing asphalt roofs will begin popping up around the country once gas tops $12. As we close in on $14, upper-middle- and upper-class neighborhoods will be thoroughly invaded by aluminum roofing. They will dot neighborhoods with increasing frequency, changing the satellite view of housetops from homogenous black to green, red, and glinty silver. Having a metal roof will become what the minivan was a generation ago or what color TV was several generations before: a fascinating novelty that, little by little, year by year, gets adopted by most of the neighborhood. The benefits go beyond mere durability. The energy conservation movement will be strong in all American households as gasoline goes into double digits. Metal roofs, because they reflect UV rays and heat, keep homes cooler in the summer and warmer in the winter compared with asphalt roofs, which, insulating-wise, are about the worst things you can top a building with.

Our Biggest Asphalt Addiction: Our Highways and Byways

Our lives come in contact most often with asphalt on our roads. We drive on it, we bike on it, we walk on it, and when it's fresh, we smell it. Asphalt is the murky, tarry gunk that's left over at the bottom of the refining vats when all the kerosene, gasoline, and diesel fuel has been skimmed off. Asphalt, kept at high temperatures of 300 degrees Fahrenheit or more, is a liquid of high viscosity that can be shaped to coat just about anything. Mixed with aggregate pea gravel and left to cool and dry, asphalt forms the dark, hard, and cheap concrete that we're all used to seeing nearly anywhere we go. It coats 94%[9] of the roads in the United States, about 4 million miles' worth.[10]

Humans have been utilizing asphalt for its malleable bonding qualities for thousands of years. Babylonians, using asphalt mined from local deposits, made roads coated in black around 625 B.C.[11] The Romans and the Greeks—whose nomenclature of *asphaltos*, meaning "secure and stable," is the root of our word *asphalt*—used it to waterproof baths, aqueducts, and reservoirs. Sir Walter Raleigh used natural asphalt deposits in Trinidad to recaulk his ships' joints in 1595.[12] The first American roads paved with asphalt in a manner similar to current methods were in front of the city hall in Newark, New Jersey, in 1870. A Belgian chemist named Edmund DeSmedt contrived the method of mixing hot asphalt with sand and pebbles, pouring and stamping the churn into a hard streetscape. DeSmedt next went on to pave a rather prominent street with his new method: Pennsylvania Avenue in Washington DC.

Laura Ingalls Wilder first encountered asphalt in a wagon journey through Topeka with her parents in 1894. She described it this way:

> In the very midst of the city, the ground was covered by some dark stuff that silenced all the wheels and muffled the sound of hoofs. It was like tar, but Papa was sure it was not tar, and it was something like rubber, but it could not be rubber because rubber cost too much. We saw ladies all in silks and carrying ruffled parasols, walking with their escorts across the street. Their heels dented

the street, and while we watched, these dents slowly filled up and smoothed themselves out. It was as if that stuff were alive. It was like magic.[13]

Asphalt is hardly magic to us anymore. Procuring it through the oil-refining process, rather than through its limited natural deposits, has made it as ubiquitous as any man-made substance there is. Its far-reaching black veins enable gasoline-powered commerce to chug about our nation smoothly. It has tamed remote reaches of wilderness, mountain passes, and dusty old Main Streets in need of tidying. The dregs of the oil bucket have become, in many ways, just as important as the more expensive stuff that gets siphoned to the engines of our cars and trucks. But getting asphalt becomes an expensive proposition during times of high gas prices. Asphalt's price, which is tightly pegged to oil and the operation of refineries, spiked like a rocket, hampering infrastructure projects from Maine to Florida to Washington State.

Towns and municipalities that were paying $50 a ton for asphalt in 2001 paid $100 a ton in 2008, removing a huge chunk of what they were able to do during a typical summer construction season. Places like Bergen County, New Jersey, paved twenty-three miles of road when their original budget called for thirty-two miles of paving.[14] Drivers noticed. During summer 2008, AAA reported 13% more flat tires for its drivers compared with other years. Lake County, South Dakota, postponed a five-mile repaving project when bids came in $150,000 more than the project's budget of $442,000. The Tennessee Department of Transportation usually paves 2,500 miles of highway a year; in 2008, it managed only 1,600 miles because of high asphalt prices. And some roads in Hall County, Nebraska, will be allowed to return to gravel strips because of escalating asphalt prices, something that will happen all over rural America in the coming decades.

The problems created in the asphalt realm by $4 gas were felt by all of society. Not only were potholes more vicious and more numerous, they were less likely to be frosted over by a fresh coat of black goop. If our paving behaviors couldn't persevere when gas was $4, what will happen when gas hits $14? More of our most vital thoroughfares will be paved with concrete, which is more than five times the cost of asphalt currently, but lasts decades longer and is less susceptible to the freeze-thaw cycles that ravage asphalt roads and cause potholes to multiply in the winter. Concrete will become popular in northern towns with the foresight to pay extra for it. Southern towns, where asphalt's only enemy is UV rays, will stick with blacktop. Ultimately, the gross mileage of our paved roads will dive every year, until only the roads in metro area cores are regularly tended to with a coating of asphalt. Rural towns used to paving dozens of miles in a year will stick to worrying about Main Street. Some of our less crucial highways will be shut down and superfluous interstate spurs will be closed. Toll roads that don't produce the requisite money to keep their tarmacs fresh will close, too.

Choosing to close some of our roads will be a choice we can make because far fewer people will be driving on the scale with which most of us motor around now. As we move to cities, prioritize our errand trips, and shop closer to home, we will drive 50% fewer miles in a world with $14 gas than we do now and there will be plenty of lonely blacktop. Some of it will simply have to be closed.

The Effects Will Ripple to All Manner of Materials

Our roads and roofs won't be the only things affected by the uptick in oil prices. Anything made from petroleum-based sources will face competition from other materials, usually those of more natural origin. Raw materials, no matter what they're made of, will cost more in a future of $14 gasoline. Carpet, for instance, covers 70% of America's indoor space and it's made of, in most cases, nylon, acrylic, polypropylene, or polyester. These carpet fibers are usually backed by a synthetic SB latex, polyurethane, or polyvinyl chloride. All these materials come from petroleum. So what's going to happen to carpet? It's going to become less popular. Hardwood, already on the comeback trail, will cover more of our floors. Carpet in the future will come from things like hemp, wool, abaca fibers (a cousin of the banana plant), sisal from the South American agave plant, or resilient strains of seagrass grown underwater in controlled farms.

Chic kitchen countertops will tend to be made of local stone rather than acrylic solids such as Corian or epoxy-filled such as Silestone. Plastics made from natural sources like that of Metabolix's Mirel will show up in more and more of our goods, lessening plastics' load on nature and its dependence on the oil trade. The plastics we do have will be recycled with a vigor once reserved for metal. Entrepreneurs will seek out and find hundreds of new uses for recycled plastics, keeping the petroleum-derived plastic we do have in circulation longer, out of landfills and places like the Great Pacific Garbage Patch.

Building materials—those beyond asphalt—will depend on the region where a project is built. Local materials will be prized for their value, as transportation costs for construction fodder become a larger and larger slice of the materials' overall price. "I think you'll see two main questions pop up with regard to materials," says Mary Ann Lazarus. "How far does it come from, and how much does it cost to move?"

Lazarus, the sustainability director at architecture giant HOK, expects builders to start seriously reconsidering the materials they put in their buildings when gas prices reach $10 a gallon. By $14, "the whole ballgame will be changing," she says. "Local materials will be king, that's for certain."

Saint Louis, for instance, sits on top of a giant clay bed, so brick making is a local industry in the area. "When you walk around the old sections of downtown Saint Louis, you notice how many of the buildings were built out of bricks simply because they were easy to get. I think we'll see more of that enter into builders' consciences," Lazarus explains. In that vein, shoppers at lumberyards in the Midwest won't see Douglas fir two-by-fours anymore, as they often do now. Douglas fir, which grows west of the Rockies and is usually logged from Oregon, Washington, and British Columbia, will stay in the West. Southern pine will stay in the Southeast, the Mid-Atlantic, and the Midwest. The forests of the Upper Midwest and New England, which have been left to flourish since we decimated their virgin timber stocks more than 100 years ago, will again be harvested in a careful, controlled manner, keeping those areas, and those areas alone, supplied with wood. "The move toward regional materials," says Lazarus, "will be pronounced."

Building supplies will be just another domino in the coterie of changes in our material world when gas prices touch $14. Voluminous retail packaging will be a thing of the past; many items will carry a price tag or a bar code in the store, nothing more. Just to recap, airplanes, those that remain in our skies, will be made of lightweight carbon fiber rather than metal. Cars, too, will feature carbon fiber and lightweight frames made from aluminum rather than steel. Plastics bred from bacteria and organic, renewable feedstocks will be firmly established in the market, displacing some conventional plastics made from oil. Newspapers and their heaping amounts of waste will no longer circulate, having moved to being strictly Web-based portals of information. Recycling will reach new heights. Household garbage cans will shrink, displaced across the country by larger recycling bins and a society that will generate 75% less waste per capita compared with current times. And Wal-Mart, the beacon of cheap disposable materialism in a globalized world, will be dead.

CHAPTER $16

The Food Web Deconstructed

It's not quite 5 a.m. We slam the rest of our grainy coffees and toss our cups into the back of the boat. Then, with a cooperative one-two-three, we push the rig into the water and hop aboard just as the water wets our boots. The sun, just now managing to get over the tree-lined horizon, appears like a foggy red traffic light, its power dispersed by the river's hazy morning shroud. The temperature is in the sixties but it will be 90 before noon. We float silently beneath a bridge stationed atop crumbling footings of limestone quarried from a local gorge 100 years ago.

"Well, dude, are you ready?" Orion Briney asks from the back of the boat. He's not talking to anyone directly. It was more of a general address to the morning. "Okay, let's go get it," Briney answers his own question.

Briney has a name befitting a fisherman and the look of one, too. He's a cross between a gruff Midwestern farmer and a hardened New England net spinner, with jolly proportions, a thick brown beard, and yellow rubber overalls that reach halfway up his belly. Briney doesn't ply saltwater. He works the middle of America on behalf of the global demand for fish.

We are floating down the calm morning waters of the Illinois

River, thirty miles north of Peoria, Illinois, where the only thing of international consequence is the headquarters of Caterpillar, the giant manufacturer of heavy equipment. Right here on Briney's thirty-foot plate aluminum boat, however, cheap oil has enabled the world to dip its net into the Illinois's shallow waters.

Briney fires up the 150-horsepower Yamaha outboard, whose growl hungers for gasoline, and we motor north up the river. Nobody talks. Jeremy Fisher, Briney's serendipitously named stepson, sits toward the front of the boat, watching for their quarry, his cigarette's red tip somehow persevering in the morning's breeze and spray. After continuing upriver for a few miles, Briney slows the boat down and stands on the back bench to get a look at the water ahead. "Nothing here," he says. "Let's try last week's spot." Fisher nods his agreement and we speed back up.

Briney pilots the boat into a calm back bay and lets the motor's throttle down to a putter. Now Fisher and Briney are both standing, scanning the waters. "Yep, they're in here," Briney says. "Big swarm of them up there three hundred yards on the left."

"Yeah, I see 'em," Fisher affirms.

To an inexperienced eye, however, there's nothing to see. Fisher points to some seemingly random ripples on the surface of the water and explains that fish make those undulations. A lot of fish. It's difficult to tell those ripples from what Fisher says are innocuous waves farther out in the river, but Briney and Fisher are sure they're on to some big ones. Briney steers the boat past the fish flock about 1,000 yards and we start dropping long lengths of net into the water, about 700 yards of net in all. The water in this spot is only three to four feet deep. Briney then doubles back to again get behind the school of fish. He guns the motor and we head straight for the fish in a long pattern of zigzags. He's herding them toward the nets. As soon as the boat is halfway there, the fishes' presence is obvious. The nets have become a rollicking boil of whitewater as the fish get ensnared in the monofilament loops.

Briney works the boat up toward the nets' chaos and gets right alongside the first net. Fisher and Briney then go to work hauling the nets in, hand over hand, disgorging them of their considerable cargo. They take the fish out of the net, almost always with two hands—these are big fish—and toss them into the middle holding section of the boat. Within half an hour the boat is teeming with writhing, bloody fish the size of logs. Getting around in the boat requires walking on top of a layer of fish three feet deep.

After another forty minutes, Briney and Fisher have the boat utterly full and Briney turns the boat around to motor the several miles back to the landing. The boat, weighed down with five tons of fish, scrapes against the muddy bottom of the back bay as it heads toward the main river channel. The sun is fully ablaze now and the river's misty cloak has been pulled away. Briney opens the motor up when the boat reaches the big part of the river. This is when things get totally strange.

The boat is under attack. Giant fish are literally exploding from the river's surface, jumping right at the boat. Nonchalant passengers risk getting smacked by a leaping forty pounder that can knock them out of the boat and unconscious. Briney keeps the motor at full throttle, giving the boat enough speed to avoid most of the jumping fish, whose leaps land them in the boat's wake. Each time the boat slows down for a turn or a narrow channel, however, the fish are able to catch up and it's time again to vigilantly guard against attack. Half a dozen fish have landed in the boat at this point and one hit Fisher in the back, making him spit out his cigarette. Luckily, it was only seven or eight pounds and not fifty. Every day on the Illinois River, Briney and Fisher catch a horde of fish and then dodge those fishes' relatives on their way back to land. The leaping fish don't know the boat is laden with their buddies. Or that's what conventional wisdom and biologists say, anyway.

These fish are Asian bighead carp. They don't belong here.

They've besieged the giant rivers of the Midwest, ransacking habitats and running off native species such as buffalo, shad, and bass. Mississippi and Arkansas catfish farmers originally brought the fish to North America to control algae blooms in their ponds. The farmers' algae munchers, which are native to Chinese rivers like the Yangtze, escaped in 1993 when a flooding Mississippi River overtook the catfish ponds. Though small in number, the fish multiplied in the Mississippi, gorging on plankton and reproducing each spring. By 1998 the fish had made it to the Illinois River, a Mississippi tributary, thriving in its placid and muddy backwaters.

The sound of a motor sends the carp launching high out of the water at passing boats, sometimes literally smacking passengers straight into the river. Waterskiing on the Illinois has become treacherous. "It's like popcorn exploding out there," says Steven Shults, a biologist with the Illinois Department of Natural Resources. A lot of popcorn. The DNR estimates 56 million pounds of Asian carp swim in the Illinois.

To most, these fish are an unmitigated environmental disaster. To Briney and a few others, the fish have been an incredible opportunity to take part in a global marketplace that's lubricated with oil so cheap that a person in Hong Kong may eat fish head soup made from an Illinois River carp. Nobody around Peoria has interest in eating the fish, which, with their flat heads and tiny eyes, look grotesque. But the fish are a delicacy to many Asians. Michael Schafer was first to figure this out. He owns Schafer Fisheries in Thomson, Illinois, a Mississippi River town 150 miles west of Chicago.

Schafer buys Briney's load for 20 cents a pound, guts, and cleans up the fish, sending the fillets and heads all over the world. The whole complicated orchestration—from the catfish farmers raising exotic carp to the environmental goof to Briney's harvest to Schafer's gutting and shipping—owes its execution to one thing: cheap gasoline. It's one of the oddest of many interesting storylines involving our food and its bizarre, faraway origins.

Briney's operation, taken strictly inside the state lines of Illinois, is a study in the world that fossil fuels enable. Briney wakes up at three o'clock each morning, usually seven days a week, packs up his nets, and drags his boat more than two hours north to the Illinois River. Then he tools around the river with his enormous outboard motor, gulping gas at a frenetic clip. Once the catch is landed and the boat back to shore, he drives his monstrous Chevy Silverado another ninety minutes, with 10,000 pounds of fish in tow, to Schafer's plant in Thomson. Then Briney gets to haul his truck and boat back home, another three hours of driving. His trucks always reach 100,000 miles inside a year's time; sometimes they last him only nine months. Briney has taken in as much as $300,000 in a single year, but his life is a hard one enabled purely by gasoline at prices below $4 a gallon.

Then consider Schafer's side of this door. He is able to buy all of Briney's catch because he has hunted out markets for a fish that isn't an easy sell in the Upper Midwest, where garbage fish such as carp are viewed as a polluting nuisance, not food. But Schafer has invested in a fleet of refrigerated semitrucks that move his carp all over the continent to Asian markets in New York, Chicago, Toronto, Los Angeles, and Vancouver. He has taken advantage of the low shipping rates to China because of the millions of containers that arrive to the West Coast full and then often return to the China Sea empty. People all over the world now enjoy fish head soup made with Asian carp that grew up, by mistake, in a landlocked river in downstate Illinois, more than 1,000 miles from any ocean. And the only reason the carp were ever in North America to begin with was because Southern catfish farmers, also enabled by cheap oil to ship their slithering crop to stores all across the continent, somehow got their hands on an Asian import that, no doubt, got to Arkansas cheaply, its travels borne on the hydrocarbon.

Asian Carp Aren't the Only Food Traveling the World on Cheap Gasoline

Briney's story is unique for its characters, but not for its theme. Peculiarities in the world's current food web abound. It's a world in which labor costs, in some corners, are exorbitant and, in other corners, are filthy cheap. And what makes all labor relevant to all markets is the price of transportation, which, relative to the flexibility it imparts to the world marketplace, is stunningly inexpensive. Cod caught in Norwegian waters get sent off, frozen, to China, where they're gutted, filleted, and packaged by workers earning a pittance.[1] From there, the spiffy cod packages return whence they came: to Norwegian supermarkets so that Scandinavians can feel good about eating their local waters' bounty. In big grocers on the famous Citrus Coast of Spain, Argentine lemons line the shelves like thousands of yellow soldiers while the region's own lemons rot on the ground in local citrus groves.[2] Italy, because it can grow kiwis when New Zealand wrestles with the Southern Hemisphere's winter, has become the world's largest exporter of New Zealand's trademark fruit.

Reshuffling the world's spidery and sometimes nonsensical food web will be one of the last tricks turned by rising gas costs. It will take a giant lever to unseat what have now become our standard and complex food networks. That lever awaits us at $16 gasoline. Everything, starting with farming, will change. The changes will ripple through to things like fish and livestock, then on to dairy and other animal products. Our fertilizers, mostly imported and made straight out of fossil fuel, will change. We will no longer eat oil. The price of everything will increase, to be sure. But these price increases will enable one to grow wheat locally where, before, it was cheaper to import.

Unfortunately for Mr. Briney and Mr. Fisher, the world

market for cheap carp fillets will eventually close to landlocked Illinoisans. Local food will again prosper, not shackled by the competing low costs of foreign land and labor connected with gasoline. Our tastes for shrimp in the United States will no longer be responsible for intractable pollution in Southeast Asia wetlands caused by shrimp farming. Europe's salmon habit will no longer defile Chile's once-immaculate coastline with millions of tons of fish farming waste.

The Crashing Fall of Sushi

There may be no dish that has better defined this culinary era and its tangled, globalized web than sushi. Sushi, of course, is the provenance of Japan, a dish that has grown with that country for centuries, from a localized method for preserving fish to a force that has reordered fisheries in every ocean on earth. Sushi has created countless millionaires, trade between unlikely partners, and new oceanic research. Sushi, too, has spawned pirates, smuggling, and international bureaucracies. Sushi's popularity has become a masthead for Japanese culture—sushi diners once signified a city's affluence; now they're merely a sign of cultural relevance, as sushi, if it hasn't planted itself in the mainstreams of all places, certainly has sidled up to the edge.

Just as Japan is head sensei in the world's sushi order, one fish sits above all others in sushi's hierarchy. Diners may order from all corners of the menu and from all different cuts of an assortment of fish, but there is one fish that defines a sushi restaurant: maguro. Maguro is tuna. And tuna, to serious sushi eaters, is bluefin. Not ahi or bigeye (the same thing) or even yellowfin; it has to be bluefin. Bluefin tuna, with its wavy, translucent fat and its exquisite texture, is the most sought-after fish in the world. The cowboys that chase bluefin take giant risks to bring its bounty back to shore. The reason, as always, is money. The biggest wild bluefin tunas, which can push 1,000 pounds, have fetched $100,000 at Tokyo's Tsukiji market, the New York Stock Exchange of world fish markets.[3]

Raw bluefin, in sashimi form, is best enjoyed fresh, inside of a week from when the migratory, muscular fish was wrested from its seawater kingdom. Fishing for bluefin can be a quixotic quest: clusters of tuna travel with the prolific tendencies of a billionaire socialite, often moving thousands of miles in mere weeks. As Japan's population grew in the 1950s and 1960s and the country's demand for maguro swelled, the country's tuna fleets, plying Northern Pacific waters, had pushed their own stocks of bluefin to the point of collapse. Demand outpaced supply in Japan, and maguro's value spiraled. The world's waters beyond Japan held more bluefin, but boats couldn't get the delicate fish to market in time from so far away.

The first piece in the unfolding puzzle that would become a truly global tuna market came in, of all places, Toronto, as detailed by Sasha Issenberg's *The Sushi Economy*. In 1971 Wayne MacAlpine worked for the cargo arm of Japan Airlines. He had been tasked to find high-worth Canadian exports for Japanese consumers. JAL cargo planes were discharging thousands of tons of gadgetry into North America, often returning home almost empty. It was bad business to run a plane full only one way. JAL executives were searching for something, anything, valuable enough to justify air transport back to Japan for consumers ready to spend a growing trade surplus. MacAlpine mentioned to his bosses, in passing, the odd tuna fishing tournament held off Nova Scotia annually. Several dozen boats would go out and, with a rod and reel, battle the monstrous northern Atlantic bluefin. The angler with the biggest fish would take home a nominal prize. What struck MacAlpine as slightly odd and what so intensely intrigued his bosses in Japan was what happened after the weigh-in: the tournament organizers fired up a bulldozer and a backhoe, dug a giant hole, and buried all the caught tuna, apparently unwanted. People in North America had no taste for tuna's red meat back then. To fishermen, the fish were enormous, fast, and fun to catch, but the only market for the meat was in pet food at cents per pound.

Within a year of MacAlpine's note, giant northern bluefin were regularly traveling, on ice, in the cargo holds of JAL planes from the East Coast to Tokyo. One big fish could mean $15,000 or more to the fisherman. New England fishing towns boomed and bristled with new entrants chasing tuna dollars. In the two decades following the first shipment of Atlantic tuna to Tokyo, there was a 10,000% increase in the price paid to tuna anglers for their catch.[4] Now bluefin caught in the Atlantic on Sunday hits Tokyoites' lunch plates on Wednesday.

Similar bouts of tuna mania have affected port towns all over the world, from Port Lincoln, Australia, to Ensenada, Mexico, to operations ringing the Mediterranean in Spain, France, Italy, Cyprus, Turkey, and Libya. Tokyo is still the epicenter of the market, and many of the most prized catches end up there. But now demand for bluefin comes from cities in every nook of the globe, from New York and Los Angeles to Shanghai, London, and Cape Town. Wherever a bluefin roams, it swims with a target on its back. The fresh tuna market, enabled by cheap jet fuel and plentiful air cargo space, has become truly global. Bluefin is almost never destined for plates anywhere close to where it was caught; its migratory ways don't end until it lands in a diner's mouth.

As the price of fuel marches up, our airspace will become less congested. Air cargo space will thin and thin some more, eradicating empty cargo holds and any hope for affordable air freight. When gas tops $16 per gallon, the availability of air freight will be a fraction of what we have now; its costs will jump more than fivefold. Transporting a 500-pound tuna, once less than 15% of the meat's value, will explode to more than 50%. The global market for bluefin, connected by planes with space to spare, will crash. Add in the increased costs of chasing these brutes about the ocean in high-powered fishing boats, and the cost of a piece of fresh tuna, already expensive now, will soar to heights not tolerable for most consumers. Sushi's identity will be shaken; its foundation, its king, and its ruler, the bluefin, will cease to be a liquid global commodity. The truly rich will still enjoy luxurious, silky cuts of toro meat from bluefins' underbellies, but most of us will not see that distinctive red, translucent flare on a regular basis, if ever again.

The consumption of tuna, and of many of its fresh sushi brethren like yellowtail, eel, and the rarest of the wild salmon, will be limited to places located near these creatures' natural habitats. Mediterranean diners will see bluefin, as they have for centuries, when their schools circle through once a year. The same goes for people in the Northeast. Hawaiian consumers will never see ahi tuna, their local variety, go away, but Chicago shoppers won't see it again behind the counter at Whole Foods for $20 a pound, a price that seems steep now but will, in the future, be harkened to as a bargain.

Sushi restaurants, in their number and frequency, will dwindle in an environment where their core offerings of fresh, raw seafood have jumped astronomically in price. The few sushi restaurants that do survive in places far from natural fish stocks will either be of gourmet ilk and very expensive or they will rely heavily on rolls made with artificial crab, farmed salmon, and cooked or tempura fried fish that were deeply frozen.

The bright side of this coming sunset for the globalized seafood market is that the world's fish populations, especially the fragile stocks of fish such as bluefin, cod, snapper, and salmon, will get a chance to heal, repair, and renew. It's estimated that our oceans' fish stocks have been depleted by nearly 50% in the last fifty years. The world's bluefin fishery has been pushed near the brink already; many of the tuna's most frequented hangouts, the North Atlantic, the Mediterranean, and the South Pacific off Australia, have already seen their catches crash by more than half in the last twenty years.

The so-called ranching of tuna, where younger fish of about fifty pounds are netted in the wild and raised to become large in pens, has helped keep world bluefin markets lubricated with protein, but their economic model is already prone to capricious swings and those fish still travel on airplanes, in most cases, to reach markets. Tuna ranching has accelerated the depletion of tuna schools, because it removes the adolescent fish that should become the schools' reproductive mainstays. Luckily for the tuna, high gas prices will end tuna ranching as we know it, putting the ranches' faraway markets out of reach.

The only question is what will give first: the tuna, or gas prices? The race for tuna's survival pits energy prices against dwindling stocks of the fish worldwide. The longer it takes for gasoline to make its inevitable, giant price climb, the longer the global tuna fishery will be exploited and pushed near the brink of an irreversible crash. There are two scenarios for the future of sushi:

1. Gas prices rise only moderately during the next five years, allowing us to eat sushi often and relatively cheaply until the world's fisheries collapse.
2. Gas prices advance rapidly during the next five years, saving fisheries and ensuring that future generations will get to eat bluefin indefinitely, albeit only on special occasions.

The race is on.

Many American Farms, Faced with High Gasoline Costs, Will Go Local Again

Tim Fuller is something of an expert when it comes to soil health. He can tell dead soil from vigorous soil the way a normal person can tell sand from clay. Fuller, a farmer, also knows that our soils across much of North America have been nutritionally bankrupt for decades on account of our industrialized methods of farming. The only thing that keeps crops rising from our flaccid soils year after year is the liberal application of fertilizers. Fertilizer has become the key to human population. Without it, humankind simply wouldn't have enough food. And as with most things in our current world, fertilizer has more to do with oil than most think.

Fuller slumps to a knee, burrows his hands into the loosely packed soil, and digs out a weed that's infiltrated his neat and flourishing row of onions. He flicks the invader away from his crops and pulls his faded hat from his head, rubbing his bald pate with a look of contemplation. Fuller's fingers, stained brown like his compost-rich soil, smooth out the dirt like a carpet salesman proudly petting his wares.

"I'll tell you, there wasn't a living thing in this soil when we got here, far as I could tell," he says. He rises up, puts his hat on his head, and points out at the homogenous sea of soy that surrounds his farm on three sides. "It was all like that, mass-farmed, sterile, and bombed with herbicide three times a year." His disdain for big-business farming, like that which surrounds him, and its chief enabler—Saint Louis–based Monsanto—is plain. Fuller reclaimed this plot to grow produce for local customers and restaurants in 2001. It took two years of tilling in compost, manure, and dried molasses to resuscitate the beat-up soil. "There's nothing worse you can do to farmland than what they have going here." He again raises his arm and sweeps it toward the fields of soy.

About fifteen feet from Fuller, a weed stalk at the edge of the big soy field crawls with several dozen large, lumpy, disfigured insects that look like giant brown ladybugs with patches of mold-like fur dotting their shells irregularly. Fuller fingers one of the critters and gives it a squinty examination. "Well . . . isn't that gross. These things have survived three cycles of Roundup this summer." Roundup is a popular herbicide made by Monsanto, the agriculture giant. He turns one of the bugs over in his fingers and rubs his head again with his free hand. "Hmm. Well, I think they're Colorado potato beetles, but these are the weirdest-looking ones I've ever seen."

Farming is not Fuller's first career. He's sixty-four. He has an MBA from the University of Chicago and taught business school classes there for seven years. Before farming the Illinois prairie, Fuller owned a management consulting business that, while it paid better than willing green beans from dirt, left him unfulfilled. A longtime Northern Californian, he reveled in the aura of the cultural revolution cradled in Berkeley's 1960s. Its echo never quite left him. Fuller grew organic crops in his yard for several years and found an outsized amount of satisfaction in that compared with his lucrative consulting business. So in 2002, he pushed all his chips into his hobby and opened up Erehwon Farm, a six-acre plot fifty miles west of downtown Chicago. He's at ease milling about his hand-tilled produce rows. "I'm broke," he says, chewing on a tomatillo he just plucked, "but I'm happy."

Small farmers of Fuller's ilk are few. But their day will come in a world of $16 gas, when our transportation networks for produce become untenable and volume loses out to vicinity. Fuller's farm is ideally located for a future world. One side of his field straddles the start of hundreds of miles of megafarms that stretch west all the way to the Rockies. The other side of his farm borders the burgeoning exurbs of Chicago. Fuller grows a little bit of everything: sugar snap peas, Swiss chard, eggplant, arugula, raspberries, blackberries, strawberries, spinach, and an uncountable variety of tomatoes. "It's challenging," he says. "It's the most complicated thing I've ever gotten involved with. Our mission is to see if we can run a local, sustainable farm profitably. It's elusive. But that's what I need, something that's impossible."

Fuller's operation, at a mere six acres, is small for any farm, but especially compared with the multi-thousand-acre spreads that supply much of our grain and produce. Because gasoline comes so cheaply, compared with the price of produce, it currently makes perfect sense to grow tomatoes in California and Mexico for consumers in Minneapolis, Cleveland, or Boston. "I was talking with some shipping companies about what it costs to get produce from California to Chicago," Fuller says. "The numbers were under fifteen cents a pound. Fifteen cents a pound? That's nothing when you're talking about produce prices of one to two dollars a pound."

The price of moving food mingles with other costs, too, the biggest of which are storage and refrigeration. When a tomato is picked in California, it's nabbed from the vine long before it becomes ripe so it can weather the tumbling, chaotic journey from its remote Western field to an East Coast grocery store. The tomato needs refrigeration, sometimes during its voyage, and almost always upon arrival, because local stores may not yet be ready to put it out. So the tomato travels across the country hard and green, surviving roads' potholes, handlers' drops, and forklifts' shakes. Upon arrival, it waits and waits until its number is called, which rescues it from the age-defying chill of deep refrigeration. What grocery store shoppers are left with at the end of this process is a round, red fruit with a spongy interior and a wisp of tomato flavor that can be teased out with some granulated sodium chloride. "Consumers think salt is taste," Fuller laughs. But for most consumers, salt *is* taste, when without it your tomato tastes like an irradiated watermelon.

All that trucking, refrigeration, and storage costs money. But it's not enough money, Fuller points out, to outweigh the rewards of growing produce in mass quantities in a hospitable place such as Central California. "At what point, in terms of the price of gas, are we going to be able to overcome the advantages of the year-round growing season in California and other parts of the world?" Fuller says. "I'll tell you one thing, it's going to be a high number, nothing as low as ten dollars a gallon. It will be closer to twenty."

The ultimate disrupter to our food web, outside of natural

disaster, Fuller says, will be the price of energy. Rising gasoline prices will be the incorrigible gorilla that trashes our complex weave of food producers, shippers, and wholesalers, ultimately changing the equation for good at $16 per gallon. Ferrying Central California's bounty to New York will be economically unsavory. The year-round growing seasons of places like California, as Fuller says, gives them large advantages in maintaining hegemony of our produce supply. But the world's ebbing oil supply will force the price of transportation from these places to far-off coasts past a tipping point. When gas reaches $16, packing a piece of produce from California to the Midwest will cost $1 a pound or more.

"Will we get to a point when human labor becomes cheaper than gasoline-powered machinery for some tasks?" Fuller asks. "I think that's possible." Couple that with the transportation costs that $16 gas brings us, and there won't be many Spaniards grinding up South American lemons for a post-siesta refreshment or an evening aperitif. They'll grind Spanish lemons. And fish won't likely be crossing Asia twice on their way from North Sea waters to Norwegian restaurants. Our food world will condense.

"What I think will happen is this," Fuller says. "Cities like Chicago will be ringed by a series of farms that go from ten acres to a hundred acres, maybe even to five hundred acres. Not nearly as big as the biggest farms today, but big enough to take advantage of scaling their costs," he explains. "Each one of these farms will specialize in something. One might be tomatoes, one might be peppers, I'm sure several of them would grow all sorts of greens."

The farms' fields would fill the landscape wherever the urban clutter of people and their homes stopped. They would displace fields of corn, soy, and wheat close to cities, relegating those crops, for which freshness isn't paramount, to places where barge and train transportation can be fully leveraged. So Atlanta would get its tomatoes, its cucumbers, its carrots, and its greens from farms all within a hundred miles. The economics of avoiding transport from

Mexico, the West Coast, or even locales farther away will usher in an era of freshness and proximity for American produce consumers. It will be yet another chapter in this strange saga of mass-scale economics and globalization that has pushed our food farther and farther away from us, only to reverse field at the point of exploding energy prices and $16 gasoline.

Americans will still be able to enjoy French goat cheese, Italian olive oil, and if there's any left, Hawaiian bigeye tuna. These are luxury items that already carry premium price tags; their prices will simply become more premium. The higher-priced items, in general, will weather the deglobalization of food. It's the commodities, the staples of rice, wheat, soy, and apples, that won't be cutting Magellanic wakes through the world's oceans, as they do now.

Maintaining the Crops We Know in a Shrinking Food Web

Things like potatoes will go from the ground, to a train car, to a market, to your dinner table. The whole operation might take one to three days. The costs of massive distribution networks will no longer be levied on the consumer. The fingers of radiating farm rail services will facilitate an elegant, simple supply chain from maker to user.

Albertsons or Safeway will no longer set the price of a sweet potato; rather, the local market will. If cantaloupes fared poorly in the Upper Midwest one summer, they would be more expensive in Chicago, but the price of melon in Charlotte would remain unaffected. The question, of course, then becomes: What foods can grow where? Will I still get tomatoes during winter in Chicago? Will there be red peppers in New York's January?

The answer is yes. These fruits and vegetables that can't be grown easily outside of comfier climates will cost more, surely, but their supply won't dry up. Fuller and others see a movement to grow produce through the winter in so-called hothouses—greenhouses that can be easily assembled and temperature managed so that produce growing in the Upper Midwest and Northeast can persevere all year long. We won't be piping natural gas into these places or firing up kerosene stoves to keep our crops cozy, not with the price of gas at $16. Old-school methods will make a comeback, aiding our farmers in a quest to supply winter produce, minus the costly highway miles.

A hothouse, cheaply constructed, is a narrow greenhouse framed up with metal or wood spans. Plastic is stretched tightly on the outside edges between each member, enclosing the space. A second layer of plastic is stretched across the inside edges of the trusses, forming an insulating sandwich of air between the two sheets of plastic. The sun pours in all day, utterly unabated, as the whole structure is effectively a big window. When built with a little care and sealed tightly, the sunlight alone is enough to keep the atmosphere inside comfortable, even in climes like Detroit's or Cleveland's. "Light's not an issue," Fuller points southwest toward the sun. "We get tons of light here, even at this latitude in Illinois. We're dead even with the South of France, latitude and light-wise."

The humid air inside the hothouse and the resulting condensation, however, can lead to deadly frost on deeply cold nights. For that reason, the hothouses will need a source of heat other than the daytime sun. Fuller, the old-schooler that he is, buries compost that is at the height of its decomposing process under a shallow layer of dirt inside his hothouses. The compost, which is biodegrading and making heat, will keep the hothouse warm enough for most of the winter. This method was used by farmers going back more than 100 years ago.

"This here is what we use," grunts Fuller, climbing up a giant pile of compost at the back end of his farm. With a backhanded flip, he brushes off the outer layer of dry, flaky compost, revealing a dark, rich, and steaming core. He burrows his hand in, up to his wrist, and quickly pulls it out, like someone testing the waters of a scorching hot tub. "That's a hundred and fifty degrees, I'd say. Hot enough that you can't hold your hand in there. Can't be much hotter than that, or the critters [bacteria] making the heat would be dead," he laughs.

Fuller's compost heaps include manure, tree mulch, some straw, and a mix of farm waste—corn husks, damaged veggies, weeds, etc. Fuller gets as much manure as he wants free from small local horse farms that don't want the stuff.

In the future, hothouses on most farms will not run on hot compost, but on passive solar heating that keeps warm water flowing through pipes buried beneath the greenhouse. The energy won't cost anything, once the capital costs of installing the system are retired, and it will keep Northerners in fresh tomatoes, peppers, and cucumbers through the winter.

Closer Produce Means Better, Healthier Produce

These changes to where our produce comes from will benefit our bodies. Our food will be closer, crunchier, and because it will be picked closer to full ripeness and have to endure a far less arduous journey to our tables, it will be healthier, containing more of the vitamins and nutrients that our produce, when grown right, is supposed to contain. Many of the vegetables and fruit in our produce aisles currently were picked green and hard so that they could endure marathon truck rides and the vibrations of commercial traversing. When picked so early, produce gets less time to develop its full range of nutrients and minerals. Signs of ripening, like a red hue, may manifest on the outside of your store-bought tomato, but the nutrient value will be inferior to that of a fruit allowed to fully ripen on the vine. The very act of transport, with its rollicking exposures to heat and light, can further degrade produce's nutrients, in particular the fragile ones like vitamins C and B1 (thiamin).

With $16 gas, your tomato won't need refrigeration and it won't need to be picked green and hard. And its taste will be like that of a tomato, not odorless squishy pink foam.

Fuller's customers come to him because they abhor mealy, bland vegetables. They buy shares for the growing season, usually for $35 or so per week for twenty weeks. This entitles them to a piece of the harvest, which they can pick up from the farm weekly or, if they live close enough, the farm will deliver it to their door. With $16 gas, local farms brokering these kinds of arrangements will prosper. And they will be needed. America will call for a new breed of farmers, who don't base the whole of their operation on hydrocarbons for transportation to their far-off customers and for mass-produced feed for their plants. New blood, like Fuller, will reinvigorate small farming. The knowledge we need to farm this way still exists, though it's rarely handed down through generations of families as it once was. Libraries brim with books on small, sustainable farming. But not even books will be necessary to educate America's next farming generation. "I pretty much learned everything on the computer," Fuller says. "Thank god for the Internet."

Fuller and organic farmers of his type prefer natural fertilizers from local sources, which lend their produce a rich, hearty taste. But as romantic as manure is to naturally minded farmers, there simply isn't enough of it to keep the whole world in crops. That's why, in a future of $16 gas, we will face challenges beyond where our food comes from geographically. The most vexing question: how to feed our food.

Fertilizing Our Way to Scarcity

For two centuries, the world's agriculture barons have shown an incredible penchant for finding unsustainable crop enhancers. When one fertilizing agent became depleted or insufficient, a new resource was found, exploited, and exhausted. Today is no different. We have repeated history's folly once again. But this time technology may bail us out.

In 1800, manure was the key player in the reinvigoration of our agriculture fields. But as the human population ballooned and our need for crops and sustenance grew exponentially, manure's relevance fell away. Farmers couldn't sustain the number of animals needed to churn out a proportional amount of dung. Replacements were found.

Justus von Liebig, a German chemist, came to this conclusion in 1840: "A time will come when fields will be manured with a solution . . . prepared in chemical factories."[5] If Liebig only knew the enormity of his prescience.

In 1843, Englishman John Bennet Lawes began experimenting with crops, yields, and fertilizers on his family's Rothamsted Farm, just north of London. Rothamsted still operates as an experimental farm today, its bottled crop samples fully intact and dating back more than 160 years. Rothamsted confirmed and chemically elucidated what some farmers had figured out on their own: applying mixtures of nitrogen and phosphorus can radically improve crop yields, even beyond those of a thoroughly manured field.

This realization and wide recognition of the chemistry behind crop yields led to some of the more bizarre twists in world history. In the 1600s, Europeans hauled back boodle from newly discovered continents and islands that consisted of gold, spices, silver, and gems. Two hundred years later, Europeans and now, too, Americans, pillaged the Southern Hemisphere and Pacific islands not for gold, but for bird poop, bringing it back by the shipload.

Europeans and North Americans spent the better part of 100 years, beginning in the mid-1800s, separating countless islands and their civilizations from magnificent hoards of phosphorous and nitrates. In many cases, ships sailed to tropical waters for that one reason: to mine poop. Ancient guano, left from centuries of migrating seabirds, had accumulated on these islands, forming thousands of layers of chalky deposits that, in some places, were 200 feet thick.

The first guano hit American shores in 1824 when John Skinner, who was the editor of the *American Farmer*, imported two casks of Peruvian guano to Baltimore.[6] With thirty times as much nitrogen as ordinary manure, guano's utility became clear immediately. Crops flourished and farmers from the Carolinas up through Maryland clamored for it.

By the 1850s, New York ports welcomed guano shipments regularly and the United States and England imported a combined one million tons a year. As guano grew in value, it even set off wars. The War of the Pacific pitted Bolivia against Chile in a scrap for control of guano deposits on the Pacific Coast. When the war ended in 1883, Chile's victory left Bolivia landlocked, as it exists today. Bolivia's current navy, the world's largest for a landlocked country, remains an odd legacy of that long-ago war fought over bird shit.

By the 1930s, we had exhausted most big deposits of guano, leaving more than one island in ecological ruins as their own nutrient pyramids had been hijacked to subsidize European and American growth.

Where we would turn for our next source of soil-enhancing nutrients would be almost academic. As petroleum-powered machinery took over farming, so, too, did petroleum-based fertilizers. Our fertilizers would now come from the same sources that supported a twentieth century of astonishing technology advancements. That model—thanks to cheap fossil fuels—remains in place today. Almost all of our nitrate-rich fertilizer in the United States now comes from natural gas. After using all the manure we could find and depleting the world's ecologically marvelous stores of guano, our farming practices have now contributed, in not a small way, to the whittling of our precious fossil fuel supplies.

Most of the world's fertilizers are built mainly with ammonia, which is a molecule comprised of one nitrogen atom and three hydrogen atoms. Humankind manufactures more ammonia than any other chemical compound on earth. Its creation demands a giant amount of the earth's resources. Making NH_3 sucks up 1% of the world's power supply and 4% of the fossil fuels that we burn. The compound also goes into refrigerants, cleaning solutions, and fuels, but its main use—nearly 89%—is for fertilizers.

Ammonia has become the building block on which the world feeds. When you eat an ear of corn, you are eating fossil fuel. Not just because it took an enormous amount of fuel to plant and harvest the crop, but because the nitrogen compound that made it possible for that ear of corn to grow was derived from natural gas. When you eat corn, soy, a tomato, or a potato, you're eating natural gas. Yum.

The nitrogen for NH_3 comes easily; it's simply plucked from the air we breathe, which is 78% nitrogen. The hydrogen in ammonia has always been the tricky atom to wrangle. In 1910 German chemist Fritz Haber patented a method using high temperatures and extreme pressures to bond hydrogen atoms with nitrogen from our air. Soon thereafter, Carl Bosch, working for the German chemical company BASF, commercialized the process, making it applicable on a massive scale. Their method, called the Haber-Bosch process, won the pair Nobel prizes and is more responsible for humanity's population explosion in the twentieth century than anything else. Haber and Bosch showed the world how to grow more food.

For a few decades, water was the main source of hydrogen for making ammonia through the Haber-Bosch process. Electrolysis—passing giant amounts of electric current through H_2O to split the molecule into hydrogen and oxygen atoms—was used to obtain the hydrogen. Norway constructed the 60-megawatt Vermok hydroelectric plant for the sole purpose of splitting water molecules to make ammonia. That plant furnished most of Europe's ammonia needs up until the Second World War.

The use of electrolysis and water in making ammonia all but

stopped with the advent of cheap and bountiful natural gas in the 1930s. That's because it takes far less energy to simply strip the hydrogen out of natural gas (CH_4) than to split water molecules. But the price of natural gas is inherently tied to the price of oil and gasoline, and it will increase to the point where getting our fertilizer from water molecules rather than hydrocarbons will make sense. And here in the United States, we have burned off much of our easy-to-get natural gas already. As a result, we now import 80% of our fertilizer from nations like Qatar, Mexico, and Russia, where natural gas is more plentiful and cheaper. That's a higher import percentage than oil, which we import at a 67% rate. And arguably, the ammonia fertilizer is every bit as important as our oil, perhaps more so.

Surging Fuel Prices Will Compel Us to Find an Alternative to Eating Fossil Fuels

When the price of gas reaches the heights of $16, natural gas's price, too, will have become exorbitant. Peak supplies of oil and natural gas have been reached in our current world. We will not see major increases in these supplies ever again. "People tend to forget that our cars and our industry aren't the only things competing for fossil fuels," says Steve Gruhn. "It's also our mouths. China is using more gas because they're building more cars, sure, but they want to eat better, too." To sustain human life as we know it, we must have ammonia-based fertilizers. "People can live without cars if they have to," points out Gruhn. "They can ride bicycles. But they can't live without food."

And they won't. The answer to what will become one of humanity's gravest questions in the future—how to feed the multitudes of billions without fossil fuels—is, as Gruhn likes to say, "sitting at the end of our nose." We used water to make ammonia 100 years ago and we will once again. Better yet, we won't burn mountains of coal or exhaust enriched uranium to do it, Gruhn says.

Gruhn is the president and co-founder of Freedom Fertilizer, a company bent on subverting the natural gas model the world uses to make fertilizer. Gruhn started his outfit in Spirit Lake, Iowa, in February 2008. The premise is simple: Leverage the abundant wind power in Northwest Iowa and Southwest Minnesota to use electrolysis to make ammonia from water and nitrogen. Gruhn's education in the ways of fertilizer and power came naturally. He grew up on an Iowa farm that remains in his family. In 1998, the state of Iowa conducted a wind survey to determine the best possible locations for future wind power development. The Gruhn family farm, it turns out, was on the windiest spot in the state. "When I saw that, I knew that at some point, somebody was going to approach us about putting up turbines on the property," Gruhn explains. "So I wanted to be prepared."

Gruhn immersed himself in the grittier points of wind power, learning everything he could. Having been a farmer his whole life, Gruhn, forty-eight, already knew the pressures surrounding fertilizer production, having seen it shift from the United States to overseas quickly as our gas supplies dwindled. "The more I found out about wind, the more intrigued I became," he says.

Gruhn lives near a geographic feature in Iowa known as Buffalo Ridge. Upper Midwest winds tear through the Dakotas and slam into the ridge all year round, making it one of the better spots in all of the United States for wind power. But the problem inherent in placing windmills in places like Buffalo Ridge and the gusty Dakotas has been that, because very few people live there, the power has to be carried out on high-voltage lines to cities such as Chicago, Omaha, and Minneapolis, if not farther. Those lines would cost billions to erect. In addition, when electricity is transported across great distances, a good chunk of it gets lost to resistance in the transporting wires and cables. In the case of shipping wind from Iowa and the Dakotas, 50% of it could be gone before it gets to its users.

The beauty of Gruhn's vision keeps the wind power working locally, cranking out juice to separate hydrogen from oxygen. Northwest Iowa also happens to be roughly in the center of North America's farm belt. To the east sit the cornfields of Wisconsin, Illinois, Indiana, and Ohio. To the north, the farms of Minnesota, the Dakotas, and the spreads of Manitoba and Southern Saskatchewan. To the south and west are the fields of the Great Plains: Nebraska, Kansas, Oklahoma, Texas, and Eastern Colorado. Much of the nation's ammonia supply already has links to Northwest Iowa, as two pipelines for the stuff pass through here. "You can roll into small towns around here and not find a gas station," Gruhn says, "but you will find an ammonia distribution facility."

Each acre of corn grown here requires 150 pounds of ammonia fertilizer. Making that requires more energy than the act of tilling, seeding, harvesting, and transporting the crop to market. And making a single ton of NH_3 out of natural gas produces 1.8 tons of carbon dioxide, the main culprit in global warming. Generating a ton of NH_3 from coal produces 3 tons of CO_2. Using wind power to strip water of its hydrogen produces no carbon dioxide. It does, though, produce pure medical-grade oxygen, a valuable and marketable product.

Using wind power in this kind of a local capacity—to make something that we desperately need—makes more sense than deploying turbines randomly and piping the electricity to urban areas at enormous cost. Gruhn has already attracted the attention of the USDA, which awarded Freedom Fertilizer a $100,000 grant to research his proposal further.

Iowa's place in our grid of energy solutions has been rising steadily. "If I stand on my rooftop here, I can see four hundred megawatts of wind power and three hundred million gallons of ethanol production and a couple of biodiesel plants," Gruhn says. Of the millions of dollars that the USDA doles out in grants, 10% have been going to innovators under the jurisdiction of the department's Storm Lake, Iowa, office, near Gruhn. A full 30% of USDA grants have been pouring into Iowa. The state that straddles the progressive Upper Midwest and the more conservative Great Plains finds itself the epicenter of green energy's new core. Most of the new wind towers going in here are beasts reaching 400 feet above the ground and beyond. They have the capacity to generate 2.5 megawatts. When wind consistency and speed are factored in, the turbines should deliver the equivalent of 1 megawatt of continuous juice, which equals the needs of about 800 American homes.

Electricity sold on the grid in Iowa for owners of turbines averages about 4 cents per kilowatt-hour. That means that each tower that produces 1 megawatt is worth $960 a day. That rate means turbine owners will pay off their investment in nine to ten years, with a useful life on the turbine of about twenty-five years. Not a bad scenario, which explains why so many turbines are now popping up across Iowa and the Great Plains.

But if those turbines were supplying power for electrolysis to create ammonia using the conventional Haber-Bosch process, the returns could be greater. Gruhn can make 2.72 tons of ammonia per day per megawatt of windpower. The recent spot price for ammonia was $1,200 a ton and has been steadily and quickly rising during the last few years. Its price closely follows that of fossil fuels because ammonia is, in essence, a fossil fuel. One turbine, therefore, can produce $3,300 worth of ammonia per day with the only feedstock for the process being water. Considering it took $960 worth of electricity to make the ammonia, if Gruhn can keep his other costs below $2,300 a ton, he's making a profit. "That's not a problem," he insists. And that's not to mention possible income from capturing the pure O_2 created in the process.

Gruhn would load his ammonia onto rail car tankers bound

for farms across the country or, better yet, "We could build this on top of one of the existing pipelines and just dump it into there," he says. Water, luckily, is not a threatened resource in Northwest Iowa as it is in the Great Plains of Kansas, Oklahoma, Western Nebraska, and Colorado. "Our annual rainfall keeps us pretty rich up here," Gruhn boasts. Iowa's rain and wind bounty would, in effect, become our food. The same kinds of operations could be started in water-rich Minnesota, Wisconsin, and Michigan.

Another beauty of the system is that ammonia could easily be made from graywater, which is the effluents from residential sinks, showers, and floor drains. The treated effluent from sewage plants could be used as well. Wastewater could become the feedstock of our fertilizer, which, of course, is the feedstock to our food. An elegant circle. Water could also be captured in gathering basins on site. A four-acre basin, during a one-inch rainstorm, would yield 452 tons of water for the creation of ammonia.

The Choice Is Ours: Get Our Future Fertilizer Dirtily, or Get It Cleanly

When the price of gasoline reaches numbers beyond $15 and on up to $16, one of two things have to happen for the world to stay fed: We will make our fertilizer from water, or we will make it, in a much dirtier way, with coal. If catastrophe—such as a widespread Middle East war or disaster in Russia—were to strike today, the coal option would likely roll into place because, right now, it's the easier method to install. We would face an inordinate amount of additional air pollution from burning this coal, from which we would strip hydrogen to make ammonia with.

Fortunately, momentum suggests that natural gas will be able to carry us for several more years. By the time a crisis-like shortage comes on the natural gas front, our electrolysis technology, our wind farms, and our farmers will be ready. For every cent that natural gas's price increases, the bounty from creating ammonia from water and renewable energy becomes more lucrative. When there's money to be made, somebody always steps into the breach. Perhaps the venture capitalists of California's Sand Hill Road, so many of them now pledging their allegiance to green causes, will see ammonia's promise and its far lesser environmental impact compared with ethanol, a commodity they have backed thus far with glee.

Making ammonia carries with it the bilateral incentive of its use as a fuel—the stuff actually burns. It takes heat of 1,200 degrees for ammonia to combust, but when it does, it's a clean reaction, leaving behind nitrogen and water. Burned crudely, there is risk of creating nitrous oxide (NO) and nitrogen dioxide (NO_2), which can cause acid rain and smog, but those hazards can be mitigated by clean engine technology. Gruhn's dream is that cleanly made ammonia pops up as a competitor to gasoline. "Ammonia could literally be the smelling salt that jars our economy awake," he says. "Why send our money abroad for fuel when we can spend it right here?"

Precedent exists for vehicles being propelled by ammonia. In World War II, the Nazis, desperate for fuel to keep their war machine churning, stripped Belgium of all of its gasoline stores and resources. Belgians, trying to keep Brussels running as it did before its occupation, converted the city's buses to run on ammonia. "We can make ammonia fuel for about the equivalent of three-dollar-a-gallon diesel fuel," Gruhn points out.

A world beyond $16 gas could usher in a new farming economy borne almost fully on the fumes of ammonia. Our abundant wind would be converted to food grown on local farms along rail tracks leading into cities. The farms' produce and grains would ride to urban consumers along sleek, dedicated rails towed by purring locomotives spewing not the smoke or particulates of diesel fuel, but nitrogen and water.

CHAPTER **$18**

Renaissance of the Rails

A mere seventy-five years ago, a man named Ralph Budd placed the United States firmly at the fore of train travel and technology. The passenger train industry in the early 1930s, like most everything else, was struggling for customers and for relevancy in a bleak economic landscape. Budd was the president of the Chicago, Burlington and Quincy Railroad, better known as the Burlington. Budd had been searching for a way to excite America's taste for train travel, which had been ebbing thanks to the automobile's rise and the dire state of the economy. He wanted a marvel that would sell newspapers, set spectators agog, and most of all, get more people back on the rails.

Budd's solution was to build the fastest, most advanced train in the world, something that would compel people to ride. And this train would be no prototype. Budd's rig would carry paying passengers. He needed a builder, someone who could make his mind's spectacle a reality. In one of those coincidental twists of history, Ralph Budd of Burlington met Edward Budd of the Budd Company in 1932. Edward Budd, while no relation to Ralph, was something of an innovator himself.

Ralph Budd had been spending some of his leisure time plying the pages of *The Canterbury Tales*.[1] Inspired by the book's re-counting of Zephyrus, the wind out of the west, Budd named his new yet-to-be-created train the Zephyr. He had engineers design the outside of the train's cars to be sheathed in stainless steel, which lent the locomotive and its trailers an exotic flash. More importantly, stainless steel is light, compared with the old hardened steel and wood cars that roamed the world's rails at that time. Less mass meant the engine could pull the same number of cars with less energy, leaving more of its torque to advance the train to high speeds.

Consistent with the art deco movement of the era, the train was streamlined, its edges rounded, and its countenance, caboose, and passenger cars tailored to a smooth finish. The front locomotive resembled a knight's helmet, bent forward and charging toward a foe. This not only gave the train a futuristic look that galvanized passengers' excitement, but also reduced drag forces by a third compared with the Zephyr's contemporaries. This further aided the Zephyr in its quest to go faster with less effort. The Budd Company came upon another breakthrough when it built the Zephyr's cars to share wheel trucks. Instead of the traditional couplings which would connect each car to the next one, Budd's idea was to have each end of each car rest on a set of two wheel axles, leaving the other end of the wheel axle platform for the next car, connecting the cars together. This eliminated the heavy coupling mechanisms and reduced the number of wheel trucks needed under the train, further decreasing the Zephyr's weight. The Budd Company received yet more patents for the fluting that ran along the sides of the stainless steel cars, reducing their drag and strengthening the panels at the same time. A 600-horsepower, 447-kilowatt engine from the Winton Motor Company powered the train.

Budd and Budd had built a wonder of engineering. They planned to unveil the sleek beast at the Chicago World's Fair in 1934. But it wasn't enough to just plop the train down in the middle of the festivities. Burlington wanted splash. Ralph Budd planned a record-breaking trip from Denver to Chicago that he dubbed *The Dawn to Dusk Dash*. Budd and Budd, along with a train full of passengers, set out on May 26, 1934, from Denver at 7:04 a.m. The train pulled into Chicago at 8:09 p.m., 13 hours and 5 minutes later. That trip took normal trains 25 hours. The Zephyr averaged an amazing 77 mph on its trip and, at one point, hit 112.5 mph, a record for a train carrying passengers on normal track.

The Zephyr became a celebrity machine. It toured the country, drawing 2 million people out to see its gilded flourishes. Burlington then sent the Zephyr into regular service, which it toiled dutifully at for twenty-six years and more than 3 million miles. Its last on-duty run went from Lincoln, Nebraska, to Kansas City, Missouri. The iconic train then continued on to its old cradle of fame in Chicago, where it now sits on display in the city's Museum of Science and Industry. Amtrak immortalized the Zephyr name in 1971 with its California Zephyr route, which travels from Chicago to San Francisco and still operates today.

Amtrak didn't canonize the Budds' creation simply for its notoriety. What the Budds did was make a machine upon which almost all of the world's current high-speed train travel is based. "Almost everything we know about high-speed trains came from the Pioneer Zephyr," says Rick Harnish, the executive director of the Midwest High Speed Rail Association. "The stuff they use today in France, China, Japan—most of it comes straight from lessons learned on the Zephyr."

There's irony in the fact that Amtrak would name a run after the Zephyr, a train whose technology led the world to a revolution of train travel but whose home country, the United States, lags far behind the rest of the developed globe. Amtrak, of course, is the last guardian of long-haul passenger rail service in this country. And the Zephyr, as glorious a triumph as it was, marked the last time the United States led innovation on the rails. Since the Zephyr's ride to prominence, the U.S. rail system has largely stagnated, ignored by a government bent on other pursuits and a public that, for good reasons, relies on trains as transportation of the last resort in all but a few cases.

In a future of gas prices of four or five times what we're used to, traveling across the United States' vast share of North America will be a tough proposition. Going by car will be very expensive, and will require laborious tenacity behind the wheel. Plane travel will be limited and not a workable option for most people. The best solution is obvious and already exists across much of the rest of the world: high-speed trains. Not only are modern high-speed trains fast and efficient, but they run on electricity, not gasoline or diesel. A high-speed train is effectively a transportation instrument—a highly proficient one—that runs on whatever we want it to: nuclear, hydro, wind, coal, solar, or cow farts.

The Dire State of the Network

Traveling by train from Chicago to New York these days isn't for those low on patience. The Amtrak trip consists of a maddening crawl along aging tracks, inadequate switching stations, and insufferable, inexplicable pauses in the middle of nowhere. It takes more than twenty hours. In America, this is what train travel between our two most important business centers, and indeed, most of the country, has become: a joke. But things weren't always like this.

The disintegration of the U.S. passenger rail system has been decried from many corners for decades. It has been a slow and steady schlep to the bottom of the heap for U.S. trains. We've dug quite a pit. The reasons for our train system's demise are numerous, but there's one common stitch that binds all of them together: cheap oil. Cheap oil has enabled Americans to live where they want on their own terms. Sprawling metros, enabled by cheap gasoline and the automobile, have pushed far away from centrally located train stations. Car travel itself, with the decrepit state of our rails, can be just as swift as riding a train, and the independence that car travel affords appeals to that Jeffersonian side of most Americans, the idea that we're in charge and we'll say when we go and when we come. Plane travel, too, has subverted the chances of an American high-speed train network.

The advent of a true high-speed train network in America will be the ultimate sign that our world has adapted to oil's scarcity. Its existence would signal our country's collective recognition that the world has changed forever according to energy's terms. Fire-breathing jet engines and carbon dioxide–sputtering cars will fade off into history, part of another era of transportation for an evolving human race and civilization. Creating a high-speed train network across the vast lower forty-eight states will take a combination of overwhelming public will, government leadership, and private enterprise cooperation. The number and size of the barriers to high-speed train travel in America are huge. And the money needed to create such a system occupies heights in the hundreds of billions, and likely trillions, of dollars. For that reason, it will take gas prices of the most compelling magnitude to make widespread American high-speed rail a reality: $18 per gallon.

People will cling to their steering wheels and their airline seats until their fingers are pried off by sheer financial behest. But people won't simply ride trains because they've become the only affordable form of traveling long distance. They may very simply just stop traveling, a phenomenon that would be devastating for our economy and our national fabric. So how can we ensure that doesn't happen? It starts, says Alex Kummant, with giving people service that's enjoyable, dependable, and of course, fast. Kummant was the CEO of Amtrak until November 2008. He oversaw the Amtrak revival of 2006 through 2008 that witnessed the service's trains packed as high gas prices and plane fares sent new riders running to Amtrak. Kummant left Amtrak amid disagreements with the service's board of directors regarding Amtrak's direction and philosophies. (Most of the board had been appointed by President Bush, who tried to wean Amtrak off government funding to operate more like a private business and less like the successful national high-speed train networks across the world, all of which depend on some form of government support.)

A high-speed network of American trains will bring cities closer to one another, enabling easy travel and seamless business. An encompassing high-speed train network will give us the general sense that—after seeing our world shrink thanks to the slow atrophy of our plane and car options—our world encompasses more than our immediate city. In a world of $18 gasoline, high-speed rail is necessary for America to stay relevant to other world powers, some of which have a large head start on electrically powered bullet trains. Stagnant societies tend to stay stagnated; vibrant ones adjust, adapt, and move forward. The building of the American high-speed rail network will keep our country in the latter group rather than regressing to the former.

We will build networks to become more like the British and the French, who have the Eurostar train that rockets from London to Paris (part of the journey passes underneath the English Channel) in just over two hours. We will build projects like those of the Chinese, who are connecting Beijing and Shanghai with a new high-speed line that will cut the travel time between the two from fourteen hours to five. These two stalwart cities of China are 800 miles apart, farther away from each other than Chicago and Jackson, Mississippi.

Our trains will run more like those in Japan that make the complicated 800-mile trek from Tokyo to Fukuoka in less than five hours. We will finally catch up with the likes of the Koreans, who flit between Busan and Seoul on their country's KTX train that can travel at 215 mph. Americans will experience travel like that of the Thalys line, the maroon train that whisks passengers 200 miles

from Paris to Brussels in 80 minutes. We will know what it's like to
travel on the German ICE train from Munich to Hamburg at 180
mph. Even the Russians have been busy, building a 400-mile high-
speed line from Moscow to Saint Petersburg that now carries people between that country's two most important cities.

The Lone Bastion of American Speed

The United States does have one high-speed train. And like the
ceaseless stations of New York's subway system, it's heavily ridden
and highly appreciated. Amtrak calls it their Northeast Corridor. It
travels from Washington DC up the Eastern Seaboard to Boston.
Its prominent stops include Baltimore, Philadelphia, and New York.
The line is better known as the Acela, which is the express train that
runs on the Northeast Corridor's tracks.

Boarding the 6 a.m. Acela Express train in New York's Penn
Station offers little excitement. The train is dark, the people are
quiet. There's no security and no assigned seats. Passengers simply wander down to the track, step aboard, pick a seat, and settle
in. The cars are pleasant and roomy; the passengers, largely, are
professionals. There's even a quiet car where cell phone use and
loud conversations are banned. The train gets moving out of Penn
Station with little fanfare. It glides through the tunnels of Manhattan, under the Hudson River, and out into the darkness of
New Jersey. A conductor makes sure people don't dawdle when
boarding in Newark, then again in Philadelphia and Baltimore.
The train runs quietly with only the whoosh of the electric motors and a smooth and forgiving suspension system mellowing out
the track's clacking. The train tilts into turns, allowing it to stay
traveling at more than 100 mph while slightly veering to the right
or left.

The Acela's path leads it through quaint shoreline towns,

past harbors brimming with tall masts and the occasional Atlantic lighthouse. South of Wilmington, Delaware, the towns give way to a deep deciduous wood, a mix of New England autumnal color and Mid-Atlantic greenery. The route follows the woods through Maryland and reenters them again after Baltimore, ushering riders from the depths of the forest to the heart of U.S. bureaucracy in a matter of minutes. The train usually pulls into Washington DC's Union Station on time and just about full at 9 a.m., giving riders a wide open itinerary to tackle business in the capital. In the scant matter of three hours, passengers travel from the frantic bustle of midtown Manhattan with its swirling crowds, noisy sidewalks, and red-eyed absorption through the sea towns of the Mid-Atlantic and its pastoral woods of unsullied countryside into the seat of federal power. As the train glides slowly to a stop, people close their laptops, unplug their phone chargers, rub their eyes, and switch out of relaxation mode into full-tilt business mode. Glib passenger conversations abruptly end, suit jackets are donned, and countenances change from a passive tranquillity to fierce intensity.

For Americans, the Acela is excitingly fast; there are times on the trip from New York to DC that it goes 130 mph. In the world of high-speed trains, however, the Acela is not particularly fast or, by some standards, even high-speed. There are many trains in Europe, Asia, and Japan that routinely top 200 mph.

Like the New York subway, the Acela typically runs close to full. Unlike the subway, the tickets aren't cheap. I paid $340 for a round-trip ticket on the Acela on a normal October Tuesday. Plane fares are cheaper. But planes take close to twice as long and are less dependable. A plane traveler leaving from Midtown Manhattan to central DC has to spend one hour on public transit or $40 on a cab to get to LaGuardia, Newark, or JFK airports, arrive ninety minutes before their flight, spend an insufferable twenty-five minutes getting through security, and then pray the flight is actually on time, far from a slam dunk for New York metro airports. The plane is airborne for less than an hour, but most flights land at BWI or Dulles airports in the DC area, putting travelers another expensive cab ride or an hour-long public transit ride outside the central capital. The Acela runs on time, has no time-consuming security gauntlets, and goes straight from Midtown to central DC. Getting out of Union Station in DC takes about two minutes of walking. Same thing for New York's Penn Station. Similar things can't be said, obviously, for the towns' respective airports. All these reasons lead 65% of travelers going between New York and Washington to Amtrak rather than one of the dozens of daily flights offered by Delta, American, United, or Continental, flights that are often cheaper than Amtrak.

The Northeast Corridor is what the rest of American train travel can be. And it's what it will be when gas prices approach $18 per gallon. Our current anemic train networks make it easy for millions of passengers to skip the rails when it comes to choosing among trains, planes, and automobiles. But what about when a line as appealing, as efficient, and as fast as the Acela is installed? People will come around to the train, and they'll come around quickly. The numbers behind Amtrak's revenues are revealing and astonishing. Amtrak captured $1.73 billion in revenues during its fiscal 2008; $950 million of that came from the high-speed Northeast Corridor trains. More than half of Amtrak's total haul—54%—came from a 450-mile double stretch of track that only carried 37% of Amtrak's 29 million riders in 2008. That's what frequency, speed, and comfort can do for ridership. Imagine if train service of that caliber or even better were installed in much of the rest of the United States. The effects on commerce, regional relations, family connections, and the general mood of the public would be profound. A renaissance of the rails, indeed.

Amtrak's Feeble Status in the Federal Hierarchy: Meet Me at the Side Entrance

Architect Daniel Burnham, the protagonist of Chicago's record-setting World's Columbian Exposition in 1893, intended for Washington DC's Union Station to be the grand entrance hall to one of the world's most important cities. When the station opened in 1907, most people agreed that Burnham had succeeded. Union Station's polished Great Hall and its muscular arch-filled façade pack enough bombast for a narcissistic monarch. The station is the southernmost stop for the high-speed Acela train and connects directly to Washington's beautiful subway system. The station also houses Amtrak's headquarters.

But even in what should be Amtrak's throne, the agency has been relegated to an unceremonious spot that requires walking out of the station's Great Hall, past a steakhouse, and through a set of outside doors. Once outside, those seeking Amtrak's door can find it a few giant columns to the left, behind a nondescript entrance that requires visitors to be buzzed in by a security guard in a drab front room, like a walk-up apartment. You could be entering a single-room-occupancy joint on the Lower East Side, or it could be the headquarters of our nation's passenger rail system. An average Starbucks is more impressive.

Perhaps the lean home office instills a sense of slender pragmatism to Amtrak's leaders, an attitude that's necessary to lead an organization so bereft of adequate funding when compared with its contemporaries around the world. Alex Kummant, though he can dream big, always kept his focus on incremental gains, small gains, any gains. "The world we have to live in here at Amtrak is a pragmatic one where we say what we can reasonably get done in the next five years," Kummant explains while sitting at the conference table of his office at Union Station. "And building high-speed corridors, without a different kind of public commitment and without billions and billions of dollars, just isn't possible."

There's almost an annoyance on the part of Kummant, and Amtrak executives in general, with the perception, held by many Americans, that high-speed rail is the only rail worth having. But Kummant acknowledges that speed is something that, in and of itself, can draw people back to the rails. "Give me single-digit billions in single-digit years and I can make some of these high-speed corridors happen," Kummant says. "We could do the Chicago to Detroit corridor for one billion dollars—and we could have trains going a hundred and ten miles per hour on the route."

For maybe double that price, Amtrak could make the corridor a 200 mph zone, getting travelers from Illinois to the shores of Lake Saint Clair in ninety minutes. But nobody would complain about a three-hour trip, either. Not when driving takes five to six hours with light traffic, and flying, with all of its airport shenanigans, takes just as long. The two keys to making routes like this reality, Kummant says, are a well-tuned national plan and a wholesale change on how the government supports rail.

"This is an area where national comprehensive plans matter," he says. "We don't have that. I was recently in Berlin at a conference and I said to one of my German counterparts, 'I wish I worked in a country that simply looked at rail as a necessary expenditure.'" The German, Kummant says, told him, "'You should have been here twenty-five years ago when we were down in Bonn begging for money every year. So, look, you have to understand that these things can be turned around.'"

The man was right: This can be turned around. And it will be turned around. Once gas tops $12 per gallon, Kummant foresees a public with a genuine desire for change on the rails and a government finally emboldened to do it. To get a true nationally linked high-speed network will require gasoline prices nearer to $18, but the wheels will begin turning before that. "Sometimes it takes a genuine crisis to motivate action," Kummant says, "and I have little doubt that oil scarcity is the crisis that will do it."

Kummant led the effort before Congress to secure Amtrak more funding, and he succeeded, at least for now. A new bill in 2008 granted Amtrak $2.5 billion a year for operations and capital expenditures, like repairing bad lines, of which there are many, and building out new ones. It's not enough to dream high-speed, but this bill came with gas prices of $2.50 per gallon. When the price of gas has leapt past $10, past $14, to $18, the trickle of single billions will become a flood of hundreds of billions.

The Transportation Market Is Far from a Free One

Alex Kummant had a tough job in trying to sell a country on something that it just doesn't value as much as it should. It was a very tough job. Richard Harnish's job, however, may be even tougher. And you can bet that Harnish isn't drawing the $350,000 salary that Kummant, previously an executive at Union Pacific, got from Amtrak. Harnish heads up the Midwest High Speed Rail Association. His organization runs purely on donations. As its name suggests, the association lobbies for a concentric system of high-speed rail in the Midwest spoking out from Chicago to Saint Louis, Milwaukee, Minneapolis, Indianapolis, Detroit, and Cleveland. Harnish spends many of his days in Springfield, Illinois, lobbying the state legislature to open the purse strings and make rail travel a priority. Like Kummant, some of Harnish's most successful efforts came amid rising gas prices in 2007 and 2008.

Harnish takes his trains seriously. He recently ventured to Memphis on a trip with his son. They rode Amtrak's City of New Orleans train all the way to Tennessee, which covered the 500 miles in twelve hours, hardly a blistering pace. But Harnish is a man who would rather ride a train for twelve hours than mess with planes and airports for six. His MasterCard doesn't earn him airline miles; it earns him the arcane reward of Amtrak Points. Midwest Rail's offices occupy a tranche of space above a coffee shop in a hip section of Chicago's Lincoln Square neighborhood on the city's Near Northwest Side. The office's face-nailed maple floors and room-spanning sets of double-hung windows date from a time when rail, not the automobile, was king. Harnish isn't asking for royal privileges. He just wants rail to get a fair shake. That day is coming sometime in the near future as energy prices continue to rise. But the United States is a long way from an even transportation playing field right now. Give rail that, says Harnish, and it will flourish.

"The first thing you have to realize is that there is no free market for transportation," Harnish says. "It's not as if you can go out and buy a high-speed train and just use it—you need tracks and infrastructure."

Those are tracks and infrastructure that the government does not provide. But what the government does provide is roads. Government in America spends $150 billion on road building, but they don't do much to keep up the rails. There was a time when they did, such as in the 1870s when the government guaranteed bonds issued by the Central Pacific and Union Pacific railroads to complete the transcontinental railroad. The government allowed the railroads $16,000 per mile of flat track, $32,000 per mile of track through the foothills, and $48,000 per mile of track through the mountains.[2] The subsidies, which were in fact a form of loans, totaled $53 million.[3] The railroads did get a huge handout in the form of land grants of 12,800 acres per mile of track. Not a bad deal. But railroads were still vulnerable to a fiercely competitive field of comers as rail booms-and-busts were routine in those days. Our current-day carmakers get all the benefits of free roads, no strings attached. Chrysler and GM sucked up $13 billion of taxpayer money to stay afloat in late 2008; most doubt either company will be able to repay it.

Since 1956, the federal government has sunk $3.5 trillion of our wealth into asphalt. The amount spent on our rail systems during that time is sidewalk change, less than 5% of the road total. So cars, buses, trucks—anything that drives on a road—has an inherent advantage over anything running on rails. The roads are supplied for free. Gas taxes represent some of the money spent on roads, but not nearly all of it. The 18.4 cents a gallon doesn't go too far in current times, as mentioned in Chapter $6. Our road building requires billions out of general federal funds every year. "There's a giant sucking sound of money coming out of the rest of our economy and into the pavement on our roads," Harnish says.

What the federal government has been doing, Harnish notes, is asking passenger railroads to run like private businesses while turning around and heavily subsidizing their competitors: cars, trucks, and buses. Detroit's automobile lobby has played no small part in ensuring that the balance of subsidy stays so off-kilter, Harnish says. Even so, the car companies *still* can't figure out how to make money. In a future of $18 gas, a much larger part of the pie has to go to our rail system. It will be a necessary bulwark to ensure our ability to travel in a world radically changed by energy prices.

Even freight carriers such as Union Pacific and CSX, who make money in most years, play at a serious disadvantage compared with their trucking competitors. "The railroad companies are spending north of fifteen percent of revenues on capital expenditures for track repairs, upkeep, signal improvements," says Kummant. "That's insane. But their truck competitors, they pay almost nothing for the roads. At some point, the government has to fund some of this network expansion and some of the upkeep for national railroads. It's unavoidable," he adds.

Back in Chicago, Harnish whirls in his chair and points at a picture of a double-decker commuter train whizzing past cars stuck in traffic on Chicago's Kennedy Expressway. His finger homes in on the train. "Who is lobbying for this?" he asks. "Not Union Pacific.

They own the track but they'd just as soon see the passenger trains get off of them because of their high liability issues. It's not the steel companies who make the rails—those last fifty or sixty years. And the rocks under the rails come from a UP-owned quarry. Other than that, there are a handful of little contracts for signals and what-not, but not much. But that's the beauty of rail."

Harnish then moves his finger to point at the four lanes of southbound Kennedy traffic. "But over here, you have the carmak-ers, the oil companies, the tire companies, the giant construction companies that build these highways, the companies that make these huge light posts by the million, the companies that mow the midway grass . . ." He trails off. "The list is endless. That's a hard thing to fight."

The Future of U.S. Rail Will Again Turn Bright with the Realities of High Gas Prices

The lobbies, the jobs, the fact that change, typically, is detested by the public—there's a panoply of reasons why it will take a very high price per gallon to change how our government funnels our trans-portation dollars. But that's what has to happen for our country to be zigzagged with high-speed rail. What Harnish suggests is that new highway building be stopped completely. "We need to stop highway construction and go into a pure maintenance program," he explains. "We have enough roads already. And in a future that will probably have fewer people driving cars, we won't need any more roads. We should be shifting our resources into railroad im-provements and mass transit improvements."

Harnish likes to highlight projects currently on the docket that, he says, should never be completed. One such venture is U.S. Route 20 in western Illinois. The state and the federal gov-ernment have plans to make the fifty miles of two-lane Route 20 between Freeport, a town of 25,000, and Galena, a town of 3,500, four lanes all the way. The cost: almost $1 billion. That's $18 million a mile to widen an existing highway between two rather small towns. The same $1 billion could build a high-speed train corridor from Chicago to Milwaukee or from San Diego to Los Angeles or San Francisco to Sacramento or more than halfway from Portland to Seattle. Instead, the momentum of our government's road-building machine may build a road that few will know about, care about, or use.

The federal government spends $40 per Amtrak traveler. That sounds like a nice bump. But Washington doles out $500 per car passenger in the form of road subsidies. "That imbalance is unlike anywhere else in Western Europe or developed Asia," says Harnish. "The American people have to realize, at some point, they won't be able to drive or fly everywhere they want to go."

The people of Europe have realized this for a long time. Gas taxes across much of the continent have brought Europeans to use about half as much oil per capita as Americans. The multiplication and spreading of high-speed train networks has been part of Europe's metamorphosis toward a society less reliant on gasoline. The changes began in the 1960s and 1970s amid the first Arab oil embargoes and continue to this day. The European train experience gives us a preview toward what to expect as gas prices increase in the United States and the rest of the world. In the end, the American network will be just as widespread and just as fast as any other in the world.

Spain, up until the late 1990s, was not among the European elite when it came to their train system. But with a government bent on fighting aimless sprawl outside Madrid and bringing the whole country within a three-hour train ride of the capital, Spain's train system has progressed with astonishing speed. What's happened in Spain is a testament to how quickly projects as daunting as country-wide high-speed rail can be licked when the whole nation, spurred by the government, mobilizes for the cause. Spain's transportation budget is now evenly split between rails and roads. The Spanish government has authorized $360 billion worth of infrastructure during the next fifteen years, with half of that, $180 billion, going to rail.

Madrid has been linked to dozens of cities with 200-mph train lines, linking that country with affordable, safe, and comfortable transit. Spain's intensely undulating topography has made many of the high-speed installations tricky and expensive, but the efforts have changed the lives of many Spaniards. The train trip from Madrid to Barcelona, which is 310 miles as the crow flies but 429 miles as the train goes because of terrain features, took 7 hours and 30 minutes in 2001, when ten trains made the trip daily. Now there are twenty trains daily that make the same trip in a scant 2 hours and 40 minutes. That's farther than Los Angeles to San Francisco, or about the same as New York to Cleveland. As part of Spain's improvements, the country has teamed with France's TGV high-speed network to offer a train that goes from Madrid to Paris in 7 hours—that's the same distance as Chicago to New York.

If Spain can do this, the United States can do this. The United States should be able to do this even better, in fact. Spain has committed ten times as much money as the United States has even considered committing to its train system. Spain, with only 41 million people, has a gross domestic product of $1.4 trillion, or $34,000 per capita. The United States, with 300 million people, has a GDP of $13.8 trillion, or $46,000 per capita. The U.S. military spends more money by itself than Spain's entire government, which has expenditures of $570 billion. America is a sleeping rail giant.

Rocketing gas prices will have the giant at full attention, and the United States' ratio of road to rail spending will reach a 50-50 balance when gasoline hits $18. Considering where we're at now, that suggestion sounds impudent, but our world will have undergone a vast renovation. We will live closer together, our cities will be vibrant, manufacturing will have been reborn, our food will be more local, and our trash production will be cut in half. What will be missing from this world is the old function of the airports: an overlaying transportation system that binds our country together as one, keeping our wonderful diversities tied together through the simple physical ability to change places quickly. A country such as ours will require a cohesive rail system as grand as our ideals. This will be the final step in our country's transformation from times of cheap oil largesse to competitive oil scarcity. We will live differently, but we will live well. Easy travel across our nation will again be at our easy disposal when high-speed rail spreads across the nation.

It will start in California. California's voters took the step in late 2008 of passing a measure supporting $10 billion in state-backed bonds that would jump-start construction on a 700-mile network of 220-mph trains. The tracks would stretch from San Diego to Los Angeles, up through Fresno, and then north to San Francisco and Sacramento, cementing together our country's most populous state with a train network as advanced as any in Europe. The project will take cars off California's choked highways, pollution out of its smoggy valleys, and lend convenience, affordability, and speed to Californians. The state's High Speed Rail Authority estimates travelers will pay $55 to get from San Francisco to Los Angeles in 2 hours and 38 minutes, making the train cheaper and faster than flying, when accounting for time spent at the airport.

The California project still faces many hurdles. The state has faced consistent fiscal crunches with annual deficits projected in the multibillions that could impede the state's creditworthiness. But nothing will help California's efforts like rising gas prices. Voters passed the 2008 bill with the memories of $4 per gallon gas fresh in their minds from the summer. In the face of even higher gas prices, this project will get done. It will serve as a template for the rest of the country to follow. The California effort will also, in a way, dress down the federal government and Amtrak, who will have been thoroughly upstaged by a state agency with, theoretically, far smaller resources.

This will galvanize the federal government to get involved with more high-speed rail planning, especially when people, as Harnish and Kummant predict, flock en masse to a finished line that runs up half of our West Coast.

Other states will swivel into action as well as the price of gasoline shoots into the double digits, headed toward $18. Texas, the second-most-populated state, will be right behind California, as it will look to link Houston, Dallas, Austin, and San Antonio in a neat triangle of electrified rail, with extensions reaching the Gulf Coast at Galveston and Corpus Christi. Oklahoma will chip in for a stretch linking Tulsa to Oklahoma City down to Dallas, helping solidify these cities' transformations from sprawl to true urban centers replete with modern transit. Kansas, in turn, will support a link from Oklahoma City to Wichita on up to Kansas City, Missouri.

Following Texas's lead will be Florida, another one of our five most populous states. The Sunshine State will send high-speed rail north from Miami to Fort Myers, then to Tampa, east to Orlando, and north to Jacksonville. Georgia will meet Florida's network there, bringing track south from Atlanta.

Gas prices of $18 will spur action in the Midwest, where high-speed rail will spill out of Chicago in all directions, linking it to Milwaukee, Minneapolis, Saint Louis, and Indianapolis. Missouri will link Saint Louis to Kansas City, giving the Midwest network access clear down to Houston and the Gulf of Mexico.

Harnish believes that a high-speed Chicago to New York corridor could be the first big initiative taken up outside California's independent movement. "The current situation is just shameful," he says, referring to the twenty-one-hour marathon required of Chicago to New York train riders.

Such a project would unite the Upper Midwest with the East Coast as never before. It would give these regions, which have such similar demographics, cities, and neighborhoods, a transcending transit link that will step into the void left by the dozens of shuttle flights forced to shut down when gas reached $8 per gallon. The corridor would go from Chicago to Toledo (with a short connection to Detroit here) to Cleveland, southeast to Pittsburgh, across Pennsylvania to Philadelphia, and then up to New York, linking with the Northeast Corridor. The trip from Chicago to New York would take less than six hours.

In the Mid-Atlantic, North Carolina will link Charlotte to Greensboro to Raleigh, which will, with Virginia's help, connect to Richmond, which will then connect to the Northeast Corridor at Washington's Union Station. The Northeast Corridor, at this point, will be the slowest high-speed track in the nation, prompting the Capitol Hill check writers to authorize a massive revamping of the Northeast Corridor, giving it 220-mph capability. The federal government will have a hand in all these high-speed developments, as a planning commission will finally be put together, giving the United States the comprehensive rail plan it's never had.

California's network will eventually conspire with the feds to link with high-speed track to Portland, Oregon, which will connect with Seattle. Los Angeles will connect with Las Vegas. A strong national plan will be necessary to get rail west from Chicago to Denver, continuing out to Salt Lake City, and from there, to Reno and San Francisco. The completion of this route will solidify a nation acclimated to high-speed train travel.

Our world will have been thoroughly altered by the scarcity of petroleum and its rising cost. The changes will be good and bad, depending on one's outlook. High-speed trains, however, will be unequivocally good and welcomed by all. They will simplify our lives and they will improve our lives. A college student home for break in Chicago will be able to have Sunday breakfast with her parents, take a short ride on the subway from her family's home in the city's Lincoln Park neighborhood to Chicago's Union Station and board a 10 a.m. express train for New York, back to school. She will pass through Illinois, Indiana, Ohio, Pennsylvania, New Jersey, and lower Manhattan. Indiana's steel mills will flit by in a one-minute blur. The barns of Ohio and Pennsylvania, pretty in the nascent spring light, will be flashes of art, held by her eye for a half-second, no more. A one-mile-long tunnel through one of Pennsylvania's sharp, scaly hills will be a concise sixteen seconds of blackness. She'll nap for three hours and find, disappointedly, that she left herself only three hours on the train to work on her paper that's due in two days. Luckily for her, she will be in her dorm room at Columbia University, on New York's Upper West Side, by 6 p.m., with plenty of time to conjure prose and cram research.

In a world of $18 gas, the legacy of the innovative and unrelated Budds will finally be picked up, dusted off, and carried on toward a better-linked America. The completion of this modern marvel of track, no doubt to be finished off by some large, hydraulic tool mounted on four wheels, will prove as momentous as that of the first transcontinental railroad when a tired but triumphant Union Pacific worker hammered in the final spike at Promontory Point, Utah, in 1869.

The U.S. Military at $18 per Gallon

The B-52 bomber has been flying missions for the U.S. Air Force since the 1950s. Not much has changed on the old bird. Sure, the cockpits are crammed with updated circuitry and gadgets, and its bombs might be a bit more accurate, but the giant warplane still takes off, flies a long way rather slowly, and drops its deadly ordnance from several miles above the earth. The plane uses not two, not four, but eight screaming Pratt & Whitney jet engines, each summoning 17,000 pounds of thrust. The engines, in fact, aren't much different from those that propelled the 1950s plane. Better technology exists, but the Air Force is comfortable with its workhorse.

The U.S. Air Force is like an old curmudgeon who started

smoking in the 1950s and still, in the face of all the dire warnings, won't give up his habit. But like the old man, who, of course, has managed to stay alive all these years, the Air Force remains. It takes a lot to change an old man's mind. The Air Force is the same way. Gasoline prices approaching $18 per gallon, however, will get the Pentagon's attention the same way $25 packs of cigarettes would motivate the old man. Every $1 increase in the cost of a gallon of gasoline costs the Defense Department $5 billion. The trip from $4 per gallon to $18 per gallon would mean $70 billion in extra costs.

The B-52 flies for twenty-four straight hours sometimes to make a bombing run and get back home. The plane truly is, as its military moniker says, a Stratofortress. The airplane is 160 feet long with a wingspan of 185 feet. It's 40 feet high. Empty, it weighs 185,000 pounds. At takeoff it can hold 310,000 pounds of jet fuel plus another 70,000 pounds of bombs.[4] It takes a crew of five to operate. The Air Force launches sorties to the Middle East from as far away as Guam and North Dakota. In one hour of flying, the B-52's eight engines gobble up 3,334 gallons of jet fuel.[5] With $4 gasoline, that one hour of fuel costs $13,300. With $18 gas, it increases to $60,000 an hour. A mission on the other side of the world would cost $1.4 million for the fuel alone. The B-52, despite its simple lines and its graceful, arching wingspan, is a flying pig. It's the biggest hog, in fact, in the cabal of fuel gluttons that the U.S. military employs. The B-52 has flown and fought in every major U.S. conflict since it joined our airborne ranks almost sixty years ago. The B-52's reign will be in jeopardy in a world of $18 gas as the military and its machines evolve to use less fuel for reasons of money and security.

"Any sort of situation with high oil prices is going to affect everything the military does," says Michael Levi, who is the director of the program on energy security at the Council on Foreign Relations. But the U.S. armed forces won't stop doing their jobs when gas reaches $18. If the Pentagon wants to bomb something, the price at the pump will not stop them, Levi says. What high fuel prices do, however, is force the military to spend money on fuel that they'd rather spend on capital costs, such as new planes, boats, missiles, etc. The military spent more than $15 billion on energy during 2008, more than half of that on jet fuel. To keep its capital procurement program running, the Pentagon has already begun to think about a world of gasoline prices in the double digits. After all, what's a military without new toys?

In addition to the money pressures, says Levi, the military has never been comfortable relying on fossil fuels that largely come from countries that don't consider the United States among their staunchest of buddies. High gas prices, put simply, are a security threat. The Pentagon's answer to that threat will be, simply, to use less fuel while striving to stay as relevant as it has always been on the world's tactical stage. Levi says the military will spearhead its efforts not with decreased missions, but with technology. "They would try to do what they do now at a much higher level of efficiency," Levi says. "The military will try and curb its costs primarily through innovation and applying new technology to old tasks. This has been an on-again, off-again focus of the Pentagon for years," he adds.

That is, on again in times of high fuel prices, off again during times of $1 gasoline. In a future of gas prices on a bumpy climb, the military's focus will become permanently in on-again status. Planes like the B-52 would not survive in any type of great numbers, and the ones that did would be retrofitted with four high-efficiency engines instead of eight guzzlers. The Air Force will also introduce new, highly efficient versions of its C-5 transport planes and its airborne radar system planes, which stay in the air for much of their lifetimes, through peace or war.

In a further effort to keep its fuel lines flowing in times of strife in oil-supplying countries—a situation that becomes more likely with high gasoline prices—the Air Force has been experimenting with synthetic fuels made from natural gas and coal. This is a costly process, but one that can be done domestically. The Air Force hopes that by 2016 it has the capability of supplying half of its 3 billion gallons of jet fuel with synthetic versions in case of a supply cutoff from foreign sources.

The Navy is also a guzzler. The Air Force and the Navy together account for 85% of the military's fuel use.[6] Some representatives in Congress have been pushing the Navy to make its fleet more nuclear. Currently, only the Navy's submarines and aircraft carriers run on fission reactors, about 80 of its 300 ships. Representative Roscoe Bartlett, a Maryland Republican who crusades for energy conservation, says the break-even point for an all-nuclear fleet is near oil prices of $100 per barrel. The Navy says nuclear cruisers make sense at $80 per barrel and destroyers at $200. Regardless of who is right, the price of oil surpassing both of these points is inevitable and so, too, is a U.S. Navy that is powered exclusively with on-board nuclear reactors. Being all-nuclear will also keep U.S. ships safer and less vulnerable. The USS *Cole*, when it was hit with a ship packed with explosives in Yemen's Port of Aden, was on a scheduled refueling stop, a stop it wouldn't have required had it been nuclear powered. The explosion blew a forty-foot hole in the *Cole*'s hull and killed seventeen American sailors.

Navy ships that have good lives left but no nuclear power will see their electrical and diesel systems upgraded and made radically more efficient. A 2001 Navy study found that its Aegis cruiser, the USS *Princeton*, uses $10 million worth of diesel fuel a year to get around the world.[7] That's $25,000 for each member of the boat's 400-person crew. When gas is $18, the fuel cost for each sailor on the USS *Princeton* will be $225,000. Almost half of that fuel goes toward creating 2.5 megawatts of electricity for the boat's electric systems, while the rest goes to supply 80,000 horsepower to its propellers. The study found that modernizing the ship's electrical systems and exchanging outdated coolers, pumps, fans, and filters could save as much as 50% on electricity, drastically cutting back on fuel costs. The Navy has been dragging its feet on these kinds of retrofits, but in a world of double-digit gasoline prices, every ship in the fleet will get a turn in the dry docks to have its electrical systems overhauled.

The U.S. Army, when it's in full ground-attack mode, slurps energy and gasoline by the bucket. The Army's main workhorse, the seventy-ton Abrams tank, has a voracious appetite. Its gas turbines can get the rig moving across rough terrain at 40 miles per hour. The tank's fuel efficiency, however, isn't measured in miles per gallon, but in gallons per mile (the tank spends three gallons to go a mile). Exacerbating the Abrams's gluttony, the Army often likes to use helicopters to get fuel to advancing tanks in battle, raising the cost of the delivered fuel to $500 per gallon. So getting the Abrams on some kind of diet will be high on the Army's errand list in a future of $18 gas. Levi says the Army won't get rid of its tanks, but will probably install higher-efficiency turbines inside new tanks in an effort to double their fuel efficiency. The current turbines are based on 1960s technology.[8]

Other Army vehicles, such as Humvees and personnel carriers, will see changes, too, as their frames are switched over to titanium and carbon composites. The Army is already testing vehicles powered with hybrid diesel-electric engines. Vehicles running these efficient technologies won't be merely a part of the regular Army at $18 gas; they will dominate.

In addition to ferrying gasoline to tanks via choppers, the Army runs giant, inefficient diesel generators to power its forward command stations that can be set up on the fly. In the future, the Army plans to use a new generation of tactical hybrid power station, which will accompany command tents and utilize on-board wind turbines and solar panels to supply the center with power. It's green power, but the Army loves it because it's portable power; no helicopter flights for barrels of diesel fuel here, just pure, unattached mobility and energy.

The Pentagon will not cease to be a force in the world with gas priced at $18, but it knows that it can't stay relevant in a world of ever-advancing technologies if it's blowing half its budget on fuel. That's why the military is actually ahead of many other sectors of the government and the economy when it comes to looking toward a future of high gas prices. It can't afford to be complacent. Nor can the rest of us.

CHAPTER $20

The Future of Energy

Greener Than Green: Curbing Our Energy Waste

The Kanawha River Valley of West Virginia roils with gritti-ness. Slag piles, coal mounds, and sooty mineshafts have been ubiquitous here for more than a century, as this valley's coal has powered our society from an agrarian muddle to a wondrous ex-hibit of technology and progress. The hills of Appalachia climb with immediacy near the Kanawha River's edge, culminating 1,200 feet above in peaks dabbed in hardwoods and crumbly rock faces. Many of the steep hillsides here bear the scars of our energy scavenging—tunnel mouths and roughly cut roads etching the greenery with their brown switchback patterns. Coal trucks rumble down the two-lane blacktop. Their cargo, prone to the bounces and curves of the road, flecks the highway shoulder with obsidian streaks of black. The air smells of dust and metallic soot. It sticks in the mouth and tastes like a mild bloody lip.

The Kanawha River, sometimes rollicking, sometimes tran-quil, often pools up behind frequent dams that supply hydroelec-tricity to nearby smelters and refiners. Giant coal plants, perched on the river's banks, belch smoke and steam that drifts east toward the mountains. The electricity flows out of the plants on giant high-voltage wires that skip from one bank to the other, and occasionally get footing on an island. The river long ago ceased being a crystalline byway, its waters having been sacrificed for electricity, coal, and heat. The West Virginia Bureau for Public Health advises fishermen to eat none of the carp, catfish, suckers, or hybrid-striped bass they catch because of the high levels of dioxins these fish absorb from the river's muddy bottom. Industry has reigned here ever since boulders and rock islets were removed from the lower part of the Kanawha in 1840 to facilitate barge traffic and easier access to the local coal deposits.

This valley—with its coal, its hydro, its mines, its hardened work force, and its remote locale—is the heart of old American energy. Half a dozen generations here have grown up and grown old mining coal and sucking dust. Things here have worked the same way for more than eighty years. Mine coal, burn coal, make steam, turn turbine, make electricity. Same goes for the hydro dams: Dam it up in the spring and slowly let it out all summer long, turning the turbines as the water gets released. This valley is old-world energy with all its grungy foibles.

So it may seem odd that one of the most significant conservation efforts in America has been taken up right here, a mere 100 yards from the Kanawha's east bank. What's happening here is a blueprint for our future, a future of higher energy prices in which we value every last drip of power and loathe its waste like a miser. Here in the unincorporated town of Alloy, thirty miles southeast of Charleston, the state capital, beneath a towering, steep slope of hardwoods, is the world's most prolific silicon factory. West Virginia Alloy annually makes 72,000 tons of the shiny metal at this plant, and to do so, it ingests titanic amounts of energy. The factory requires a steady stream of 135 megawatts, enough juice to sustain 120,000 American homes. The electricity feeds the plant's arc furnaces, whose centers glow white with heat at 6,000 degrees Fahrenheit. In the furnaces, West Virginia Alloy melts a mixture of Alabama quartz, local hardwood chips, and local coal. Quartz is composed of silicon and oxygen: SiO_2. The scalding heat seeks out the oxygen that's in the quartz and strips it out, leaving behind pure silicon that pours out from the furnace's bottom into small rail cars. Chemically, the process is known as a carbon reduction because the oxygen in the quartz bonds with the carbon from the coal and the wood. Silicon goes into a spectrum of products from circuit wafer boards to shaving cream to caulk to cosmetics and kitchen utensils.

The energy conservation efforts here are mammoth—this plant will produce more green energy—50 megawatts—than $300 million worth of large windmills or $2.8 billion worth of solar panels. And it will cost only $75 million. The project focuses on the plant's furnaces that currently belch heat as promiscuously as a raging bonfire; getting closer than twenty feet threatens gawkers' eyebrows. The company warns visitors not to wear polyester, whose low melting point could be eclipsed during a walking tour. Near the upper half of the furnace, where the wood, coal, and quartz get mixed together by what amounts to a giant spatula attached to a small forklift, the heat feels like standing in Death Valley sun on a 130-degree scorcher of a day. Moving inside of thirty feet for a better look, at the behest of my factory guide, I stuffed my notebook into my pocket because its pages felt close to igniting.

The furnace is left open to vent heat any way possible to avoid melting parts of the furnace that aren't supposed to melt. Just like a car engine requires cooling, so does the furnace. In addition to the random venting, the furnaces' innards are water-cooled by two-foot-wide radiator pipes that dump their heat outside in three rows of twenty-three loops, each 100 feet high. This giant radiator is clearly discernible on Google Maps. Just zoom in on Alloy, West Virginia, and you'll see it. This kind of cooling system allows the furnaces and the plant to run constantly with few work stoppages.

To Tom Casten, chairman of Recycled Energy Development (known as RED), this extensive and complicated radiator system amounts to a massive pile of waste. Its sole purpose is to dissipate heat. "Heat," Casten says often, "is energy. So why waste it?" Casten founded RED in 2006. It specializes in capturing heat that's otherwise squandered and doing something useful with it. Casten isn't one for wasting words, either; he bores straight to the point. That could come from his time as a Marine Corps engineer or from his MBA from Columbia, where he was valedictorian. Casten has spent most of the last three decades working and profiting from making our energy use more efficient. He has become one of the world's masters of energy efficiency. Casten can look at a building or a factory and immediately begin to process where easy energy gains can be had.

Casten started several companies that were so successful at making money from wasted energy that they became takeover targets for larger companies. Casten lost Trigen, a company he helped take public on the New York Stock Exchange in 1994, to a hostile takeover bid from France's Suez; he lost Primary Energy, which pursued the same business as RED, when Canada's Epcor bought it in 2006 for $330 million. Casten did well on those deals but felt he never got those companies to the heights he'd envisioned. He wants to take RED public one day, while still maintaining control. But Casten, sixty-six, feels a tug far beyond money when it comes to this fight. Cutting back on waste is the next frontier in the energy battle, he says. "We will move toward a future of higher efficiency or we will face the consequences of global warming and decreasing resources," Casten explains.

Grabbing the Low-Hanging Energy Fruit

For the silicon plant in West Virginia, that means no more radiator system and no more open venting. To optimize the plant for heat capturing, RED will decrease the amount of air to the furnaces, which will raise the temperature of the exhaust to 1,400 degrees. The furnace hoods and electrode arms will be changed from mild

steel to stainless steel, which holds up better to higher temperatures and the constant induction from the 70,000-amp firing phases.
The open section of the furnace, a five-foot gap all the way around
where the wood-quartz-coal mixture glows and condenses, will be
enclosed. Plant workers won't need the now-omnipresent seven-
foot-tall fans to keep cool. The project should be finished in 2010.

There will be, in effect, a giant vacuum system of ducts that
pulls the 1,400-degree exhaust away from the furnace to make
steam in an old building onsite. The old building is where the company once burned coal to crank steam turbines and create electricity. The steam turbines are still in there, some of them so old that
their imported pipes carry the swastika of Nazi Germany. Using
steam made from the furnaces' excess heat, RED will turn one of
those same turbines and send its electric load 100 yards back to the
silicon plant, creating 50 megawatts where before there was only
heat pouring into the atmosphere.

About 40,000 American households can run on 50 megawatts—
and here is RED, in a coal-driven valley in West Virginia, plucking
50 megawatts straight out of the air. West Virginia Alloy couldn't
be more smitten, of course, because they're going to save a giant
pile of money. When RED's project finishes up, this West Virginia
plant will not only be the largest silicon plant in the world, but will
also be the silicon producer of lowest cost in the world. Even with
all of China's cheap labor advantages, WVA president Arden Sims
says this plant's cheap and efficient electricity will make its silicon
less expensive than Asia's. "We've known for years that we've been
blowing energy out the door," he says in a West Virginia twang.
"But we didn't capitalize sooner because the price of energy has
been cheap. You'll see more of this across the world, I think, as the
price keeps going up."

The new efficiencies introduced at the West Virginia plant
have convinced WVA to reopen its factory in Niagara Falls, New
York, with a similar setup. Once that plant, which WVA shuttered

owing to Asian competition three years ago, is running, Sims says, it will result in a movement of manufacturing jobs from China, where a giant share of the world's silicon is made, back to the United States, where WVA will have become the low-cost supplier of silicon.

"There's no reason that the United States can't reestablish itself as a manufacturing heavyweight if we get smarter about how we use our energy," says Casten. He calls factories such as the one in Alloy the "low-hanging fruit." He adds, "There's plenty more where that came from."

Casten deployed similar strategies at the labyrinthine Mittal Steel plant in East Chicago, Indiana, one of the largest mills in North America. It employs 10,000 people. The project there captured the 2,000-degree exhaust coming off the mill's massive coke ovens, turning that into 1 million pounds of steam an hour and 95 megawatts of juice. The project ran $165 million, but saves Mittal $100 million a year in electricity costs at their Indiana plant.

As the price of gasoline marches upward toward $20, the United States will need to, finally, orchestrate a comprehensive energy plan that secures our country's supply of electrons far into the future. A big part of that plan will be not only finding new sources of supply, such as more wind and nuclear, but also shoring up the massive amounts of energy waste that take place every day. The massive buildings beneath the country's towering smokestacks are the best place to start. Before we start pouring concrete on a new coal or nuclear plant—or even a footing for a new wind tower—we should, and we will, be scouring our current infrastructure for, as Casten says, the low-hanging megawatts.

There are a lot of easy megawatts to be had. They're everywhere: steel mills, drywall plants, paint factories, glass manufacturers. Every time you pass a paper mill or a power plant or a refinery of some type that is billowing steam or a flame into the air—and there are tens of thousands of plants doing this across the United

States—you're watching raw energy spewed into the atmosphere. All for the simple reason that buying additional energy supplied by fossil fuels has been the cheap and easy choice for these factories to make, before energy prices began their climb. Think about this: You're drinking a beer in the living room. You get up and have a seat in the kitchen to eat, accidentally leaving your beer behind. When you realize you've left your beer in the living room, you would go and fetch it, obviously. But what if a beer cost a penny instead of a dollar? You might just stay in the kitchen and reach for a new beer in the fridge, leaving your half-finished and perfectly tasty brew to grow warm in the living room. That's effectively what American industry, and indeed, the world's industry, has been doing for a century when it comes to energy.

That will change. As gas prices push $20, America's industry will take every conservation measure they can. The change from that will be more drastic than any windmill project or solar panel array, no matter how many acres either may be. The U.S. Department of Energy says that, by recycling industrial waste heat, the country could reduce its CO_2 emissions by 20%, the equivalent of taking all the cars and light trucks off our roads. That's an awesome boon to the environment, clearly. As we make the changes to cut our energy costs, the earth will be a prime, if unintentional, benefactor.

Reigniting the Fires of Manhattan

As we capture and use our wasted heat, power, and energy, we will be moving back toward the efficiencies we knew more than 100 years ago. Our electric grid, small as it might have been in 1910, operated at 65% efficiency. That means that 65% of the power we made eventually got into the hands of end users. From then until 1957, the efficiency of our national power grid eroded to 33%, which is where it is today. "I can't think of another industry that hasn't improved its efficiency during the last fifty years," Casten says. "Industries that don't get more efficient typically die."

RED's formula of capturing and using excess heat from manufacturing processes hardly constitutes new science. Thomas Edison did the same thing with the world's first power plant on Pearl Street in Manhattan when he sold the exhaust from his coal-fired plant to his neighbors to heat their buildings. Cheap energy, however, drew the world away from such efficiencies. Those days are fleeting, however. "We're at the start of something that should have been done long ago," says Casten. By capturing waste heat just at the U.S. manufacturing level, we could bring 65,000 megawatts back into the grid, enough for 50 million homes. It's energy we're already making and that comes cheaply—cheaper than wind, solar, nuclear, or even coal.

Casten and RED would like to see things taken a step further with more local energy generation—similar to what Edison employed in Manhattan. For instance, using a natural gas–powered turbine to make electricity to power a city block. The exhaust from burning the natural gas, which is 900 degrees, can be used to turn a steam turbine to make more electricity or, in the winter, used for heat. Structuring things this way yields efficiencies greater than 90%, about three times as good as our current grid.

RED will use this process to help gypsum giant USG reconfigure some of its drywall plants, which are notorious energy gulpers. At the plants, mined gypsum arrives in raw form, aboard rail cars. The gypsum gets crushed and blended into a slurry that's slathered onto the paper shell we all recognize as drywall. The wet sandwich gets dried out at 700 degrees inside ovens the size of football fields. Ovens that big require copious amounts of energy. Currently, USG fires them up with natural gas, like you would with a gas oven at your house, and powers the rest of the factory on electricity from the grid. RED will instead install natural gas turbines that will burn gas to create electricity for the plant and use the 900-degree exhaust to cook and dry the sheetrock, more than doubling the efficiencies of USG's plants and, of course, saving the company a heap of cash.

The Department of Energy says there exists 135,000 megawatts of opportunities in the United States for combined heat and power, also known as cogeneration, where the result would be more than a doubling of current efficiencies. That's like getting a free 67,000 megawatts. That's not a trivial amount; the whole U.S. generating capacity stands at 1.1 million megawatts. With a future of high energy costs and gas prices pushing well into the double digits per gallon, local generation will again become part of the solution.

Picture a Manhattan block in mid-December, crammed with high-rise apartment buildings full of lights, people, and warmth. Several thousand people live on the block. All of their electricity, the fuel for their daily lives, comes from a compact natural gas turbine running in an underground installation in the center of the block. The heat produced from the turbine is used to create hot water and warm the entire block. Each one of these people would have an energy footprint with an efficiency above 90%, compared to the current 33% Americans now live at. That means the same energy-intensive life a Manhattanite lives now, with the same perks of entertainment, climate control, and lighting, would require only a third of the energy it currently takes.

The power of localized generation is enormous. The reason is simple: Heat doesn't travel well. You can't pipe it more than several hundred yards without bleeding off much of its warmth. When we burn coal or natural gas at remote power plants, that heat is utterly wasted. "You're cutting up the cow and throwing out the T-bone," Casten says.

Localized combustion won't be the answer to all our energy ills, but it will certainly become more and more relevant as the price of gas climbs. It will become reality in some places when the price of energy and gasoline goes past $14. That's roughly three to four times what we pay now—more than enough to spur local generation projects. Casten expects other kinds of proven resources, such as anaerobic digestion, to be more readily utilized as the price of energy creeps higher, too. Anaerobic digestion takes place when microorganisms break down human and organic waste, producing methane (natural gas) that can be captured and used as fuel. Casten often refers to farmers in Nepal and how they power their lights and stoves with gas supplied from the anaerobic digestion of their animals' dung. Casten has talked to Chicago officials about digesting the human waste at the city's O'Hare International Airport, usually the first or second busiest airport in the world. "No reason to waste it," he chuckles.

O'Hare has 77 million passengers a year passing through its terminals. In addition, it handles the sewage from the thousands of planes that dock there on their way to somewhere else—the airport is a hub for both United and American. Casten's son, who is RED's CEO and has a biochemical engineering master's degree from Dartmouth, figures the average person spends 1.5 hours at the airport and that most people spent 3 hours on their incoming flights and relieved themselves accordingly on their aircrafts. Assuming O'Hare installed the needed tanks to hold and digest the waste, it would give the airport an annual biogas-generating capacity of 81 billion BTUs—enough to heat 1,125 Midwestern homes. Not a giant amount, but it's energy that now goes unused. Imagine: Every time a passenger went through the decidedly unpleasant process of using an airplane washroom, at least he would know he was helping solve America's energy problems.

Our Energy Future: Hydro Aperitif, Wind Appetizer, Nuclear Entrée—The Rest Is Garnish

John Rowe's brand-new office uses 50% less energy than his old digs. Its appointments—stone floors, lacquered burlwood tables and shelves, large LCD screens—hardly look spare, but Rowe is a man who can afford to be efficient and comfortable at the same time. Rowe's green space, with its occupancy sensors, recycled building materials, and low-flow water fixtures, expounds on his declarations that the easiest way to mitigate America's coming energy crunch is to find power savings within our current infrastructure. It's not a novel theory, but it's a welcomed one, considering it comes from Rowe, whose business is selling energy. Rowe's office view from 700 feet up off the corner of Madison and Dearborn in Chicago's Loop is worthy of a tourist's gape. Looking through the double-paned glass that runs next to his conference table, one can see north along Lake Michigan to Chicago's North Shore and beyond toward the Wisconsin border. Southward, the view clearly shows the lakeshore hooking east through Indiana, on its way to Michigan's beach towns.

Rowe's stellar view befits his place in the energy world. He is perhaps the most powerful man in American energy outside the oil industry. As the CEO of Exelon, Rowe sits atop the largest nuclear empire in the United States. Exelon operates seventeen reactors at eleven nuclear sites across the country, concentrated in Illinois and Pennsylvania. Exelon's nuclear fleet accounts for 20% of the United States' 100,000 megawatts of nuclear capacity. Its total energy portfolio creates 24,000 megawatts.

At the very moment I'm sitting down with him, Rowe is tangled in a cutthroat Wall Street poker match. Two days before, Exelon had submitted an unsolicited bid to acquire NRG, a New Jersey energy firm, for $6.2 billion. NRG's board was reviewing the proposal; news could break at any moment.

"I checked the wire before I came up and I didn't see anything—and I have to assume there's nothing going on or else you wouldn't be sitting here talking to me," I say to Rowe.

"Well," Rowe laughs, "don't be so sure. Sometimes I'm the last to find out what's going on."

That would be humble hyperbole, of course. Rowe and Exelon were not able to acquire NRG on this pass at the company, but Exelon's eyes continue to wander the energy landscape for additions to their nuclear stable.

Rowe was trying to grow by acquisition at a time when energy companies, according to analysts and market prognosticators like Warren Buffett, were undervalued. But Rowe was also looking to snare NRG's share of a major nuclear plant in Texas and capitalize on NRG's plans to build two new reactors in that state in the near future. Exelon owns 1,400 megawatts' worth of coal production, but Rowe is not a coal man. Those coal assets are a mere 5.8% of Exelon's 24,000-megawatt energy bag. As most energy men do, Rowe talks about the future almost exclusively. What happened in the past and what works now are immaterial.

When Rowe talks about the future, he talks about nuclear. And perhaps to the surprise of many that don't follow the power industry, Rowe is one the most dogged supporters there is of a carbon cap and trade system—a carbon tax—for American industry. Rowe, of course, has Exelon's interests in mind here. Exelon gets 70% of its power from nukes—a source that emits almost no carbon. Most of Rowe's competitors depend far more heavily on greenhouse gas–spewing coal, such as Ohio's American Electric Power, whose 35,000-megawatt portfolio is 70% coal.

The role of nuclear power will have to increase in a world of higher gasoline and energy prices. Double-digit gasoline prices will thoroughly restoke America's nuclear fires. As we replace the gas in our cars' tanks with electrons in our cars' batteries, we will need more juice from the power plants of America. There are four main ways to generate new power: there's coal, natural gas, renewables (wind, solar, and geothermal), and there's nuclear. The latter will become the clear choice to provide the majority of our energy as our fossil fuel sources ebb and the concern with global warming becomes more acute.

Our Future Energy: Where It Will Come From and Where It Won't

At $20, the pressure of plug-in cars will stress our electric grid. The exploding price of heating oil will push more people in the Northeast and Mid-Atlantic to more-affordable electric heat, further increasing the strain on our power plants. Electricity will become more expensive as the cost of transporting coal spikes and the supply coming out of our giant coal basins in Wyoming and Utah gets maxed out. Brownouts, an unacceptable by-product of a fractured electric grid, will sweep the nation.

To continue furthering a civilization resembling our current one will require abundant and affordable energy. The high price of oil will push us toward renovating our grid, updating our power plant infrastructure, and changing the way we look at energy. We will waste less and generate more efficiently. Electric cars, becoming more frequent in our garages and on our streets, will mark a true turning point for our society as it goes from one powered by fossil fuels to one powered by generated electricity. We've already got one foot in the right sandbox. More than 60% of our GDP comes from services and industry that run on electricity. More than 85% of our country's energy demand growth since 1980 has been met with electricity, not oil. We will go from gas-fired ovens, heaters, and cars to devices that, one way or another, plug in. Electricity, compared to oil, is cheap. That fact will propel electricity forward as our fuel of choice. We spend about $350 billion on electricity—half the amount of cash we pack out for oil.[1]

All in all, we garner far more utility from a dollar spent on electricity than a dollar spent on oil. And that electric dollar stays in the country instead of flowing overseas. We have the resources in North America to tip the energy balance heavily in favor of our electric grid instead of oil. It will take decades, but it can be done. It has to be done. We will not eliminate our use of oil; those who say we can are simply deluded. But we can vastly cut our economy's dependency on it. There will always be some things, like keeping a jet or helicopter aloft or powering a giant mining truck, that oil can do better than anything else. But for the rest, we will revert to a world powered by electricity.

Coal

Coal works. It supplies about 50% of U.S. electricity. But coal is dirty. And mining and transporting coal, a very bulky medium for energy storage, is gasoline-intensive. Coal is good at one thing: burning. When it burns, it emits monstrous amounts of CO_2. World energy production dumps 33 billion tons of CO_2 into the atmosphere every year—and that figure is going up. More than 40% of that carbon came from burning coal for electricity. If the trends of today continue, we will continue adding more coal capacity to our power generation footprint. But if the earth's nations are serious about climate change, coal's role in the future will be diminished as it yields to the faint carbon footprint of nuclear power.

What makes coal so attractive is the simple fact that we have a lot of it, and because of that, it's cheap. Coal's cheapness will be undermined, however, by the rising cost of the gasoline that's required to mine and transport it. Coal's affordability will be further damaged by the almost certain addition of some kind of carbon tax in developed countries like the United States that will be placed on industries that burn coal.

The idea of clean coal sounds nice, but with the technology we know of now, it's wildly expensive and it depends on the sequestration of CO_2 in the ground, a technique that's unproven and may not work for the long haul. Clean coal is a Hail Mary pass. It's coddled by politicians because it's a concept that would, theoretically, solve all our problems. Everybody knows we have a lot of coal in the United States; people also know that conventionally burning coal is harmful to the climate, the environment, and our own bodies.

The idea behind clean coal: the emissions (CO_2) from coal combustion would then be captured and injected into salt domes and other spaces thousands of feet below the earth's surface. A lot of things have to go right for carbon gas to be snared from the smokestack without any vapors escaping and then for it to be injected into deep cavities in the earth without any of it escaping through Earth's porous crust. The number of places CO_2 can be sequestered—especially places near power plants—is finite. We can't pump the earth with CO_2 indefinitely and expect it not to come out. It's irrational and irresponsible. And even if it worked, the cost of clean coal is at least three times the cost of nuclear. In addition, nuclear doesn't require the wild bet that the earth won't cough up what we pump into it. "Nature did invent a perfect and efficient form of carbon sequestration," Exelon's Rowe likes to say. "It's called coal."

Hydropower

Hydropower is our most dependable green energy source. It supplies almost 10% of our electricity and some places, like Washington State, get nearly 80% of their electricity from water moving from higher elevations to lower elevations. Hydropower doesn't have an abundance of friends in environmental circles, as it tends to disturb ecosystems and, in some cases, introduce erosion. But hydropower prevents floods, and it can be counted on twenty-four hours a day, for most of the year. It's a splendid resource that emits zero CO_2. But we've largely exhausted the prime spots for hydropower in North America. Hydropower will remain an important piece of our energy picture, but its role isn't likely to increase.

Solar

Solar power, in narrow applications, can be very useful. It will never become a sizable part of our generating capacity, however, for one simple, obvious reason: The sun disappears for half the day. But powerful solar arrays in places like California, Arizona, and Nevada can, and will, help keep juice flowing during peak demand times, which occur roughly from 2 p.m. to 7 p.m., when the most people are active and when the temperatures are hottest. Conveniently, the warmest places that use the most air conditioning are also the places where the sun shines brightest and most often.

Solar energy, in one form or another, is responsible for most of the energy we know. Oil and coal are the result of millions of years of compressing and concentrating organic compounds that originally existed thanks to their ability to capture solar energy. Oil is the ultimate manifestation of millions of years of solar power decanted into an easy-to-transport and easy-to-burn medium. It only makes sense that we would try and harness the source of oil's power from its original spigot, that being the sun.

There has been a kind of land rush in the Mojave Desert in California, Nevada, and Arizona, to stake claims for property and permits to make solar power. About 100 claims have been filed with the Bureau of Land Management for more than 60,000 megawatts of solar capacity.[2] Most of that will never be built; California, the hungriest of states for energy, uses 33,000 megawatts, only half the energy represented by the applications. Some projects will come on-line, such as Arizona's Solana generating station that will crank out 280 megawatts of solar power upon its completion in 2011. Solana, if in service today, would be the largest solar plant in the world. But the fact remains that you can't light Los Angeles at night with solar power. There's no getting around that limitation. Solar doesn't come cheaply, either. To install a megawatt of solar capacity can cost three times what a megawatt of wind costs. And wind, though it doesn't always blow, often blows both at night and during the day.

Wind

Aside from capturing the thousands of megawatts we waste, as RED is doing in West Virginia, wind power is the most promising avenue to increasing our use of green energy. Wind turbines are colossal works of wonder. Their presence across the country has not yet become ubiquitous, but turbines dot enough states that most Americans have seen their giant fiberglass blades whumping with the wind.

Wind turbines face some of the same generation fluctuation issues as solar panels. Sometimes the wind just doesn't blow. But in our country's best spots, like western Iowa, Minnesota, North Dakota, and the ridges of Texas, the wind blows more often than not. Wind also enjoys a decided cost advantage when compared with solar power. Wind power can be competitive, says Exelon's Rowe, at 8 cents a kilowatt-hour; most of the nation pays more than that for its electricity. A kilowatt of wind power can be installed for $1,700, a price similar to new installations of coal power. In fact, the only generation that comes cheaper is natural gas, which can run as low as $1,100 per kilowatt to install, but then requires expensive natural gas to burn. Wind is free.

Wind towers' affordability is clear; they're sprouting up like weeds across the heartland down into Texas and as far east as New England. In 2007, the United States added 5,300 megawatts of wind power, increasing its wind capacity by 46% in just one year. That increase accounted for 35% of U.S. generation additions in 2007. No country has ever brought on the amount of wind power in one year that the United States brought on in 2007. Better still, we broke our own record in 2008. The American Wind Energy Association says the United States added 8,400 megawatts in 2008, giving it 25,000 megawatts of wind capacity and vying with Germany for the world lead. After 2008, the United States will have led the world in wind power installation during four straight years—and that's after not registering a blip in 2004. As the United States has headed the world pack, Texas has been our frontrunner. Of the 5,300 wind megawatts added in the United States in 2007, Texas had 1,700 of those, 32% of the total. Among foreign countries, only Germany, Spain, and India have more wind power than Texas and its 5,500 megawatts.

We will continue to lead the world in added wind capacity. And while the United States may soon have more cumulative wind power than any other country, it plays much less of a role in our energy puzzle than it does for many other smaller countries. Denmark, the king of wind, derives 20% of its electricity from gusts; Spain is at 12%; Portugal is near 10%; Ireland is at 8%; and Germany at 7%. The United States gets 1.4% of its electricity from wind. For our country to get to 5%, we would need an additional 46,000 megawatts of wind power, an amount that's twice as much as we or anybody else has at this point. But considering what we've done during the last three years, getting to 5% within the next decade would seem quite possible. And—as we get better at installation and manufacture more of the parts here in the United States—getting to 10% could happen within the next fifteen years. Bold plans, but in truth, wind by itself won't be enough.

Geothermal

Energy derived from the depths of the earth is not new science. We've been tapping hot springs in places like Iceland for more than a century to turn turbines and to heat homes. The east side of Boise, Idaho, is rife with homes heated with nothing more complicated than pipes carrying spring water through their radiators. The only costs to the users are the upkeep of the pipes. For the cozy homeowners, there's no fuel expended and no utility bills.

Places where hot springs bring forth the earth's core energy and allow us to easily tap it don't dot the planet often. Outside of those spots, we have found clever ways of capturing the ambient heat in our soils with geothermal furnaces that, in the winter, collect heat from the unfrozen dirt below the frost line and, in the summer, cool our homes by using the 55-degree deep soil as a heat sink for the hot air in our house. But those systems need assistance from traditional fossil fuels and electricity in times of extreme cold and heat, and they can be very expensive—more than $20,000—for homeowners to install.

A new turn in geothermal energy technology, though, holds large-scale promise for the future of renewable energy. In Australia, a company called Geodynamics is working on a project to drill a set of wells more than 16,000 feet into the rock underlying the hot climate of the central continent. The project will use dozens of wells to heat water that will run turbines and make electricity as part of a 50-megawatt installation that will supply power to Australia's grid. The power plant, whose wells will be spread around a 400-square-mile swath, will cost $250 million to build. That comes to $5,000 a kilowatt, more than twice the cost of wind power installations. The big difference, however, is that these geothermal power plants aren't at the mercy of the wind's whims; they'll produce twenty-four hours a day. And that price of installation will fall as companies hone geothermal building techniques.

Geothermal power plants won't work everywhere, but a 2007 MIT study said that 100,000 megawatts of large geothermal projects could be brought online in the United States by 2050, a tantalizing prospect. We have yet to take the full plunge into wholesale geothermal power, but it could prove to be a clean and reliable resource that we can't ignore, given the dependability flaws with wind and solar and the environmental destruction spewed by burning coal.

Natural Gas

Natural gas–fired power plants currently supply 20% of our electricity, and as mentioned above, they account for much of our unused or cushion capacity. Natural gas's role in the near term is likely to increase for several reasons: The plants are cheap, it can be fired up fast, and perhaps most importantly, plants that burn natural gas are the easiest to build politically. Nobody wants a coal plant near their town, with good reason. And perhaps even fewer people want a nuclear power plant in their backyard, even though nuclear plants, as built today, pose far fewer health risks than coal plants. Natural gas plants, however, can be built almost anywhere. The natural gas industry has built itself an environmentally friendly image. That's a credit to the industry's marketing savvy. Natural gas, it's true, burns cleaner than coal and does not emit the particulate pollution that's especially harmful to human lungs.

At its roots, natural gas is a fossil fuel that greatly contributes to the carbon buildup in our atmosphere. Natural gas is methane, CH_4. When it's burned, the carbon bonds with atmospheric oxygen, just like the carbon in coal, to create CO_2 that contributes to global warming. Natural gas will not escape future carbon taxes that are sure to come. And natural gas, just like oil, is a finite resource. Supplies in the United States passed their peak more than two decades ago. We import the stuff from anywhere we can: Canada, Venezuela, Qatar, Russia—more stable suppliers than those of oil, on the whole, but not exactly the most dependable group of nations, save for Canada. But natural gas, just like oil, will become a commodity of increasing scarcity. As that happens, its role in our energy future will eventually decline.

Nuclear—Our Holstein Cow

Nuclear power is elegant. All the energy one person would ever require in the form of enriched uranium fits in a tuna can. Four pounds of enriched uranium has as much energy as a million gallons of gasoline. And there are no sooty nuclear emissions.

Nuclear power plants create electricity by allowing uranium-235 to split into two smaller atoms. When that happens, two or three neutrons, the bonding elements of atoms, are released. Those neutrons go on and smash into another two or three uranium atoms, releasing more neutrons, restarting the process. Under the right conditions, a chain reaction unfolds quickly and neutrons are spraying everywhere. Every time a neutron splits an atom, it releases an enormous amount of energy. This is where Einstein's $E = mc^2$ comes in, which says, in simplified terms, that the energy released is directly related to the mass forfeited by the atom (the neutrons) times the speed of light squared. Neutrons don't weigh much, but they don't have to when there are billions of them all multiplied by the squared speed of light. You can see how the energy piles up quickly. Nuclear power plants simply take the heat (energy) made during this reaction to create steam, which turns a turbine, which makes electricity.

Nuclear isn't considered green energy, but perhaps it should be. According to a British government report, nuclear energy has a carbon footprint close to that of wind energy. The study accounted for emissions that occur building the plant, mining the uranium, enriching the uranium, operating the plant, and deconstructing the plant. Even with all this factored in, the study found that nuclear energy has a carbon footprint equal to 5 grams of CO_2 per kilowatt-hour of electricity produced.[3] About 40% of nuclear's CO_2 emissions trace to the mining process. Wind checked in barely lower at 4.6 grams of CO_2 per kilowatt-hour, most of its CO_2 coming from the fabrication and installation of the wind towers. Coal, of course, is public enemy No. 1, with 1,000 grams of CO_2 released per kilowatt-hour. Just as important, almost half of the world's uranium ore comes from deposits in Australia and Canada, friendly countries.[4]

Nuclear power, at least outside of Russia, where safety standards were long nonexistent, has been very safe for humankind. The only major accident in the United States—a partial meltdown of the reactor at Three Mile Island near Middletown, Pennsylvania—resulted in zero deaths and no human exposure to harmful radiation. Coal power, on the other hand, where the United States derives 50% of its electricity, is not only responsible for billions of tons of CO_2 entering the atmosphere, but it kills an estimated 25,000 Americans a year due to complications from its sooty particulate pollution, according to the EPA.

The sole issue that continues to dog nuclear power is the question of what to do with its waste. Currently, we store most of our spent fuel rods onsite at nuclear facilities in cooling ponds. That system, for all its faults, has never resulted in any serious accidents or harmed any part of the outside population. Clearly, a centralized storage place for our waste would benefit the nation and nuclear power. The site at Yucca Mountain in Nevada stands just about ready to go. Only political hand-wringing and environmental fear-mongering stand in its way. Even if Yucca were to leak some waste, which, considering the massive nature of the mountains there and the design of the site, isn't likely, there would be little damage to the surrounding populations. The groundwater aquifer is just about nonexistent and nobody lives on top of the mountain itself. The risks of continuing down a path of coal burning grossly outweigh any risks we might face with a nuclear waste disposal site such as Yucca Mountain.

Exelon's Rowe, who helms one of the largest power companies in the world, has applied with the federal government to build one new nuclear plant, in Texas. Rowe would build more, but constructing the reactors is simply too expensive, even for a giant like Exelon. "Building just one fifteen-hundred-megawatt nuclear installation will cost six billion dollars," Rowe says. "We could apply for two, but that would be an outlay of 12 billion dollars—which is more than the total book value of my company," he chuckles.

There hasn't been ground broken on a new nuclear power plant in the United States since the 1970s. That will change. It has to change. As the kilowatts of America's power lines stand in for the sloshing gallons in our gasoline tanks, and as our population grows and our dirtiest coal plants are retired, we will need vast amounts of new power generation capacity. And it will have to be cleaner generation, not simply more carbon-belching coal plants. Nuclear provides us a clear avenue to clean energy that can be massively scaled, dependably managed, and supplied without fears that geopolitical strife will interrupt it.

The plants are extremely expensive, however, and until costs to build them are mitigated by scale and familiarity (we haven't done this in thirty years), the industry will likely need an assist from government, in the form of guaranteed loans or subsidies. But we shouldn't be opposed to supporting nuclear technology—the lone dependable source for clean energy that can power a majority of our grid. "If we're going to subsidize wind, solar, and clean coal, why not subsidize the technology that stands the best chance to make the biggest impact on a low carbon energy future—and that's nuclear," Rowe says.

$20 EPILOGUE

Sometime in the Twenty-First Century—
Brooklyn, New York

Bill lives in a world where gasoline, where it can be found, costs $20 per gallon. In Bill's world, however, the price of gas no longer rules our conversations. In fact, the price of gas isn't even in the conversation. It's a nonissue. Nobody buys the stuff, hardly, so nobody cares. In Bill's world the weather is again at the top of pedestrian gabbing fare. Nobody talks about how, last week, they filled their tank only halfway because it's all they could afford. Nor do people talk about how awesome it was to fill their tank for a mere $15. In Bill's world, there are no tanks and everything is already full, all the time.

At twenty-seven years old, Bill is typical for an American his age. He last rode in an airplane fifteen years ago and he doubts he'll ever cross the threshold of another airport gate ever again. And he doesn't care. He travels frequently, but always by high-speed train. Bill lives in New York and often rides the train two hours to visit his parents in Pittsburgh. His father enjoys regaling him with tales of airports and trips to New York that took the family six hours door to door. It all sounds so ridiculous to Bill, the schlepping, the airports, the delays, the baggage hassles. But he appreciates his dad's amazement with the nation's train network, even if he sees it as just a utility that's always been there for him as an adult.

Bill rides the train for an hour to see his sister in Boston or for two hours for a weekend getaway on the French streets of Montreal. He often treks to Chicago to spend long weekends with his older brother, who also shows up in New York quite often. When he's on the go, and that's fairly often, Bill expects to be sitting, or sometimes standing, on a train before anything else, whether it's in a subway car slicing its way downtown or a train that blurs the passing scenery of upstate New York.

Like 70% of the people his age, Bill has never owned a car. Gasoline cars are around, but he doesn't ride in them too often. There are just as many electric cars plying the streets of his city now, too. But owning one of these, while attractive and a bit glamorous, isn't cheap and just isn't needed. His Chicagoan brother, two years his elder, doesn't own a car nor does his Boston-living sister, two years his junior. None of them, in fact, ever expects to own a car. Bill's parents, who live in the Mount Lebanon area of Pittsburgh, own a small electric sedan that they love, but Bill's father keeps making noises that they will ditch their car, the garage, and the house and move into central Pittsburgh, which is once again a bustling, vibrant city core that would have reminded Bill's late grandfather of the city's glory days decades ago.

When Bill rides the train through the New Jersey landscape to the west or the near upstate terrain to the north, he passes by acre after acre of produce farms. Some of this land, just twenty years ago, teemed with cheap subdivisions. Some of it boasted corn and grain crops. But now this land supplies New York and its close-by neighbors with tomatoes, zucchini, peppers, cucumbers, spinach, romaine, and just about anything Bill might find in the fresh produce aisle at his neighborhood shop. The high-speed train line is shadowed by a normal freight line that brings the vegetables and fruit into the city every day. The same ring of farms surrounds all U.S. towns now, big and small. Food, for Bill, has almost always been local. America farms as much as it ever has, but its crops are spread evenly around the country, distributed regionally rather than nationally. Illinois grows less corn and has more wheat, apple orchards, greenhouses, and potatoes. California, conversely, grows more corn and wheat while cranking out fewer avocados and citrus fruit. Food is just too expensive when it has to be shipped cross-country.

Bill lives in a four-story building in Brooklyn's Park Slope neighborhood. It's an old building, built near the beginning of the twentieth century, but it pulses with technology. Bill's hot water and half of his electricity come from solar panels on the building's roof and upper walls. The solar panels operate a system that mimics the photosynthesis process in plants. The energy harnessed by the cells during the day, which splits water molecules into oxygen gas and valuable hydrogen atoms, can be used by the homes at night through a fuel cell that recombines the hydrogen and oxygen and harnesses the energy released during their bonding.

Flat roofs in New York, Pittsburgh, California, or anywhere else, that aren't used for solar cells often have gardens or grass installed. Six inches of dirt nourishing an overhead collection of plants helps keep buildings insulated in the winter and cool in the summer. The green roofs displace less water, which helps keep sewage plants from being overwhelmed while their insulating effects allow power plants to produce less electricity. Many homes, including many walk-up buildings in New York City, boast extensive produce gardens on their roofs. The gardens are often maintained by a tranche of companies that have cropped up solely for the purpose of keeping the building's inhabitants deep in sustainable and fresh vegetables throughout six months of the year. It's the ultimate supply-chain reduction.

When Bill turns on anything in his house that's sucking power from an outlet, he can track its exact power usage down to hundredths of kilowatt-hours. In a $20 world, many homes in America will be equipped with an energy-monitoring system. Bill can track the usage of each light socket and outlet throughout his apartment. He knows that watching that last hour of television cost him 80 cents. These systems, in a $20 world, have been mandated in places like the Northeast and California to help consumers conserve energy and prevent grid blackouts. The strategy has worked brilliantly; when people can see exactly what it costs them to leave that extra light or that unwatched television on, they quickly wise up, encouraged by savings they can see and realize instantaneously.

When Bill gets outside his apartment door and locks the bolt from the outside, the electronic lock relays the signal to the home's interlinked electric system, extinguishing all the lights and turning off air-conditioning systems. During times of peak demand, a small LED light glows on all the light switches and outlets in Bill's flat, reminding him that electricity is more expensive at that moment. Little prods like that help American homes in a world of $20 gas use 50% less energy per capita than they did in a world of $2 gasoline.

In his kitchen, Bill brews tea heated by the energy of the sun. Bill's kitchen cups are not plastic made from oil, but plastic made from the sugar of a corn plant grown in Ohio. The spent water from Bill's building is recycled to flush toilets or to water back- and front-yard plants. Bill jogs in athletic shirts made of finely knit wool, not polyester, which is used less and less because of its high costs. Bill's running shoes have natural rubber bottoms—as in tree rubber—since the composite petro-based materials that used to be made from petroleum and were so common in the past's sneakers are all but forgotten. Bill's street has been paved with concrete as part of New York's plan to get its small streets on a twenty-year pavement plan.

Without as much car traffic, the streets can survive longer. If they're concrete, they can withstand the rigors of winter better than asphalt, which has seen its main advantage—cheapness—erode. Along the concrete streets, New York has installed fee-based electrical outlets for the charging of cars. Trolley cars have returned to the streets of Brooklyn, Chicago, Sacramento, and dozens of other towns, serving as bridges between some cities' subway-deprived warrens and their newly expanded, glistening and efficient underground lines. During rush hour, when the trolleys come frequently, people boarding a trolley car can usually see another car up the street within two blocks and one down the street within the same distance.

Bill lives in the original heart of American urban density, but 90% of Americans also call high-density urban centers home now. City land speculators have struck it rich while exurbian landlords have been ruined.

Bill's girlfriend wears lipstick made from argan oil from a Moroccan ironwood tree rather than petroleum. Bill's wine, and most wines, come in boxed membranes that take far less energy to produce than glass bottles. Much of Bill's newer furniture, his flooring, and some of his summertime barbecue wares—biodegradable plates, knives, and forks—are made of bamboo shoots and fibers that come from plantations in Florida and Texas. The bamboo plant builds mass more prodigiously than a tree could ever dream of and has, along with bioplastics, helped replace many oil-based plastics around the house.

Bill works for a company that designs tidal power stations all over the world. Such installations can be seen all along the East and West Coasts now, as well as much of the developed coastline in the world. The seas' constant swirl is an energy source that, once an efficient method for harnessing it came about, could not be ignored. Bill's job is one of millions that have been created for a new world built on a new energy paradigm, one that's not centered on oil, but instead on a multitude of energies coming from things as disparate as the earth's molten core to the sun coming from the center of our solar system.

Bill's gig owes its existence directly to innovative companies that, during the last twenty years, have been powering our rapid tap dance of adaptation as our oil use diminishes. The global economy, once powered by crude, is now powered by trade in materials and devices to capture and preserve the energy we have. Cargo ships still cross the oceans, but not with the rush-hour regularity of before. Now they're full of solar arrays, wind turbines, massive batteries, millions of electric cars, and thousands of new high-speed train parts.

In Bill's world, cargo ships have evolved into gargantuan nuclear-powered islands that measure 4,000 feet long and 400 feet high, and weigh more than 1 million tons. The *Queen Mary 2,* by comparison, sits at 1,100 feet long and weighs 150,000 tons. These new ships' cavernous bellies will be ten times larger than the standard container ships of today. These massive ships evolved not out of additional amounts of international trade, but out of exorbitant diesel prices. These ships will revive trade between the world's giant economies after some aspects of globalization were stymied by the high costs of moving anything. Many people now take trendy cruises to cross the Atlantic in four days on a nuclear-powered megacruise ship rather than pay twice as much to fly. European vacations don't disappear for Americans, but they come less often, and when they do, they last two or three weeks rather than just one.

These nuclear ships will be, in Bill's $20 existence, the latest manifestation of nuclear power's democratization. The United States's current policy of keeping nuclear power away from anybody but our closest allies will be incompatible in a world of rapidly expanding energy demand and decreasing crude oil supplies. Hundreds of new nuclear plants will dot the globe from South America to the Middle East to Southeast Asia. The multinational companies that build these reactors, such as GE, will revel in a worldwide nuclear renaissance. The reactors will be built to generate as little high-level nuclear fodder—the stuff of nuclear bombs—as possible, but tight international policing will still be needed. The world won't have any other choice, as these changes will be dictated from an economic pulpit, not an emotional one.

The future energy world, and hence, the modern world, will be ruled by strict efficiency metrics, not mere it-works-so-don't-fix-it methodologies. The world's route to energy equilibrium will be determined by sets of equations that determine utility, worth, and function. The same equations will replace our gluttonous American model for life with an elegant one, a model so innovative that our world, while recognizable, will be far, far from the same. These energy equations will render McMansions defunct and SUVs dinosaurs. These equations will fill our ridges with wind turbines and thin cars from our roads. These equations aren't expressed through indecipherable statistics, but through one simple modern idiom: dollars per gallon.

Acknowledgments

This book's verve, direction, and concept would not be as they are without the help of David Fugate, my literary agent. He never seems to tire of supplying helpful criticism, even when he's read a chapter several times in several different manifestations. His counsel proved invaluable when contemplating the direction of this book and its tone. David also proved to be a steady hand in negotiating the wild world of publishing, a realm I had no familiarity with whatsoever. This project simply wouldn't have happened without him.

David knew exactly the editors who would be most excited about my proposal. Among them was Rick Wolff at Grand Central Publishing, whose belief in my book was ardent from the start. Rick is the editor that every writer wants: generous with his praise, measured and smart with his pen. Rick wasn't bashful about telling me when I'd wandered from the point or gotten gratuitous with my detail. His even judgment is evident throughout the preceding pages.

Dozens of people assisted me in traversing the major facets of our lives and how they will change with the price of gasoline. Uttam Shivhare did a splendid job illustrating how rapidly developing parts of the world, such as Shivhare's India, want nothing more than to emulate the lives we already have in America and to pump gasoline and drive cars, just like us. Keith Bradsher, through his insightful book *High and Mighty*, helped me understand and explain how SUVs took over America. David Grabowski's research and his colorful explanations illustrated how fewer Americans will die in crumpled cars when gas prices increase. Charles Courtemanche, through his work and his time with me, showed how America will become healthier and skinnier in a future of higher gasoline prices. J. Paul Leigh's research tells of cleaner air in a world of high gas prices.

By spending a day with me examining some of Chicago's train bridges, Professor Joseph Schofer of Northwestern University helped me understand the dire shape of our infrastructure and the reckoning we're headed for when gas prices permanently increase. Nobody's business better exemplifies the boom-bust nature of the airlines than that of Mike Potter. His good-natured and thoughtful insights helped me understand the life of a commercial jetliner and its limitations. Vaughn Cordle, with decades as a pilot and financial analyst, helped me illustrate how gasoline prices can ruin an industry. Aerospace behemoth Boeing, by letting me on their factory floor in Washington State, helped me show how the industry is trying to combat a future of higher gasoline prices with technology.

UPS is one of the largest companies on the planet; it's certainly one of the most ubiquitous. In my experiences, UPS is also one of the most cooperative, transparent, and innovative big companies in the world. By allowing me to work a day on one of its electric trucks in Manhattan, UPS not only showed me how it orchestrates, daily, one of the most complex tricks in logistical engineering, but also how it has acknowledged its gasoline dependency and how it is preparing for a future of using less fuel.

Shai Agassi has shared his theories on revolutionizing the world's car fleets with more people than me, but that doesn't make his quest any less compelling. His vision gives us a base point for optimism in a future of thinning oil supplies. Metabolix CEO Rick Eno helped me understand that plastics needn't come from oil now or in the future. Civil engineer Edward Kennedy of Hatch Mott MacDonald showed me the amazing netherworld of New York City and what it takes to extend its labyrinthine reach. Bill Pedersen of Kohn Pedersen Fox illustrated the finer points of urbanism and how the design world views the future of humanity.

Stan Gale and John Hynes at Gale International were generous in their time with me explaining how they've built a city for the future out of nothing in South Korea's New Songdo City. Mary Ann Lazarus of HOK helped me understand how twisted many of our zoning laws have become under the rule of cheap oil.

Al Norman dissected the operations of a big box store and how, slowly but steadily, their abandoned stores have pockmarked America's small towns and how they will continue to do so. Marc Levinson's book *The Box* helped me understand how the shipping container has changed world commerce and how that world will have to be unfolded thanks to a silent shipment of truck trailers from Newark to Houston more than 50 years ago.

Orion Briney and Michael Schafer, by bringing me out on the waters of the Illinois River, exhibited how tightly our global food economy is woven. Sasha Issenberg's *The Sushi Economy* helped me understand how sushi's rise was enabled by cheap gasoline and globalization and how it all started with a Japanese airline and some Canadian fishermen. Tim Fuller spent a day showing me around his organic farm in northern Illinois and explaining how hard it is for local produce to compete against agriculture grown on a massive scale half a world away. Steve Gruhn explained to me our reliance on natural gas for food and how we might break that dependency in a future of higher energy costs. Through David R. Montgomery's book *Dirt*, I gained a grasp on the curious relationship man has had with different forms of fertilization during the last several centuries, including that with guano.

Rick Harnish of the Midwest High Speed Rail Association took time to explain to me the inequities of the way we fund transportation and how the deck has been fixed in favor of roads. While still CEO at Amtrak, Alex Kummant spoke his mind to me with no restraint. His approach was refreshing. I only wish that he could be at Amtrak's helm for what looks to be a renaissance thanks to new funding from the Obama administration. Kummant played no small part in establishing the legitimacy and the need for a stronger national rail system in the United States; his work put Congress on notice and helped bring in more federal money.

Tom Casten and Recycled Energy Development, at a dusty installation in West Virginia, helped me understand the colossal amount of waste in our current energy infrastructure and how, in a future of high gas prices, that waste will be used. John Rowe, Exelon's CEO, was candid with me in his remarks on the consequences of burning coal and his opinion on the role of nuclear power in our future.

My editors at *Forbes* granted me leave from the magazine so I could work on this book full time. Their generosity and understanding in this matter is especially remarkable now during troubling times in the journalism and publishing industries. William Baldwin, Tom Post, Bruce Upbin, Stewart Pinkerton, and Neil Weinberg, among others, have been supportive from the start and their confidence in me helped propel this project. Stephane Fitch and Emily Lambert, with whom I share *Forbes'* Chicago bureau, were always up for a bright conversation on sources and the book's contents and were encouraging even during my time away from the magazine. I always owe thanks to Northwestern Professor Marcel Pacatte, who has continually been a positive force in my writing career, even as the years have piled on since graduation.

Most of all, I have to thank my wife, Sarah, a gifted teacher of English, who helped hone my ragged prose and who put up with me spending more than a few late nights at the computer screen. And, finally, I'd be remiss to not thank my son, Jackson, who was born roughly when I started this project, and whose giggly smile made the hard days easy and the easy days pure joy.

Endnotes

$4 Prologue: The Road to $20 and Civilization Renovation

1. NETO Financial Group: http://www.netofinancial.com/2008/08/10/the-50-trillion-investment/.

2. Jeff Rubin, "The Age of Security," *CIBC World Markets Report*, April 2008.

3. Kevin Phillips, *Bad Money: Reckless Finance, Failed Politics, and the Global Crisis of American Capitalism* (New York: Viking, 2008).

4. Ali Samsam Bakhtiari, "The Century of Roots," April 2007; http://www.sfu.ca/~asamsamb/.

5. Jad Mouawad, "As Oil Giants Lose Influence, Supply Drops," *New York Times*, August 19, 2008.

6. Ibid.

7. Brian Hicks and Chris Nelder, *Profit from the Peak: The End of Oil and the Greatest Investment Event of the Century* (Hoboken: Wiley, 2008), 42.

8. Ibid., 43.

9. Matthew Simmons (founder of Simmons & Company International), "The World's Giant Oilfields," a white paper, January 9, 2002.

10. Alan Weisman, *The World Without Us* (New York: St. Martin's Press, 2007), 136.

Chapter $6: Society Change and the Dead SUV

1. Amanda Ripley, "10 Things You Can Like About $4 Gas," *Time*, July 2, 2008, 38.

2. Jonathan Welsh, "Want a Used 'Econobox'? Better Get in Line," *Wall Street Journal*, July 16, 2008.

3. Keith Bradsher, *High and Mighty: SUVs—The World's Most Dangerous Vehicles and How They Got That Way* (New York: Public Affairs, 2002), 4–20.

4. Bernard Simon, "US Goes Hybrid as Prius Sales Pass Ford Explorer," *Financial Times,* January 11, 2008.

5. Malcolm Gladwell, "Big and Bad: How the S.U.V. Ran Over Automotive Safety," *New Yorker*, January 12, 2004.

6. Bradsher, 89.

7. Ibid., 76.

8. Ibid., 101. Also see Bradsher page 60 for Ford Explorer mpg data.

9. Michael Shnayerson, *The Car That Could* (New York: Random House, 1998), xiii.

10. Ross Werland, "Navigating Italy by GPS," *Chicago Tribune*, July 27, 2008.

11. Gladwell, "Big and Bad."

12. David C. Grabowski, "Is There a Silver Lining to Rising Gasoline Prices? (Rapid Response)," *Southern Medical Journal* 101.8 (August 2008): 775(1).

13. Charles Courtemanche, "A Silver Lining? The Connection Between Gasoline Prices and Obesity," dissertation paper (December 19, 2007). Courtemanche did the work while a Ph.D. student at Washington University in Saint Louis. He is now a professor at the University of North Carolina, Greensboro.

14. US EPA Office of Air and Radiation, "Particulate Matter: Health and Environment"; http://www.epa.gov/particles/health.html (accessed February 18, 2009).

15. J. Paul Leigh and Estella M. Geraghty, "High Gasoline Prices and Mortality From Motor Vehicle Crashes and Air Pollution," *Journal of Occupational and Environmental Medicine* 50:3 (March 2008): 249–254.

16. Christopher Conkey, "Funds for Highways Plummet as Drivers Cut Gasoline Use," *Wall Street Journal,* July 28, 2008.

17. Craig Karmin, "Leasing of Landmark Turnpike Puts State at Policy Crossroads," *Wall Street Journal,* August 26, 2008.

18. All facts on London toll system: Environmental Defense Fund, "Taming Traffic in London," April 5, 2007; http://www.edf.org/article.cfm?contentID=6159.

19. Craig Karmin, "Leasing of Landmark Turnpike Puts State at Policy Crossroads."

20. Daniel de Vise, "Fuel Costs May Force Some Kids to Walk," *Washington Post,* June 23, 2008.

21. Ibid.

22. Ray Henry and Jessie L. Bonner, "More Kids Will Walk to School," Associated Press, August 19, 2008.

23. David Leon Moore, "Have Globe-Trotting Prep Basketball Teams Gone Too Far?" *USA Today,* February 9, 2007.

24. Ibid.

25. Todd Holcomb, "Gas Prices Have Georgia Schools Rethinking Sports Travel," *Atlanta Journal-Constitution,* July 1, 2008.

26. Shaila Dewan, "As Gas Prices Rise, Police Departments Turn to Foot Patrols," *New York Times,* July 20, 2008.

Chapter \$8: The Skies Will Empty

All airline information gleaned from financial documents filed with the SEC.

Chapter $10: The Car Diminished but Reborn

1. Jonathan Fahey, "Hydrogen Gas: GM's Wild Hydrogen Gamble," *Forbes*, April 25, 2005.

2. BJSOnline.com, "Seven Miles Down: The Story of the Bathyscaph Trieste," *Rolex Deep Sea Special*, January 2006.

3. Alan Weisman, 121–123.

Chapter $12: Urban Revolution and Suburban Decay

1. Alan Weisman, 24.

2. Figures from U.S. Census.

3. National Association of Home Builders, Median and Average Square Feet of Floor Area in New One-Family Houses Sold by Location, November 2008; http://www.nahb.org.

4. Gus Welty, "Chicago Revives an Ailing 'L'," *Railway Age*, July 1, 1996.

Chapter $14: The Fate of Small Towns, U.S. Manufacturing Renaissance, and Our Material World

1. Anthony Bianco, *The Bully of Bentonville: How the High Cost of Everyday Low Prices Is Hurting America* (New York: Doubleday Press, 2006).

2. Allison Tarmann, "Revival of U.S. Rural Areas Signals Heartland No Longer a Hinterland," Population Reference Bureau, January 2003.

3. Association of American Railroads, Policy and Economics Department, "Overview of U.S. Freight Railroads," May 2008.

4. Marc Levinson, *The Box: How the Shipping Container Made the World Smaller and the World Economy Bigger* (Princeton, NJ: Princeton University Press, 2006).

5. Ibid.

6. Jeff Rubin, CIBC World Markets Report.

7. Bill Siuru, "New Study Makes a Strong Case for Natural Gas Garbage Trucks—Alternative Fuels," *Diesel Progress,* North American Edition, November 2003.

8. National Association of Homebuilders Research Center, "From Roofs to Roads: Recycling Asphalt Roof Shingles into Paving Materials," 1999.

9. 94%: National Asphalt Pavement Association, "Asphalt Pavement Overview"; http://www.hotmix.org/index.php?option= com_content&task=vie w&id=14&Itemid=33.

10. 4 million miles of U.S. Road: Federal Highway Administration, "Our Nation's Highways: 2008."

11. 625 BC: National Asphalt Pavement Association, "History of Asphalt"; http://www.hotmix.org/index.php?option=com_content& task=view&id=21&Itemid=57.

12. Ibid.

13. Laura Ingalls Wilder, *On the Way Home: The Diary of a Trip from South Dakota to Mansfield, Missouri, in 1894* (New York: HarperCollins, 1962), 51.

14. Nate Schweber, "Cost of Asphalt Rises, Affecting Repaving," *New York Times,* June 29, 2008.

Chapter $16: The Food Web Deconstructed

1. Elisabeth Rosenthal, "Environmental Cost of Shipping Groceries Around the World," *New York Times,* April 26, 2008.

2. Ibid.

3. Sasha Issenberg, *The Sushi Economy: Globalization and the Making of a Modern Delicacy* (New York: Gotham Books, 2007).

4. Ibid.

5. David R. Montgomery, *Dirt: The Erosion of Civilizations* (Berkeley: University of California Press, 2007), 183.

6. Ibid., 185.

Chapter $18: Renaissance of the Rails

1. Museum of Science and Industry, Chicago, Illinois, http://www.msichicago.org/whats-here/exhibits/pioneer-zephyr.

2. Stephen E. Ambrose, *Nothing Like It in the World: The Men Who Built the Transcontinental Railroad 1863–1869* (New York: Simon and Schuster, 2001) 80.

3. *Great Trans-Continental Railroad Guide* (Chicago: Crofutt & Eaton, 1870).

4. U.S. Air Force, http://www.af.mil/factsheets/factsheet.asp?id=83.

5. Steven Komarow, "Military's Fuel Costs Spur Look at Gas Guzzlers," *USA Today*, March 8, 2006.

6. William Matthews, "Department of Defense Seeks New Energy Sources," *Defense News*, Army Times Publishing, January 1, 2007.

7. Ronald O'Rourke, National Defense Congressional Research Service, Testimony before the House Armed Services Committee, subcommittee on projection forces, U.S. Congress. Hearing on Alternative Ship Propulsion Technologies, April 6, 2006.

8. Matthews.

Chapter $20: The Future of Energy

1. Peter W. Huber, "Energy Policy and the Environment Report: The Million-Volt Answer to Oil," Manhattan Institute for Policy Research, October 2008.

2. Todd Woody, "The Southwest Desert's Real Estate Boom," *Fortune*, July 11, 2008.

3. Parliamentary Office of Science and Technology, UK, "Carbon Footprint of Electricity Generation," *Postnote* 268 (October 2006).

4. World Nuclear Association, http://www.world-nuclear.org/info/inf23.html.

Index

Agassi, Shai, 97–104
Airbus, 70–71
Air France-KLM, 67
Airline Forecasts, 61–62
airlines and aviation industry
   air freight, at $16 per gallon, 178
   airlines likely to disappear, 61–65
   airplane graveyards and resale, 52–56
   airport closings and downsizing, 68
   Boeing's new 787, 71–73
   change of descent patterns, 88–89
   cost, intercontinental flights, 67
   demise of, at $8 per gallon, 56–71, 73
   demise of, at $20 per gallon, 247–48
   Eastern Airlines and Pan Am, 55–56
   flawed precedents of late 1990s, 58–61
   foreign carriers, 67
   future of, 66–69, 201
   jet fuel, 56, 57–58, 59, 73
   lack of regional flights, 66
   losses, 2001, 60
   prediction of jobs lost, 69–70
   pricing of seats, new criteria for,
     68–69
   trouble for Airbus and Boeing, 70–71
air pollution, 35–37, 42. *See also* coal
   gas prices and reduced, 36–37, 104
   tolls on vehicles and reduced, 41–42

All Nippon Airways, 67
all-terrain vehicles (ATVs), 107
alternative fuels, 88, 93, 95–96, 197
American Airlines, 64, 65
American Electric Power, 235
American Wind Energy Association,
   240
Amtrak, 200–203, 215–17
   Acela, 204–6
   government support, 203, 207–9, 213
   high speed trains, future, 208–9
Archer Daniels Midland, 110
Artesia High School, 47
Asiana Airways, 67
Asian bighead carp, 170–76
Aspen, Colorado, 76
asphalt
   history, 165
   road surfacing, 43, 164–67, 211
   roof shingles, 163–64
Atlanta, Georgia
   cheap oil and growth, 121
   hydraulic hybrids used in, 91–93
   mass transit, 117, 118, 120, 136, 138
   rail transportation, 216
   urban renaissance and, 135, 140
Austin, Texas, 216
Australia, 32, 44, 103, 178, 179, 242, 244

automobiles, 17–32
  air-powered, 93–95
  America's love of cars, 81–84
  automobile ownership, 8, 9–10, 104
  decreased miles driven, 2008, 2, 19, 29
  demise of cities and, 137
  diesel engines, 28–29, 92
  electric vehicles, 26, 84–104, 120,
    130–31, 235, 248
  fewer vehicles, gas costs and, 5, 19,
    104
  government bailouts/subsidies, 210–11
  hybrids, 17, 20, 23, 87, 90–91
  hydraulic hybrids, 91–93
  hydrogen-powered, 95–96
  lobbying by Detroit, 211–12
  middle class growth and, 8
  pickup trucks, 26–27, 31–32, 107, 174
  resale values, 20
  safety, 25, 29–32, 104
  startups, 105
  SUVs, 4, 17, 19–27, 30, 31–32, 253
  Tata's Nano (The People's Car), 9–10
  taxes on, 103
  tolls in cities, 41–42
  urban renaissance and one or no car
    families, 138, 248

Bakhtiari, Ali Samsam, 12–13
Bergen County, New Jersey, 166
Bethune, Gordon, 65
Better Place, 98–104
bicycles, 35, 46, 51, 105, 107, 119, 122,
    128, 131
Bisignani, Giovanni, 58
Black, Norman, 89
Bloomberg, Michael, 42
bluefin tuna, 176–80
BMW, 28
Boeing, 70–73
Boise, Idaho, 241
Bolivia, 13
Boston, Massachusetts
  density of population, 124
  mass transit, 19
  quality of life, 124

return of the foot patrol, 51
subways, 138
urban renaissance of, 132
BP, 13–14, 15
Brasilia, Brazil, 123
Briney, Orion, 170–74, 175
British Airways, 67
Budd, Edward, 198–99
Budd, Ralph, 198
Burnham, Daniel, 123, 139
Bush, George W., 203

California
  air quality and gas prices, 35–37
  rail transportation project, 215–16
  school buses, 46
  solar energy, 238, 239
Capistrano United School District, 46
carbon footprint
  biodegradable plastics and, 111
  cement and, 125–26
  coal and, 237, 244
  nuclear power, 235, 244
Cary, Illinois, 130
Casten, Tom, 226–33
Charlotte, North Carolina, 138, 217
Chevron, 13–14
Chicago, Illinois, 121
  Asian markets, 174
  density of population, 119
  elevated trains, 137–38
  Exelon office, 234
  infrastructure problems, 39–40
  mass transit, 19
  O'Hare Airport, human waste at, 233
  probable tolling spots in, 42
  rail system, 153, 209, 211–12, 216, 217
  return of the foot patrol, 50
  Skyway, 44
  trolley cars, 251
  urban renaissance of, 132, 133
China
  automobile ownership, 8, 10
  as consumer market, 158
  ending of cheap imports from, 144,
    156, 157, 160, 161

high speed trains, 203
manufacturing in, 156
middle class growth, 8
Shenzhen, 159
Wal-Mart and, 145
China Eastern Airways, 67
Chrysler
government bailouts, 211
Jeep Cherokee, 22, 26, 27
losses, rising gas prices and, 27
SUVs, 23, 24
Cintra (Spain), 44
cities. *See* communities
Cleveland, Ohio
rail transportation, 209, 217
urban renaissance of, 132, 133, 134
coal, 16, 224–25, 237–38
carbon tax and, 237
"clean," 237–38
damage to health and environment,
224–25, 237, 244
diminishing supply, 236
electric power from, 235
rising cost of transporting, 236
West Virginia, 224–25
communities, 4, 5. *See also* housing;
mass transit
bike lanes and path networks, 105
city planning and redesign, 133–37
density, 119, 120, 133–34, 251
exurbia, disappearance of, 119, 130,
136
great cities, 121–22
infrastructure revamping, 40–44,
119–20, 136
local marketplaces, 134, 135, 139, 144
megaburbs, 4
new city created, Songdo City, 122–27
parks, 124
police departments, 49–51
rebirth of Main Street, 152–54
rebirth of old buildings, 134, 139,
152, 249
small town renaissance, 141–54
splurb, 147
suburbia, 2–6, 128, 131, 148

tolls levied on vehicles in cities,
41–42
urban renaissance, 120–40, 247–53
zoning laws changed, 138–40
consumer goods
bamboo for, 251
carpets, 167–68
change to sustainable sources, 163,
250, 251
ending of cheap imports, 143–45,
160, 161–62
items affected by oil prices, 2
middle class and, 8
petroleum-based, 3–4, 8, 162–64
plastics, ecofriendly, 107–12, 250
personal care items, 3, 111–12
repair vs. disposable, 151, 160–61,
163
roofing materials, 163–64
Continental Airlines, 61, 63, 64–65, 67,
69
Cordle, Vaughn, 61–62, 65
Coshocton, Ohio, 142–43
Courtemanche, Charles, 33–35
CSX railroad, 211

Dallas, Texas
cheap oil and growth, 121
density of population, 119
mass transit, 118, 136, 138
rail transportation, 216
urban renaissance and, 140
Davenport, Thomas, 96
Davis Monthan Air Force Base, 55
Delta Air Lines, 61
Denmark, 103, 104, 241
Denver, Colorado, 119
density of population, 119
mass transit, 117, 138
rail transportation, 217
urban renaissance and, 140
DeSmedt, Edmund, 165
Detroit, Michigan
rail transportation, 209
urban renaissance of, 133, 134
Dewitt, Nebraska, 159

diesel engines/diesel fuel, 43, 45, 47, 56, 85, 86, 87, 88, 89, 92, 115, 162, 164, 197, 201, 221, 222, 252
    biodiesel, 195
    clean, 28–29
    hybrids, 222
dirt bikes, 107
Disney World, 78
Drucker, Kenneth, 126

education, 4
    changes in airline travel and, 74–75
    high speed trains and, 217–18
    school buses and, 44–46
    state universities, 75
    urbanization and, 135
    youth sports and transportation, 46–48
electric vehicles, 26, 95, 96–104, 248
    braking energy, 92, 125
    commercial trucks, 84–90
    competitors for, 91–95
    cost and availability, 130–31
    impact on power supply, 99, 101, 236
    limitations of, 120
    lithium-ion battery recharging, 97–104
    three problems, 100–102
employment, 5, 158
    airlines and aviation industry, 69–70
    American manufacturing, 158–61
    commuting by car and, 130, 149
    innovative companies, 252
    repair people, 151
    small-town jobs, 149
    telecommuting, 150
    urban renaissance, 122, 123, 128, 134
    walking, biking, or mass transit to, 105, 134
energy, 224–49. See also oil
    ammonia for combustion, 197
    anaerobic digestion, 233
    brownouts, 236
    capturing/reclaiming waste heat, 224–33
    coal, 16, 224–25, 235, 237–38, 244
    cogeneration, 232
    drywall plants, 231–32

electric grid, U.S. inefficiency, 230–31
electricity, sources for, 236–46
    geothermal, 235, 241–42, 252
    hydropower, 238
    local generation, 231–33
    low oil prices and house size, 129
    megawatts needed per 40,000 households, 228
    natural gas, 235, 242–43
    nuclear power, 234, 243–46
    oil prices and rising price, 16
    power savings and, 234
    scenario at $20 per gallon, 249–53
    silicon plant, 225–29
    solar energy, 186, 235, 238–39, 252
    tidal power, 251
    wind power, 193, 235, 239–41
Eno, Rick, 111, 112
environment
    air quality and gas prices, 35–37
    asphalt shingles in landfills, 164
    biodegradable plastics, 109–12, 250
    carbon dioxide emissions, from fertilizer production, 194
    carbon tax and, 235
    cement manufacture and greenhouse gases, 125–26
    chemical herbicides and, 181–82
    coal and damage to, 224–25, 237, 244
    damage from plastics, 109
    depletion of fish, 179–80
    fish farming waste, 176
    garbage, reduction in, 161–62
    green buildings, 249
    green cities, 125–26
    guano collection and, 189–90
    hydropower as green energy, 238
    landfills, 112
    North Pacific Subtropical Gyre, 111, 168
    nuclear power and, 244
    pollution from shrimp farming, 176
    recycling, 168
    sustainable sources for consumer goods, 163, 250, 251
Epstein, Ronald, 72

Erehwon Farm, 182
ethanol, 16
Exelon, 234–35, 238
Exxon Mobil, 13–14

Fairfax County Public Schools, 45
farming. *See also* food
    changes at $16 gallon, 175–76, 184–85
    compost, 181, 186, 187
    distribution of produce globally, 183,
        185
    fertilizer, 175, 188–97
    hothouses, 186–87
    industrialized, 181–82
    local, to supply cities, 184–85, 248–49
    organic, 180–81
    return of the small farmer, 182, 188
    USDA grants, Iowa, 194–95
    wastewater use, 196
Fisher, Jeremy, 171, 175
Florida, 48, 216
food, 170–97
    distribution globally, 175–76, 183, 185
    global demand for fish, 170–80
    imported, 185
    locally grown, 151, 175–76, 184–85,
        187–88, 248–49
    more nutritious, 187–88
    organic, 148, 154, 180–81, 188
    storage and refrigeration costs, 183
    sushi, 176–80
Ford, Henry, 97
Ford Motor Company, 27
    Expedition, 24, 26, 27
    Explorer, 4, 22–23, 32
    Fiesta ECOnetic, 28, 29
    Focus, 27
    Model T, 97
    pickup trucks, 26
    plug-in hybrids, 90
    production changes, 27
Freedom Fertilizer, 193, 194
Fuller, Tim, 181–84, 185, 186, 188

Gale International, 123–24, 125–26
garbage trucks, 161–62

gasoline
    air quality and gas prices, 35–37
    annual fuel costs per family, at $10
        per gallon, 105
    diesel fuel vs., 28–29
    low prices, airline boom, late 1990s, 59
    low prices, disintegration of passen-
        ger trains and, 201–2
    low prices, fishing and, 173, 175–76
    low prices, food distribution, 175–76
    low prices, pickup truck boom, 26–27
    low prices, SUV boom, 26
    low prices and urban sprawl, 121
    obesity and price, 33–35
    percentage of oil imports for gaso-
        line, 2
    price per gallon, 1998, 26
    taxes, 32–33, 38, 40–41
    why prices will climb, 6–16
Geodynamics, 242
geothermal energy, 235, 241–42, 252
globalization
    container ships, demise of, 155–58
    ending of cheap imports, 143–44
    foods and, 175–76
    return of, $20 per gallon, 252
    reversal of, 157–58
GM (General Motors)
    Chevy Volt, 90
    electric car, EV1, 26
    government bailouts, 211
    hydrogen-powered cars, 95–96
    losses, rising gas prices and, 27
    pickup trucks, 32, 174
    SUVs, 22, 23, 24–25, 27, 32
Grabowski, David, 30, 31, 32
Greensboro, North Carolina, 217
Gruhn, Steven, 192–96

Hall, Robert, 88
Harnish, Rick, 200, 209–13, 216
health
    air quality and gas prices, 35–37
    gas costs and changes in, 4
    locally grown food and nutrition,
        187–88

health (*continued*)
 nuclear power and, 244
 obesity and gas prices, 33–35, 104
Hickman, Marty, 47, 48
HOK, 126, 139, 168
Honda
 Civic, 20
 Insight, 90
 plug-in hybrids, 90
housing, 4, 5
 central city, 134
 city development, at $12 gallon,
  135–36
 countertop materials, 3, 4, 168
 downsizing and "stuff," 161
 end of the tract house and
  McMansions, 129, 132, 252
 flooring, 3–4, 168
 furnishings, 3, 144–45, 147, 148, 151,
  251
 heating costs, $12 per gallon, 131
 high rises, town homes, apartments,
  134, 135, 152–53
 local building materials, 168–69
 low oil prices and increase in size, 129
 metal roofs, 164
 price crash, exurbs and suburbs,
  129–30
 rebirth of old buildings, 134, 139,
  152, 249
 roofing materials, 163–64
 single-family, 128–29, 132, 134, 135
 square footage, 129, 161
 suburban ideal, 129, 148
 urban renaissance and, 132
 zoning laws, 139
Houston, Texas
 cheap oil and growth, 121
 density of population, 119
 mass transit, 136, 138
 police department gasoline budget, 49
 rail transportation, 216
 urban renaissance and, 135
Hynes, John, 124

IKEA, 108
Illinois High School Association, 47

Incheon, South Korea, 124
India, 8, 9–10
Indianapolis, Indiana, 209
International Air Transport Association,
 58
Iran, 10–11, 13
Israel, 103, 104
Issenberg, Sasha, 177

Jackson, Mike, 27
Jackson, Wyoming, 76
JAL (Japan Airlines), 177–78
JetBlue, 64, 66, 67, 69
jet skis, 107
Jones, Michael, 49–50

Kansas City, Missouri, 153, 216
Kargul, John, 92
Katz, Paul, 134, 136–37, 152
Kelling, George, 50–51
Kennedy, Edward, 114–17, 137, 140
Korean Air, 67
KPF (Kohn Pederson Fox), 128–30,
 134
Kummant, Alex, 202–3, 207–9, 216

Lake County, South Dakota, 166
Las Vegas, Nevada, 78–80, 119, 217
Lazarus, Mary Ann, 139, 168
Leigh, J. Paul, 36–37
L'Enfant, Pierre Charles, 123
Levi, Michael, 220–21
lifestyle, 5. *See also* communities;
 housing
 annual fuel costs per family, $10 per
  gallon, 105
 change from disposable goods, 151,
  160–61
 changes in airline travel, 74–75
 crime reduction, small towns, 154
 demise of destination resorts, 75–78
 end of long commutes, 130, 149
 end of the big box store and cheap
  imports, 141–49, 160, 161
 European vacations, as rarity, 67,
  252
 extinction of "Big Boy" toys, 106–7

locally grown foods, 151
local shopping, 134, 135, 139, 144
long-distance moving, 91
recreational boating, 107
scenario at $20 per gallon, 247–53
small-town life, 148–54
suburban ideal, 129, 148
telecommuting, 150
urbanization, 134–37
vacations, 67, 75–80, 252
walking, biking, and one or no car,
   105, 119, 138, 154
Lindain, Rene, 84–86
Lindheim, Mike, 101
Livingston, Ken, 41
London, England, 41, 42, 67, 68, 87–88,
   121, 128, 178, 189, 203
Los Angeles, California
   Asian markets, 174
   mass transit, 120, 136, 138
   rail transportation, 217
Lufthansa, 67

MacAlpine, Wayne, 177–78
Macquarie Infrastructure Group, 44
manufacturing
   American renaissance, 158–61
   globalization and cheap labor, 155–58
   loss of American companies, 159
   new jobs, recycled energy, 228–29
   small towns and, 159
mass transit, 113–21
   conversion of expressways into mass
     transit conduits, 136
   density of population and, 105, 134
   effect of $4 per gallon gas, 19
   elevated trains, 137–38
   new infrastructure needed, 119–20
   subways, 113–21, 137–38
   tax support for, 120
   trolley cars, 251
   urban renaissance and, 121, 132, 134,
     135, 136
Mercedes, 28
Metabolix, 110–12
Mexico, 14
Miami, Florida, 120, 138, 216

Midwest High Speed Rail Association,
   200, 209
Milwaukee, Wisconsin, 132, 209
Minneapolis, Minnesota, 132
Mirage Hotel, Las Vegas, 79–80
Mittal Steel plant, 229
Monsanto Corporation, 181
Montgomery County, Maryland, 45
Moscow, 121
Motor Development International,
   93–95

natural gas, 16, 235, 242–43
Negre, Guy, 93–95
New York, 48
New York City, 42, 121
   Asian markets, 174
   capturing and reclaiming waste heat,
     230–31, 232
   Central Park, 124
   density of population, 119, 120, 121,
     127
   electric vehicles, trucks, 84–86
   as great city, 120–21
   population growth, 119
   rail transportation, 204–6, 216, 217
   scenario at $20 per gallon, 247–53
   subways, 113–21
   trolley cars, 251
   urban renaissance and, 132, 133
Nigeria, 13
Nissan
   Maxima, 32
   plug-in hybrids, 90
   SUVs, 21, 23
Norman, Al, 147–48, 159
Northwest Airlines, 54–55, 61, 63–64,
   65
NRG company, 234–35
nuclear power, 16
   Exelon and, 234–35
   federal government support and,
     245–46
   as green power, 235
   scenario at $20 per gallon, 252–53
   Texas plants proposed, 235, 245
   waste problem, 245

oil. *See also* gasoline
  amount imported yearly, 2
  big exporters, consuming vs. export-
    ing, 10–11
  cutting back on, 236–37
  deteriorating infrastructure, 15
  dwindling reserves, 7, 12–15
  embargoes, 1970s, 1, 17
  erosion of demand for, 2008–2009, 7
  global demand for, increasing, 7–8
  middle class growth and demand,
    8–11
  multinational companies, 13–14
  peak oil, 12
  price per barrel, 14–15
  state-owned oil companies, 13
  U.S. oil fields, 14
Oklahoma, 216
Olmsted, Frederick Law, 123
Omaha, Nebraska, 153
Otis elevators, ReGen drive, 125

P&M Aircraft, 53
Paonia, Colorado, 159
Paris, France, 4, 67, 68, 121, 124, 203,
  204, 214
Parsons Brinkerhoff, 113
Pedersen, William, 128–30, 132, 135,
  138
Pennington, Tom, 113–14
Peoples, Oliver, 110
Philadelphia, Pennsylvania
  rail transportation, 153, 217
  subways, 138
  urban renaissance of, 132
Phoenix, Arizona, 119
  cheap oil and growth, 121
  density of population, 119
  mass transit, 117
  urban renaissance and, 135
Pickens, T. Boone, 13
Pike County, Pennsylvania, 130
Pinal Airpark, 54
Pittsburgh, Pennsylvania, 248
  rail transportation, 217
  urban renaissance of, 132, 133, 134

plastics, 3
  biodegradable, 109–12
  environmental damage from, 109
  grocery or shopping bags, 108
  importance of, 108–9
  price increase, 162, 163
  recycling, 168
police departments, 49–51
Portland, Oregon, 217
Potter, Mike, 52–56, 69, 70

Raiji, Ashok, 125–26
rail transportation, 198–218
  Acela, 204–6
  Amtrak, 200–203, 207–9, 216–17
  California project, 215–16
  current, compared to air routes, 205–6
  dire state of U.S. rail system, 201–3
  elevated trains, 137–38
  freight, 153, 211, 249
  high speed trains, 198–201, 203–6,
    208–9, 213–14, 247–48
  history, 96, 198–201
  lack of U.S. government support, 203,
    207–9, 210–12
  New York metropolitan area, 118
  on-grade light rail, 137
  rebirth of, 153–54, 202, 214–15
  small towns with, 149, 152, 159
  Spain, example of expanded system,
    213–14
  states likely to build at $18 gallon, 216
  subways, 113–21, 137–38
  urban renaissance and, 121, 134, 135
Raleigh, North Carolina, 217
Raleigh, Sir Walter, 165
recreation
  boating, 107
  extinction of "Big Boy" toys, 106–7
  jet ski accidents, 107
  outdoor activities, 106–7
RED (Recycled Energy Development),
  226–33, 239
Reno, Nevada, 217
Richmond, Virginia, 217
Rio de Janeiro, 123

roads, bridges, and tunnels
   asphalt price hikes, 43, 164–67
   cessation of building highways,
      212–13
   closures in lieu of repairs, 43, 44, 167
   concrete paving, 167, 250–51
   conversion of expressways into mass
      transit conduits, 136
   cutbacks on repairs, 166–67
   government paving costs since 1956,
      211
   government subsidies and, 213
   infrastructure revamping, 40–44
   model of taxing and, 104–5
   privately owned, 44
   tolling changes, 41–42, 104–5
Rosenberg, Texas, 130
Rothamsted Farm, 189
Rowe, John, 233–35, 238, 240, 245–46
Royal Dutch Shell, 13–14
Rubin, Jeffrey, 19, 157
Russia, 8, 13, 144, 145, 192, 196, 204,
   243, 244

Sacramento, California, 251
Saint Louis, Missouri
   brick making, 168–69
   rail transportation, 209
   urban renaissance of, 133, 134
Salt Lake City, Utah, 217
San Antonio, Texas, 216
San Diego, California, 49, 119, 120
San Francisco, California, 121
   density of population, 119
   flawed precedents of cheap oil, 58–59
   mass transit, 19
   probable tolling spots in, 42
   rail transportation, 217
   urban renaissance of, 133
São Paulo, Brazil, 123
Saudi Arabia, 10–11, 14, 103
Schafer, Michael, 173, 174
Schofer, Joseph, 38–39, 42–43
school buses, 44–46, 47
Seattle, Washington, 133, 217
Seoul, South Korea, 123, 124

Shanahan, Pat, 72
Shelby, North Carolina, 50
shipping
   container ships, demise of, 155–58
   cost of cargo, 154, 156
   fish, for China markets, 174
   fuel charges, 158
   nuclear-powered cargo ships, 252
   ports, 156
   small towns on major waterways, 154
shopping, 5
   end of cheap imports, 143–45, 160,
      161
   end of superstore, 134, 141–49
   local marketplaces and stores, 134,
      135, 139, 148–49
   price increase in small towns, 150–51
Shults, Steven, 173
Simmons, Matthew, 15
Sims, Arden, 228
small towns. *See* communities
Smart Car, 85
snowmobiles, 106
Solana generating station, Arizona, 239
solar energy, 186, 235, 238–39, 249, 252
Songdo City, South Korea, 122–27
South Carolina, 48, 159
Southwest Airlines, 62–63, 66, 67, 69
Spain, 213–14
Sprawlbusters, 147–48, 159
Stockholm, Sweden, 41, 42
stock market, 59, 60
Stone, Kenneth, 146
Sullivan, Louis, 139
Sushi Economy, The (Issenberg), 177
Suwanee, Georgia, 49–50

Target stores, 111
taxes
   on automobiles, 103
   carbon tax, 235, 237
   on gasoline, 32–33, 210
   for mass transit, 120
   new formula for fuel taxes, 40–41, 44
   new model for roads, 104–5
Tennessee, 48, 166

Thai Airways, 67
Thomson, Illinois, 173
Tokyo, 4, 63, 121, 177, 178, 203
Toledo, Ohio, 217
Toronto, Canada, 157, 174, 177
Toyota
    Avalon, 32
    Camry, 31–32
    Corolla, 31, 94
    pickup trucks, 32
    plug-in hybrids, 90
    Prius, 20, 23, 90, 97
    SUVs, 21, 23, 32

Union Pacific, 209, 210, 211–12, 218
United Airlines, 61, 63
University of Iowa, 75
University of North Dakota, 75
University of Oregon, 75
University of Vermont, 75
UPS
    alternative fuel vehicles, 84–90
    cost of vehicles, 88
    diesel fleet, 85
    fuel costs, 2005, 87
    hydraulic hybrids used by, 91–93
    left-hand turns eliminated on routes,
        87
    opportunities for, 89
    planes operated by, 88–89
U.S. Air Force
    alternative fuels, 220–21
    B-52 bomber, 218–21
    changes at $18 per gallon, 219–21
US Airways, 61, 62–63
U.S. Army
    Abrams tank, 222
    diesel generators, fuel needs of, 222
    hybrid diesel-electric engines for,
        222
    vehicles, fuel needs of, 222
USG company, 231–32

U.S. Navy
    military fuel use by, 221
    nuclear power, 221
    retrofitting existing craft, 221–22
    USS *Cole*, 221

vacations. *See* lifestyle
Vancouver, Canada, 174
van der Rohe, Mies, 117, 128
Vencat, Shiva, 94–95
Venezuela
    oil consumption in, 11
    oil production, 13
Victorville, California, 54–55
Volkswagen
    clean diesel technology and, 28
    Ketta, 32

Wallace, Richard, 43–44
Wal-Mart, 141–49, 169
Washington, DC, 123
    parks, 124
    probable tolling spots in, 42
    rail transportation, 204–6
    Union Station, 205, 207
West Virginia, 225–29, 239
Whitmire, South Carolina, 159
Whole Foods, 108, 179
Wichita, Kansas, 216
Wilder, Laura Ingalls, 165–66
wind power, 235, 239–41
    Europe, 240, 241
    Iowa, 193–96, 240
    to make ammonia for fertilizer,
        193–97
    T. Boone Pickens and, 13
    Texas, 240
    U.S. world leadership, 240–41
Woodmencey, Jim "Woody," 76
WVA (West Virginia Alloy), 225–29

Zero Pollution Motors, 94–95

About the Author

Intrigued by rising gasoline prices in spring 2008, **CHRISTOPHER STEINER** conceived of the concept for *$20 Per Gallon* when he wondered, simply, how will our lives change in a future of higher gas prices? A civil engineer and a staff writer at *Forbes* who regularly reports on energy, technology, and innovative entrepreneurs, Steiner researched the question. His examination roamed from Manhattan tunnels to desert plane graveyards to organic farm fields and manifested in this book, which breaks down our future and its coming changes in terms of dollars per gallon.

Before his first reporting job at the *Chicago Tribune*, Steiner worked as a civil-environmental engineer in San Francisco and Park City, Utah. He holds degrees from the University of Illinois at Urbana-Champaign and Northwestern University. He lives in Evanston, Illinois, with his wife, Sarah, and his son, Jackson.